THE MEDIEVAL WEST, 400–1450
A Preindustrial Civilization

THE DORSEY SERIES IN EUROPEAN HISTORY

The Medieval West, 400–1450

A Preindustrial Civilization

DAVID NICHOLAS

Associate Professor of History
The University of Nebraska

1973   THE DORSEY PRESS   *Homewood Illinois 60430*
Irwin-Dorsey Limited   *Georgetown, Ontario*

© THE DORSEY PRESS, 1973

First Printing, February, 1973

ISBN 0-256-01420-5
Library of Congress Catalog Card No. 72-93551

Printed in the United States of America

To my students

PREFACE

I have written this introduction to the history of the Middle Ages primarily for students in beginning college courses, but others who wish a brief overview of the essential aspects of the period between the fall of the Roman Empire and the Protestant Reformation should find it useful as well.

The text gives a survey of political, institutional, intellectual, and religious aspects of the period, but in keeping with my own scholarly orientation, I have emphasized social and economic developments. I have tried to adopt a more commonsensical approach to medieval history than is often done in books of this nature, and accordingly have noted features of daily life, technology, and popular culture that are often comparatively neglected in favor of past politics and the tremendous achievements of the theologians and philosophers of this period. I have dealt with eastern Europe, Byzantium, and Islam only insofar as they affect the history of the medieval west, which I conceive as more or less a unit. At the same time, I have noted variations between areas, for older stereotypes must give way in the light of modern research to a much more varied and complete picture of human development during these centuries.

Readers who are familiar with other surveys of medieval history will also note that I devote more time than most to the late Middle Ages and to developments leading to the modern period. This is also in part a result of my personal interest, but it stems too from a feeling that aspects of continuity between the Middle Ages and modern Europe are often neglected, while entirely too much is made of the Roman heritage of the early Middle Ages.

Acknowledgment should be made to the various historians, past and present, whose works I read and admire and who have helped shape my own view of the medieval period, unconventional though that view may be in certain respects. Such a list would be a dozen books in itself. I do owe particular thanks to my wife, Dr. Karen Schroeder Nicholas, and to Professor Jeremy duQ. Adams of Yale University, who read the entire manuscript and made numerous suggestions for its improvement. All authors should have to deal with such persons as Mr. William E. O. Barnes of the Dorsey Press, but few are so fortunate. Finally, to my students, whose probing questions I have tried here in some limited way to answer, this book is dedicated.

January 1973   D. Nicholas

CONTENTS

MAPS AND ILLUSTRATIONS

Maps

Illustrations

Part I

AN END AND A BEGINNING: THE EARLY MIDDLE AGES

1

THE DECLINE OF ROME

THE ROMANS were an adaptable, aggressive, and generally unoriginal people. They had established their domination of Italy by conquering neighboring tribes. This preeminence led them into conflict with other Mediterranean powers, particularly the various Greek kingdoms and the city-empire of Carthage, in northern Africa. Protracted wars, interference in the internal affairs of other states under the guise of protection, and outright aggression had made Rome the only significant power in the western world by the mid-second century B.C.

This change led to important modifications in Roman government and society. Italy had been invaded in the Punic Wars against Carthage, and devastation had been severe. The peasants were burdened by such depradations and by the necessity of long military service. Many returned from Africa to their farms, only to find their property gobbled up by great landlords. Some became tenant farmers of these lords, but many also migrated to Rome. An enormous proletariat had been created in the capital by the end of the Punic Wars.

The organization of the Roman state, dominated by the Senate (a cooptative body of a few hundred Italian landowners, with hereditary status) and the "tribunes" who represented the "people," was too inefficient for the government of such a vast empire. An executive was needed. Various ambitious men tried to achieve a unitary domination of the state during the first century B.C. Such a domination through an emperor was established under Julius Caesar and his successors, particularly Augustus (27 B.C.–14 A.D.). The imperial power

3

was severely contested in the first century A.D. Republicanism was by no means dead, but the motive force was more often a power struggle among generals. The difficulty of succession seemed resolved after Nerva (96–98), who began the custom of adopting as his son and successor the man whom he deemed most worthy to be emperor. Persistence of this custom was furthered by the coincidence that succeeding emperors had no sons of their own. Marcus Aurelius (161–80) had the colossally poor judgment to prepare the succession of his own son, Commodus. Commodus was totally worthless, and his assassination in 192 signaled the beginning of the paroxysm which the Roman Empire was to undergo in the third century.

Under the "five good emperors" of the second century, the empire had seen an age of apparent prosperity and peace. But there were grave internal weaknesses which became painfully obvious in the third century. The decline of Rome cannot be explained purely in the light of the changed position of the emperor. Many of the ill-fated rulers of the third century were probably more capable than some of their predecessors of the first, but they were faced with a situation which had become impossible.

The Roman Empire was drastically overextended. By the time of the death of the emperor Trajan in 117 A.D., Rome controlled not only all shores of the Mediterranean, the basis of its power and a territory which it might have been able to rule, but also substantial areas inland. These included most of Britain, all of France, Spain, western Germany to the Rhine, and the Balkans. The Romans had penetrated eastward into Germany in the first century but had been thrown back. Thereafter they established an easily defended frontier along the Rhine and Danube rivers. Roman transport and communications were excellent for their day, but they were totally inadequate for the management of such a great empire. Local authorities had to be left largely to themselves, subject only to loose control from the top.

The government of the empire was based on subdivision into provinces, under the administration of provincial governors who controlled both civil and military functions in the early empire. Often the governors were rapacious local despots. Most were from the senatorial aristocracy, although the emperors did appoint some "equestrians," men of the upper middle class. Although most provincial governors were loyal to the emperors in the second century, they became a distinct threat in the third. Many revolted under their local forces and displaced emperors.

The provinces were divided into *civitates,* city states around a central town. The local municipal aristocrats, the *curiales,* were in charge of army recruitment, tax collection, and public works. Although some wealthy merchants and industrialists were in the town governing bodies, landlords were the dominating element. These men generally owned territories outside the town as well as in the city. Their wealth came not from manufacturing but from agriculture. The municipal magistracies were often hereditary in the second century, and their administration was noted neither for great efficiency nor honesty. Lacking an adequate bureaucracy, they often leased public functions, particularly tax collection, to private entrepreneurs, the "publicans." These persons paid a lump sum to the government for the right to collect a particular tax or toll. They were obviously going to profit on the transaction, and the publicans became notorious for corruption and extortion from local populations.

Rome was troubled by a severe shortage of qualified manpower, although this was only beginning to be felt in the second century. Much of the oppressiveness of the Roman government was due to the lack of qualified officials to replace or even check on the publicans. The armies were not yet understaffed—this was a period of peace— but would soon become so. The bureaucracy would be unable to recruit qualified officials to handle the tremendous administrative apparatus which later emperors were to create.

Rome had social and economic weaknesses as well. The Romans never developed a solid industrial base. Only textiles and pottery were important in long distance trade, despite the advantages offered to trade by the economic unity of the Roman government. These are absolutely basic items; human beings must have something to wear and something to hold food and water. Beyond this, however, the Romans produced little for export between regions of the empire. Most goods were made by artisans working in small shops for local markets. Social attitudes of the Roman aristocracy also hindered economic development. Participation in industrial or even trading operations was considered degrading. There was movement upward into the aristocracy from the upper middle class, for in the last analysis wealth was the most powerful force of social mobility; "respectability" could follow after a generation. But when the aspiring aristocrat wanted to make his position firm, he invested in land, not in industrial or technological improvement. Capital thus was drained away toward an essentially passive and unproductive source. A force which made this trend even stronger was the requirement until quite late in the empire that all senators possess substantial amounts of land in Italy.

The Roman economy thus was overwhelmingly agrarian. Social values were based on a rural standard. Yet Roman agriculture was becoming unproductive even in the second century. The free peasant had lost his position under the Republic. The great estates of the rich, the *latifundia,* were farmed by a slave labor force. But the supply of slaves dwindled as the Romans ceased to conquer after the first century A.D. Slave populations do not multiply as rapidly as free ones. Much of the earlier peasant population was now on the grain dole in the cities. Particularly as money became scarce after the third century crisis, lords began requiring farmers who rented land from them to do labor services on lands which the lords retained, in addition to or in lieu of rent. The local landlords became an increasingly powerful group.

Other weaknesses threatened the empire. Even in the second century there was a striking contrast between the western regions, which were comparatively unproductive economically, and the much more prosperous east. The disasters of the third century, which hit the west much more than the east, furthered this dichotomy. The trend was to continue throughout the barbarian migrations. Even tribes which originally entered the Empire in the east tended to migrate west toward Rome.

The Crisis of the Third Century

The classic Roman empire ended in the third century. The assassination of Commodus was followed by a brief civil war. Order then was reestablished by Septimius Severus (193–211), a soldier and provincial governor. He ruled solely through the support of the army, but he did keep down rebellion and provide reasonably effective administration. His descendants, however, lost control of the situation. The extent to which the old Roman Empire had become a universal creation with no outstanding ethos or characteristic other than size is shown by the two most famous edicts of Caracalla (211–17), son of Septimius Severus. He made all free men within the empire Roman citizens and doubled the inheritance tax to which Roman citizens were subject. Large numbers of Germans began to fight in the imperial armies for the first time under the Severi. By the fifth century most armies fighting for the "Romans" were more German than Roman. The fighting by that time was between rival German bands, not between Roman and German. The same story was gradually becoming true of the imperial bureaucracy, although here also the change was only beginning in the third century.

The reliance of the Severi upon the army alone, cowing the Senate into submission, had other unfortunate implications. Armies could make and unmake emperors. The pretorian prefect, the head of the imperial bodyguard, was particularly powerful. The results of the policy became painfully apparent after 235, when the last Severus was assassinated. The Roman state collapsed completely. For half a century armies marched back and forth, laying waste the countryside, installing and deposing emperors. Average tenure of office for an emperor during this time was about six months. The emperors had two characteristics in common, other than vulnerability to assassination: almost all were from the outlying provinces of the empire, and all either controlled or were controlled by a large body of troops.

Public order broke down. Trade ground to a standstill. Even as early as the 160s Marcus Aurelius had faced incursions of Germanic tribes in northern Italy and depleted his treasury in warding them off. Now the Germans used the confusion in the empire to break the Roman defense line on the Rhine and Danube. It took some 20 years to drive them back, and even then the Romans did not completely reestablish their lines in northernmost Europe. Garrisons were depleted. There was little to stop Germans from crossing the line and settling vacant territory as farmers, particularly in the Low Countries and the Rhine regions northwest of Xanten, near Cologne. The social and economic position of the free peasant continued to decline precipitately during the confusion of the third century. In an age when the state could not protect him, he had to find someone who could. Many farmers thus became the bondsmen of powerful local landlords in return for protection. They usually gave up their land and received it back as a lifetime or hereditary tenant farm, paying a rent in produce or money for it. It was an easy step from this to serfdom.

The third century crisis had equally disastrous effects upon Roman town life. The Roman towns themselves were examples of the rurality of the Roman economy and system of values. Most were large, sprawling centers of government, and only secondarily trading and industrial settlements. Most towns, except a few along the frontier in Gaul, were unfortified. Many were totally destroyed during the third century. They were fortified late in the century, perhaps in an empire-wide program under the emperor Aurelian. The fortification cut them off from the rural regions outside, the major source of wealth of the urban upper classes. Thus turned in upon themselves, the towns continued their decline. When order was finally restored at the end of the third century, most cities were only rumps of their former size and importance. Although they continued to be used as administrative centers, they became even less important in trade than before. The Roman towns of the late third century, walled and separated from the countryside, became the models of the physical type of the medieval town.

Diocletian

Order was finally restored by the emperor Diocletian (284–305), but at tremendous cost. The very success of Diocletian is mysterious, for his chances of longevity, let alone great influence, were no greater in the beginning than those of his predecessors. Diocletian made the emperor a figure of mystery, surrounded by the oriental trappings of aspiring divinity and elaborate ceremonial. He reorganized the imperial administration. The number of provinces had grown to around 120 in the third century. Diocletian combined them into a smaller number of dioceses ruled by vicars, on the apparent assumption that a few powerful men are easier to control than many less powerful (the civil diocese of Diocletian is not to be confused with the episcopal diocese, whose territory was usually that of a *civitas*). The pretorian prefect had become a virtual dictator in the vicinity of Rome in the third century. Diocletian deprived him of his military function and confined him to civil instances in and around the city. Diocletian also downgraded the Roman senatorial aristocracy. The Senate had suffered in the third century, but it was still the major threat to the emperor's position. Diocletian used equestrians rather than senators in his bureaucracy. This situation did not last long, but it was replaced by one which was equally destructive of the Senate's function. Under Constantine (312–37) and his successors, senators again were used in the imperial administration, but the rank was broadened to the point that it was held by most country gentlemen in the late western empire, both in Italy and in Gaul. By the end of the fourth century the Senate had nearly tripled in size over the period of Diocletian, and its older prestige was hopelessly eroded. It became what the equestrian order had been earlier.

Diocletian's basic task was to reimpose order and restore the depleted treasury. His reforms, however, were designed fundamentally to stabilize conditions as they were in 284. They did not get to the root of problems. This is particularly true of Diocletian's fiscal policies. He sought to collect taxes without worrying about the tax base. The *curiales* of the cities were frozen in their positions and were made collectively responsible for the collection of taxes in their *civitates*. This was obviously a severe burden under the best of circumstances, and it was made worse by the decline of the Roman economy. The dissolution of public order in the third century meant that the government needed more soldiers and bureaucrats than before. But the population of the empire, particularly in the west, had been substantially reduced, and an astonishingly high percentage of the population in the late empire was in some way connected with governmental bureaucracy or army. The disasters had hastened the tendency of the Roman upper classes to invest in land, which is harder to tax than commercial wealth and may not bring a large cash revenue, but the government combined the head tax on persons and the land tax into an all-encompassing levy on land. Payments in kind were exacted as the use of money became less usual. Farms were abandoned. The empire fundamentally needed more revenue out of a decreased tax base, and chose to get it by freezing taxpayers to their lands and social positions. Diocletian made membership in the city craft guilds hereditary. Constantine then established viciously heavy tax rates on commercial wealth. Tenant farmers were bound to the soil by an imperial edict of 332, after sporadic attempts to do this earlier had failed. The dependence of peasants upon powerful lords, made real by the troubles of the third century, now became statutory as well.

The importance of this is not in the letter of the law, but in how well the law worked. Since the empire lacked personnel for effective control, there was always the possibility of using the most elemental of escape routes from one's obligations: flight. The hardships of the *curiales* have been overdrawn. While it is true that they rarely could collect the taxes and that the entire tax and administrative structure of Diocletian and Constantine weakened still further the always weak Roman middle class, the *curiales* might purchase membership in the senatorial order—everything, including social rank, was for sale by the imperial bureaucracy in its need for money—and thus gain exemption from taxation. The government made some attempt to control this movement. Despite the need for soldiers, *curiales* were forbidden to join the army. The church also became an outlet for persons desiring to escape the burdens of life in the world. Imperial edicts tried to stop this as well, but they had little effect. Other exemptions might be bought. Citizens of the cities of Rome and Constantinople paid no taxes. The numerous personnel surrounding the emperor were freed of most civic duties. While there was social stratification, there were avenues of escape, particularly for those who chose to invest a single lump sum for immunity rather than being subjected constantly to the needs of the state. The state, in its turn, took the short-term gain of the lump sum.

Diocletian also strengthened the imperial frontiers. Troops were dispersed into more and smaller garrisons. He increased the size of the armies. He also made more common the existing practice of using barbarian troops, particularly on the eastern frontiers. The system of *laeti* was known by this time, whether introduced by Diocletian or not; barbarians were settled inside the empire on hand which became theirs, but they and their descendants would be liable for Roman military service, the term of which was 20 years. Numerous administrative circumscriptions were named for barbarian tribes from this time because of the settlement. In this way, although totally unintentionally, Diocletian created a base of agrarian settlement for the Germans when they eventually entered the empire as large tribal groups rather than as individuals and in small bands. The imperial forces also were increased by the use of barbarian federates, tribes under a chieftain who would serve as a group, but usually for pay and not for land.

We have noted the implicit tension between the eastern and western regions of the empire. While not giving up imperial administration in the west, Diocletian saw that the east had greater potential for control and centered his activities there. In an attempt to deal with ambitions of powerful men for the imperial purple, he took on a co-emperor (*Augustus*) to rule in the west, while he concentrated on the east. Each *Augustus* was to choose a *Caesar,* who would succeed the *Augustus* as emperor when he abdicated after 20 years. The system of co-emperors did not work and was given up soon after Diocletian, but the division of the empire persisted. Although the empire was reunited at various times in the fourth century and was divided finally only in 395, the west declined and became increasingly agrarian. A serious gold drain to the east threatened, although more important factors in the declining use of money in the west were probably hoarding and eventually the melting down of gold into plate, precious objects for worship, by the churches. Although the Germanic invasions did touch the east, they were less serious than in the west. The foundation of Constantinople on the ancient site of Byzantium as a new capital by Constantine in 330 was merely recognition of the change. From this time a "New Rome" could compete with the old for prestige and wealth.

Constantine, who followed Diocletian after an interregnum of seven years, generally continued his reforms. He did make certain changes. He dispersed the legions more evenly along the frontiers than Diocletian had done. He introduced a new gold coin which was to be used even in the early Middle Ages.

The administrative changes of Diocletian and Constantine amounted to centralization at the top and social stratification at all levels, but the extent to which they had practical effect in the outlying provinces of the empire is problematical. Much still depended on the personality and abilities of the individual emperor. Most of the successors of Diocletian in the fourth century were men of reasonable ability, but the western emperors of the fifth century were total incompetents. Diocletian's reforms did provide stability in the imperial office, if not totally in the administration, which lasted at least until the Germans began migrating into the empire again in the last quarter of the fourth century. The situation was probably never again as bad as in the half-century after 235. But the cost was political and social arteriosclerosis.

The Empire after Constantine

Decline continued rapidly in the second half of the fourth century. The emperor relied increasingly on advice given by cliques of his friends and less on formally established institutions of government.

Most emperors were controlled by their generals in the fifth century, and the generals were usually Germans. The patterns change from those of the third century, however, for the emperors now were scarcely worth murdering. After the restoration of the emperor Valentinian II in 388 after a brief revolt, the Frank Arbogast was the real ruler. When Theodosius I, the last ruler of both halves of the empire, died in 395, the Vandal Stilicho was the all-powerful chief commander in the west. Military affairs were less important in the east, which was struck less severely by invasion than the west, and the situation did not arise there. The generals were able men who provided reasonably decent government under the circumstances, but there were limits to what they could do.

Affairs were in total chaos in the northern provinces by the early fifth century. The Germans definitively broke the Rhine-Danube line in 406–7, and the Roman legions were withdrawn from Britain at about the same time. From this time the sources tell of a gradual Roman withdrawal from one stronghold to another. The towns were abandoned and remained uninhabited for at least a generation. Matters were complicated by invasions from the east. Even Italy, the privileged heart of the western empire, suffered periodic invasions by Germanic tribes from the first decade of the fifth century, as we shall see. Long before the Germanic chieftain Odovacar finally deposed the last western emperor, Romulus Augustulus, in 476, the empire existed in name only. The Roman Empire in the west, shattered beyond repair in the third century, had finally come to an end.

Economy and Society in the Late Empire

Economic and social developments paralleled the political. Bound legally to the soil since 332, the peasants continued to fall toward serfdom. The total acreage of land under cultivation shrank from at least the late second century. Here as elsewhere the primary concern of the government was with the collection of taxes rather than with tillage of land. When a depopulated area could not pay taxes, its assessment was levied upon the inhabitants of the rest of the administrative unit of which it was a part. Only in the late fourth century did the government systematically encourage repopulation of deserted estates. At that time army veterans were being paid with lands abandoned by their owners. In 422 the emperor Honorius surrendered the deserted lands from the imperial patrimony in the province of Proconsular Africa; one land unit in three was vacant. The manpower shortage on the land was so severe that despite the need for soldiers, the Roman Senate successfully opposed the conscription of recruits from senatorial estates in 397, substituting a money payment instead. The physical insecurity of the time hindered productivity. Peasants and lords alike could not count on being able to save their harvests from marauding bands. A tremendous amount of land went back to forest. The decline of Roman agriculture was so precipitate that while some medieval manors later were located in the same vicinity as Roman estates, their headquarters were some distance away and the field configurations different. Only as the Germans settled down in the sixth and particularly seventh century was headway again made against the all-encompassing forest.

The decline of commerce mirrored that of agriculture. Gaul never had a thriving trade, and that of Italy was severely cramped by invasion and the threat of invasion after 400. While Italy did not decline as severely as Gaul in the fifth century, the Lombard invasions of Italy from 568 seem to have had effects on Italian commerce and agriculture parallel to those of the Franks on the north, although the results were probably less long-lasting in Italy.

Late Roman Letters

Intellectual life was not on a high level. The decline of Rome had a tremendous psychological effect on men. The city had existed for 1000 years, but now it, with the entire world order, was going under. It is not surprising that the best minds of the age were busying themselves with religious questions. As Christianity became the dominant religion of the empire in the fourth and fifth centuries, this generally meant the beginning of Christian philosophy. Whether the effect of Christianity and the Christian church on the eventual fate of Rome was good or bad in the last analysis, they were unquestionably the most original cultural phenomena of the late empire.

The Roman culture that the early Middle Ages knew was that of the late Empire. This is unfortunate, for the best of Roman literature was only discovered later. Late Rome knew only one significant non-Christian thinker, the Egyptian Greek Plotinus, who enunciated a mystical, neo-Platonic philosophy in the third century which was very significant in the early Middle Ages, although chiefly through its influence on St. Augustine. Historical writing was very poor in the later Roman period. The only historian of note was Ammianus Marcellinus, who tried to continue the histories of Tacitus, but he is important only as an eyewitness of his own age, the fourth century.

Perhaps the best work of late Roman letters was in a field in which originality was not necessarily a virtue: the collating and correction of the texts of ancient authors. Donatus and Priscian wrote grammars which remained authoritative throughout the Middle Ages. Most work in philology concerned the Christian scriptures, but the only philologist of distinction was St. Jerome.

Despite the pagan associations of the city, the ideal of Rome was venerated throughout the Middle Ages. Yet for the most part this was for its religious significance, not its political development. It is true that Christian copyists and writers preserved much of Roman thought and letters, and these were honored as being connected with Rome, although not in a Christian capacity. While some minds of the early Middle Ages thought that such pursuits were unworthy of devout Christians, this idea had been largely dissipated by the Carolingian period. The Middle Ages, however, inherited from the Romans a standard of intellectual authority and a legend, but very little of substance.

2

THE RISE OF CHRISTIANITY

THE DECLINING Roman Empire saw the development of a new religion which was to be the essential culture force of the medieval, and indeed the modern, west. Jesus of Nazareth was probably born in 4 B.C. and crucified in 29 A.D. His message was exclusively Jewish. Much of his criticism was directed at the more theologically liberal Jewish religious groups of his day. He charged Judaism with overconcentration on form and ritual and a certain prosy smugness and urged a more purely moral message. Jesus dealt only reluctantly with Gentiles. Although the stories of his life, many of them remarkably similar to the legends surrounding other cult heroes, note unusual circumstances of his birth and upbringing, the miracles which he supposedly performed, and the like, there is some evidence that he may have become convinced that he personally was a divine being as opposed to a very moral man only at the end of his life.

Palestine was an economic backwater at the time Jesus preached. There were few large concentrations of population, and accordingly it is hardly surprising that Jesus' early appeal was chiefly to the rural masses. He himself was the supposed son of a village carpenter, and his message is filled with agrarian imagery, but his religion soon became based very largely on an appeal to the poor of the cities. This change is hard to explain, but it may be due in part to the "dispersion" of Jews throughout the Roman world in the first century A.D. Christianity was spread largely by urban, Greek-speaking Jews. Certainly Paul directed more attention toward town than countryside. He was more sophisticated than many early Christians, a Roman citizen and businessman, and was instrumental in the establishment of Christian churches in such large centers as Corinth, Thessalonica, and above all Rome. Paul split for a time with Peter, Jesus' disciple, over the inclusion of Gentiles into the new religion. While Peter wanted to reserve Christianity for the Jews, Paul evolved the vision of a new chosen people, with God's choice based on moral rather than racial or genealogical criteria.

The new religion encountered some early difficulties, but they have been overplayed by Christian apologists. Considerable propaganda has been made of the early persecutions, particularly that of 64 A.D., when Nero accused the Christians of setting fire to Rome. Actually, there was little serious trouble until Christianity had become a major, although not majority, religion in the Empire in the third century. The Romans were tolerant of all religions. They struck at Christianity when they needed a scapegoat. The Christians were unpopular and somewhat "peculiar." Their secret rites in the caves around Rome became the subject of unflattering gossip, but most of their trouble came over their refusal to worship the emperor. Imperial deity was something that no one, and least of all the Romans, took seriously as religion, but it was a patriotic symbol. The official policy of the Roman government toward the early Christians was set down nicely in a letter of 113 from the emperor Trajan to Pliny, provincial governor of Bithynia: the Christians seem harmless, and as long as they do not proselytize too openly and create no public disturbances, such as over emperor-worship, leave them in peace.

The spread of Christianity was furthered by a number of conditions, some inherent in the new religion itself, others in the nature of the Roman people and empire. The Romans, ever unoriginal in speculative matters, had taken over the Greek pantheon under different names. Such a religion lacked spontaneity, to say the least, and the Romans never developed a deep faith in their own gods. Indeed, various mystery cults appeared, each with its own cult hero or heroine, an elaborate ceremonial, and the like, to supplement the Roman gods. For the plethora of angry, fornicating deities covering as many circumstances as possible, with one chief god as a sort of chairman of the board, Christianity substituted one very moral God. The moral aspect of the Christian God was important in the spread of the new religion. One might fear the power of a celestial murderer, but one could never feel that he was essentially good or the ruler of an ordered moral universe. The moral message of Christianity stands up well against other religions of recorded history.

Christianity, however, was eclectic in that it was willing to adopt some weapons of its opponents, defeating them in a sense on their own ground. Christianity was original, but it was not so strange that the Romans had to make a complete break with the past in order to adopt it. This is particularly true of church ceremonial. Nothing could be further from a highly developed ritual than the simple teaching of Jesus. Many Christian stories closely parallel those of Roman gods. Mithras, the cult hero from whose devotees the Christians borrowed most and among whom they perhaps had the greatest degree of success in the early period, ascended into heaven and was baptised in the blood of a bull. Jesus' miracles must be seen in connection with an appeal to the unlettered masses. A man who could perform feats which seemed supernatural must certainly be a god, a personage who could communicate with the spirits of the other world. Christianity also took over many pagan festivals. Easter, for instance, borrows the ancient rite of spring and is based on a calculation of the vernal equinox. Astronomers have a vague idea of when Jesus was born, but it is inexact; Christian tradition adopted the period of the festival of the Roman sun god.

Christianity later took on Germanic pagan overtones, after it had become the religious "establishment" in the Roman empire but needed to expand outside. Although not consciously, the church allowed the Germans to worship their local heroes as cult saints, incorporating them into the growing Christian conception of near deities who had lived particularly holy lives on earth. One could thus rise by moral virtue to a state of sanctity and communion with the Holy Spirit. Pagan temples were converted into Christian shrines. Pope Gregory I, the Great (590–604), made this official policy: as long as local usage does not positively contradict Christian doctrine, do not disturb it. We certainly can use the buildings. As a corollary to this, Jesus' teaching was very broad and could accommodate a variety of beliefs as long as the central aspects were not denied. This became much less the case in the fourth century, as the Church tried to define an orthodoxy, but the contradictions in the gospel accounts of Jesus' words, together with the obvious differences in tone between the Old and New Testament—the former was much more congenial to the primitive Germanic warriors—gave room for diversity. This was an age of breakdown and spiritual confusion. The Christian emphasis on the afterlife, removing the uncertainties of death and assuring the believer of a paradise, was a powerful motive in the spread of Christianity among simple and sophisticated alike. No other Roman cult was both mystery, with emphasis on an afterlife and mystical union with the cult hero through special rites, and moral, and many were neither. Christianity was combining these advantages by the late second century with the development of an extremely subtle and sophisticated theosophy which was to appeal to the educated. Christian theology was in effect placing a personal God, intervening directly in the affairs of mankind, at the apex of the Greek view of a deity as a sort of process without personality or will.

The superior early leadership of the Church was important in its spread. Although the contribution of some of the original twelve disciples was minimal, Peter and Paul were men of high intelligence, energy, and moral caliber. But the administrative framework within which these men worked was of much greater importance. The church had an elaborate organization spread throughout the empire by the early second century, although it was often underground. The metropolitan or archbishop came to the fore only later. Authority was centered in the beginning in the bishop of the local diocese. There were many lesser officials, such as deacons, acolytes, and the like. The presbyter (priest) also was important, although the diocese was subdivided into parishes under the nominal charge of one of these men only in the fourth century. As early as the late second century, a system of church councils provided a governing body, consisting of the various bishops. The first general (as opposed to regional) council, however, was called only after the church had achieved official acceptance, in 325, to deal with the Arian heresy. These councils were called more frequently thereafter to determine orthodoxy and proper usage.

Although Christianity only tried to drive out aberrant belief from the fourth century, some early theologians, such as the north Africans Tertullian and Origen, expounded doctrines of such a mystical character that eventually they were declared heretical. Such ideas, however, never seriously threatened orthodoxy in the west. In this age of cultural decline, they simply were too subtle for western minds to grasp. The east, carrying on the tradition of the ancient Greek schools, was vitally concerned with doctrinal questions, but heresies had little practical importance in the west until much later. Some later medieval heresies were reminiscent of Roman ones, but apparently grew up without being conscious of this tradition. Some of the distaste for elaborate church usage which we encounter in the twelfth and thirteenth centuries recalls the heresy of Donatus, bishop of Carthage in the fourth century, who argued that sacraments administered by an unworthy priest had no validity on high. The heresy which most disturbed the late Roman west was that of Arius, who argued that the Son was not of the same nature as the Father but was begotten by him and as such was in some way inferior although equal. Most of the Germanic tribes were converted to Christianity by Arian priests, beginning with the conversion of the Visigoths by Ulfilas from 340. But the importance of the Arian heresy was chiefly political. Clovis the Frank, converted to orthodox Christianity, justified his attacks on other tribes by their Arianism, but there is no reason to think that he understood the doctrinal implications. The great fathers of the Latin church, save only Augustine, were doers and collators, not profound theologians.

The Church Triumphant

By a sudden upturn in fortunes, the church became the religious "establishment" in the fourth century. Much of this is due to the conversion to Christianity, real or alleged, of the emperor Constantine. According to legend, Constantine became a Christian after a great victory in 312 in which he promised to become a Christian if the Christian God would give him victory—a conversion remarkably similar to that of Clovis nearly two centuries later. It has been claimed that he hoped to make Christianity a state religion to shore up declining loyalties to the state and that most of his motivation was cynical. Yet at the time of his supposed conversion a generous estimate might place 10 percent of the population of the empire in the Christian camp. Constantine's personal excesses have been cited as evidence that he did not convert. Yet there is no doubt of the later conversion of Germanic warriors whose ordinary behavior made Constantine's look saintly. Constantine certainly made Christianity a most favored religion. He participated actively in doctrinal disputes and presided at the first ecumenical council at Nicaea in 325, at which Arianism was condemned but not exterminated.

But in becoming the establishment the church lost much. As it developed an orthodoxy to defend, it became increasingly intolerant of original speculation which questioned teachings which were becoming authoritative. The church busied itself with works of conversion, but the most original and active missionaries, particularly among the Germans, were Arian. The orthodox converted the Roman population, and this ultimately was the salvation of the orthodox position, for the Gallo-Romans were the majority population in Gaul during the age of barbarian kingdoms except in the extreme north. But only when the orthodox church was forced to deal with barbarian kings as political and military forces did it concern itself overly with the salvation of German souls.

The church unquestionably became more worldly and lost spiritual fervor in the fourth and fifth centuries. The decline of the state furthered this process. St. Ambrose (340–97), one of the great fathers of the Latin church, was brought up a Christian, but had not received baptism as an adult. As a provincial governor in northern Italy, he was called in to stop a riot in Milan between Arian and orthodox. The bishopric of Milan was vacant, and Ambrose was acclaimed bishop as he entered the church. After some soul-searching, he accepted the position. Ambrose was eventually to face down the emperor Theodosius over the latter's tendency, although a Christian himself, to allow some civil rights to Roman pagan and Jewish populations in his empire. He even had the audacity to massacre a Christian population at Thessalonica merely because the Christians had massacred the local Jewish colony. Emperor did penance for his fault to bishop. The church was developing the idea that when emperors were Christian, they were responsible to the church not only for their souls' salvation, but also for their conduct as leaders of God's flock. The church took over civil functions in the diocese as the civil authorities grew ever weaker. By the fifth century the bishops had in effect replaced the secular authority of the Romans. The Ambrose case was typical and prophetic.

St. Ambrose was a sincere and moral man, but many in his position were not. Men often entered the clergy to escape civic duties incumbent on their guilds or magistracies, and the spiritual level of the clergy declined accordingly. Although the Roman state tried to forbid such enrollments, it was powerless to stop them. The church also was becoming wealthier and attracted those who desired to share the riches of the great urban churches. The increasingly Christianized population of late Rome and particularly of early medieval Europe left properties to the church in return for masses said for the soul and similar benefits. St. Augustine recommended that Christians leave a "son's share" of their property to the church, or the entire estate in default of heirs. Since by the fifth century most wealth was in land, the church built up immense estates outside the cities. As an island of sanctuary in a troubled world, the church also provided some means of protection for the weak and unsure. Although the Germans despoiled churches even after their conversion, this was unusual. Peasants buffeted about in the confusion commended themselves to ecclesiastical as well as temporal lords to obtain protection. The church eventually became all that was left of the Roman "establishment," and in this capacity it met the barbarians. The result was an inevitable barbarizing of the church as it worked out an accommodation with the world in which it had to exist.

The Rise of the Papacy

The elevation of the pope, technically the bishop of Rome, to a position of unquestioned primacy in the western church took some seven centuries. The popes were claiming universal dominion by the late fourth century, but they lost effective control of the churches of northern Europe during the confusion of the invasions. Although they corresponded with Frankish monarchs and churchmen and were instrumental in the reconversion of Britain to Christianity (see below, p. 30), they regained their full authority only in the eigth century.

Several conditions furthered the popes' aims. As bishops of the capital city of the empire, they had enormous prestige. The earliest bishops of Rome were men of considerable ability and powers of articulation. They were able to keep their community in existence even in the worst of times, and they corresponded regularly with the leaders of other churches. As the church of Rome became prosperous, its bishops were generous toward needy churches and helped found some communities. They created a series of ecclesiopolitical debts to be repaid. The bishop of Rome was asked to arbitrate some of the controversies over heresy in the fourth century, and his opinion was invariably orthodox. It is no accident that the most important heresies had spent their course by the time the popes began to obtain recognition of their claims of primacy. Orthodoxy of opinion added prestige, particularly in the nonspeculative west.

By far the most important weapon in the pope's spiritual arsenal was the so-called Petrine theory of delegated spiritual authority. Addressing his disciple Simon shortly before the crucifixion, Jesus said (Matthew 16: 18–9) "Thou art Peter, and upon this rock I will build my church . . . and I will give unto thee the keys of the kingdom of heaven; and whatsoever thou shalt bind on earth shall be bound in heaven, and whatsoever thou shalt loose on earth shall be loosed in heaven." While the Protestant interpretation of this passage was to hold that the "peter" (rock) to which Jesus was referring was Simon's statement that Jesus was Christ, the son of God, the Roman Catholic view, which was current in the Middle Ages, holds that Simon was the rock upon which Jesus chose to build his church. Since Peter supposedly founded the church of Rome and was martyred there, his successors as bishops of Rome had the "power of the keys," complete spiritual power in the world.

The earliest popes had no real way to put this doctrine into effect, but Pope Damasus I was able to claim primacy in matters of faith by the late fourth century. Rivalry increased with the patriarchs of Alexandria and Constantinople, the leading bishops of the eastern empire. The council of Constantinople in 381 stated that the patriarch of Constantinople was supreme in the east, but that he was subordinate to the pope. Damasus I refused to accept even this, on grounds that he obtained his authority from Peter, not from a council. The pontificate of Leo I, the Great (440–61) was crucial. Not only was he, rather than the emperor, the leader of the defense of Rome against the Huns and the Vandals: in 445 the emperor Valentinian III decreed that the pope was supreme over all other bishops in the west and ordered the officials of the state to assist in the enforcement of these claims.

The position of the pope nonetheless remained largely theoretical for some years. The pope could never maintain himself in barbarian Italy without protection of a secular power, but with protection came secular domination. After much of Italy was reconquered by the eastern Roman emperor in the sixth century, the popes were usually of eastern origin and orientation, recognizing the lordship of the emperor but claiming spiritual primacy over the patriarch of Constantinople. Some of the popes, such as Gregory the Great, were comparatively independent, but they lost effective authority in the west until the

eighth century, when the Franks rescued them from the Lombards
and became masters of the popes themselves.

Monasticism

The increased wealth and temporal power of the church disturbed
many sensitive persons who thought of the church's mission as the
care of souls. Men noticed the dichotomy between the simple lives
of Jesus and his disciples and the opulent church of late Rome. Many
such persons "fled to the desert," leaving the entanglements of the
world and becoming hermits. They hoped to save their own souls
through solitary contemplation; there is nothing of the social gospel
or saving others. Many of the early hermit saints were vulgar exhibi-
tionists. Their exploits included sitting atop poles, having themselves
planted in the ground as vegetables, and other means of obtaining
holiness. Others, however, were genuinely saintly persons, and informal communities developed around them. Yet the hermits were
not early monks. In principle, they lived alone and not according
to a rule.

While there were a few hermits in the west, the cenobitic or
monastic form of the Christian life spent in withdrawal from the world
was much more important. This involved life in community with other
holy men seeking the same essentially personal goal of preserving one's
own purity of soul in a world marching rapidly toward damnation.
The earliest known monastic community under a set of regulations
was founded in early fourth century Egypt by St. Pachomius.
Pachomius had little influence on western monasticism, but St. Basil,
bishop of Neo-Caesarea, compiled a set of rules which is still standard in the eastern monasteries and which was quite similar to the
rule of St. Benedict, which dominated western monasticism.

A pioneer of western monastic life was St. Martin of Tours. Characteristically, he began as a hermit, but then established a monastic community near Tours in the late fourth century. Martin, however, was
an activist who spent much of his life combatting paganism in Gaul.
Characteristically also, in an age when the distinction between monk
and priest, between regular (from *regula,* rule) and secular clergy
was only beginning to be made, there was an easy transfer from the
one to the other: for example, St. Martin was also bishop of Tours.

Indeed, most of the able and spiritually inclined bishops of the early Middle Ages were monks, although the monasteries were considered somewhat outside the episcopal hierarchy.

Martin's legacy was in his personal example and work of conversion. His *Life,* written by Sulpicius Severus, is a conglomeration of fact and fancy, stories of conversion and stories of crude miracles. It had an immense popularity in early medieval Europe and was often borrowed by others who were promoting different saints, even to the point of appropriating Martin's miracles. But Martin established no monastic rule. Monks were wandering about outside the monasteries engaged in ungodly pursuits by the early sixth century. A change comes with the work of St. Benedict of Nursia (ca. 480–543). He evidently borrowed much of his rule from an anonymous set of guidelines which circulated in the west during his lifetime, but the medieval west always thought of his as the Benedictine rule. Benedict retired at an early age to a cave to live as a hermit, and subjected himself to such ascetic rigors that his health suffered for the rest of his life. He had visions and hallucinations. Finally he realized that man is a social being and must have the company of other men to fulfill God's purpose for him. Accordingly, he founded his monastery at Monte Cassino, south of Rome. The monks were to make their establishment as independent of the sinful world as possible. They were to do manual labor in the fields and grow their own food. Regular spiritual exercises were provided for the various hours of the day, with some modifications for the change of season. The monks were to maintain contemplative silence in their cells. They were to elect the abbot, but then were to be absolutely obedient to him, even to the point of corporal chastisement. They were not to leave the abbey without his permission. The rule of St. Benedict spread gradually until it became the standard rule of western monasticism by the early ninth century.

Benedict shared with most holy contemporaries a distaste for secular learning. He made no provision in his rule for scholarship except for spiritual exercises and readings. The tradition of the monastic copyist was grafted onto the Benedictine tradition and was an innovation of Cassiodorus (ca. 490–580), a Roman civil servant who had served in the government of Theodoric the Ostrogoth (on Theodoric, see below, p. 46). A literate man and a sincere Christian, he went to his ancestral estates in southern Italy after retiring from public service and established a monastery. Throughout the rest of his long life he collected Greek and Latin manuscripts from all regions of the known world. In his *Introduction to Divine and Human Readings,* Cassiodorus set forth a program of education and copying labors for his monks. He apparently knew the Benedictine rule, but he did not establish it formally as the standard of his monastery. From his time the tradition of monastic copying as part of the exercise of godliness grew.

Many abbeys also maintained schools to train local boys in the rudiments of learning. Indeed, the monasteries had a virtual monopoly on education before the growth of urban cathedral schools in the eleventh and twelfth centuries. The abbeys were more important than the bishoprics in the preservation of Roman culture and in the foundation of the new civilization of the very localized and agrarian Middle Ages. They are certainly the distinctly medieval contribution to the church, and they performed many useful civil functions as well, such as education and poor relief. As the most conspicuous and probably the most spiritual element of the church, the monasteries perpetuated an essentially ascetic concept of personal holiness which was generally accepted as an ideal throughout the Middle Ages. Ideal, however, is quite different from reality.

Most monasteries were located in the countryside, as the monks tried to escape the temptations of the world. They thus found new pagans to convert. The Late Latin *paganus* means an inhabitant of the countryside, and the term was borrowed to designate non-Christians, for it was assumed that city dwellers were Christians or at least knew Christianity. Interior Gaul was converted by monks, not priests, during the great expansion movement of the late sixth and seventh centuries. But the rural location of the abbeys is important also in their economic history. They tended to settle along the great river valleys. As such, they had already colonized the most fertile and accessible land in northern Europe by the ninth century. Non-monastic expansion of the agrarian sector of the economy thus had to take place thereafter in largely marginal farmland. Princes and peasants alike tried to insure their souls' salvation by donating their most significant property—land—to the church, and particularly to the rurally based monasteries, which performed functions of ministering to local populations in the countryside which were only gradually taken over by parish priests in the Merovingian age. Hence the bishoprics and abbeys, but particularly the abbeys, became very wealthy. There was a corresponding relaxation of monastic discipline from around the eighth century, and an increased emphasis on worldly concerns. While the manor was probably an exceptional form of farming in the Middle Ages, most of what we know of early medieval agrarian life comes from great monastic estates. The fact that the monks could read and write had much to do with this, for only they could keep regular records, and only they had the intellectual expertise to manage their estates effectively. The amount of land under cultivation expanded tremendously in the Merovingian period under the promotion of the monasteries. The political power of the bishops cushioned the fall of the Roman empire, but the economic power of the monasteries helped to create medieval civilization.

Barbarism and Religion: Christianity and Intellectual Life

Christianity dominated the medieval intellectual experience, and some of its most important and representative figures date from the period of the breakdown of the Roman empire. Most writings surviving from this period deal with Christian dogma or moral examples. We have noted the saint's life as an important example of this. The two great historians of the early Middle Ages were Bishop Gregory of Tours and Bede, who wrote histories of the Franks and the English church respectively, but they also poured out numerous commentaries on the gospels and considered these their most important works. The decline of Roman letters in a Christian context is illustrated nicely by Bishop Isidore of Seville (d. 636), in the Spanish kingdom set up by the Visigoths in the early sixth century (see below, p. 46). In Isidore's great work, the *Etymologies,* he gave elaborate linguistic explanations of the nature of things, for he believed that the true nature of everything could be ascertained by analysis of the word used to describe the concept. He derives "man" (*homo*), for instance, from *humus* (earth), since man is made of clay. The ant (*formica*) received its name because it carries pieces (*ferat micas*) of grain. Isidore knew nothing of linguistics and wrote a work which often seems ridiculous to the modern observer, but it was the great encyclopedia of universal knowledge for the early Middle Ages. He also wrote, among other works, a *History of the Kings of the Goths, Vandals, and Suevi* which is noted neither for its historical accuracy nor its literary value. Its preface, amounting to a paean on the cattle and horses of Spain and their fecundity, replete with learned allusions from the classics, is an excellent illustration of the total lack of inspiration of the last Roman literary figures.

Earlier Christian scholars, however, were more sophisticated, and they left a tradition upon which medieval intellectuals were to build, particularly from the eleventh century. St. Jerome (ca. 340–419) in a sense is the prototype of the early Christian intellectual in both his strengths and weaknesses. A quarrelsome man, he fell out with most of the leading Christians of his day and spent his energy in polemics with them. But Jerome was primarily a linguist who loved ancient literature. He once had a dream in which God accused him of being not a Christian, but a Ciceronian. Jerome wanted above all else to unite the literary tradition with Christianity. He thought that much good could be obtained through ancient literature, although conflicts with Christianity could arise. Fundamentally, however, such knowledge was necessary for the Christians to meet the pagans on their own ground. Jerome was not a profound theologian, although his linguistic work led him into some speculation. His primary task, as he saw it, was the establishment of definitive texts, without which no amount of allegorical reasoning could be significant. If one does not know what a text literally means, how can he proceed from this to a symbolic meaning? Accordingly, he collated the ancient Hebrew and Greek texts of the Scriptures and translated them into Latin, the ordinary language of his day (and hence the term Vulgate Bible, from *vulgus,* common people). The Vulgate itself was corrupted by poor copyists in succeeding centuries. The definitive text was compiled under the direction of Alcuin, the head of Charlemagne's palace school in the late eighth century. It was the standard Bible for the rest of the Middle Ages and remains so for Roman Catholics.

Boethius (ca. 480–524) was a fundamental authority for medieval intellectuals. Like Cassiodorus, he was an important official in the government of Theodoric the Ostrogoth, but he was executed for treason. In addition to some theological works, he planned to translate the entire work of Plato and Aristotle from the original Greek into Latin, but he finished only the logical treatises of Aristotle. Only parts of this survived, but save some fragments of Plato they were the total of Greek philosophy known in the west before the twelfth century. Boethius was thus the source of much of the western classical tradition.

His *Consolation of Philosophy,* written while he was in prison, also was very popular. Philosophy personified gave consolation to Boethius in his time of trouble and led him to value totally the affairs of the mind.

St. Augustine

St. Augustine was by far the most significant early Christian thinker. With Thomas Aquinas, he is one of the two leading theologian-philosophers of his religion. He totally dominated western theology in the early Middle Ages and later rivalled the school of Aquinas. The son of a pagan father and a Christian mother, his early career was chequered. As he tells us in his *Confessions,* his early studies of secular culture led him to sinful places, and he participated wholeheartedly. He became a devotee of the Manichaean heresy, which argued that two gods, one of light and one of darkness, struggled eternally. The temporal world reflected this struggle. Only in this way, it seemed to many, could the problem be avoided in Christian theology of having a good God creating an evil world or not knowing in advance that it would become evil. Although Augustine later renounced Manichaeism, it would always color his theology, and it had a striking effect on some eastern heresies. As contacts between east and west became more intense again in the central Middle Ages, it then spread to western Europe.

Augustine eventually came to Rome, where he fell under the influence of Neoplatonism. He continued in this potpourri of religious and literary pursuits until 387, when he was baptized by St. Ambrose. He became a priest in 391, and in 395 he became bishop of Hippo, in northern Africa, an office he held until his death. During this time he wrote his major work, *The City of God.*

Augustine's first preoccupation was how men attained contemplation and communion with God. His answer was a borrowing from the Neoplatonism which influenced him so markedly. The Neoplatonists had argued that light necessarily emanated from a central source, the divinity, but in decreasing intensity until man is finally made as only a dim reflection of God. Augustine retained this basic argument, but substituted the personal creator–God of the Christians for the impersonal mechanism of the Neoplatonists. Augustine's God created and gave knowledge not through necessity, but through an act of his own free will. The problem of predestination of course enters here. Augustine had to admit that in a certain sense while God could not create evil (which was not a positive quality, but a deprivation and hence uncreated), he at least had to know of its existence and as an all-knowing being would be aware of acts of evil before they occurred.

Augustine did not emphasize the material world, but he had to deal with it. God created man and the world out of nothing. The soul of man is immortal, since it is the principle of life, and it possesses the power of reasoning and knowing. God implanted "seminal reasons" in man which contain actuality and potentiality of knowledge. Augustine leaves himself open here to the possibility that there is only one soul in which all men participate, and hence that the individual soul itself may not be immortal, but he was evidently unaware of this possible interpretation of his doctrine.

In further accord with the Greeks, Augustine found happiness the ultimate end of man and the guide of his moral conduct; but in striking contrast to them, he considered happiness attainable only through the contemplation of God. Man seeks the supreme good, the love of God, by an act of will. The will is free and can turn toward God or toward the material world, and it therefore can operate against divine law and will. Man can fulfill his nature only by turning toward God, but his will allows him to do otherwise. Augustine here as elsewhere has difficulty with the all-knowing and all-powerful God in combination with the ability of sinful man, created by God, to act contrary to the law of God by an act of will.

Hence mankind, both individuals and the collectivity, witness a sort of Manichaean struggle between two principles, the love of God and the love of the world. History, the framework within which man's destiny is played out, sees the City of Jerusalem pitted against the City of Babylon. The pagan state was embodied by Babylon, while the church was the City of God or Jerusalem, although in addition to having concrete meaning in history these are abstract moral and spiritual principles. A Christian who does not show himself to be part of the city of God in his conduct is part of the city of man. The state is founded upon justice. Justice, according to Plato, is the giving to each his due. The Roman state was no state and hence fell because it failed to give God his due. Augustine thus explained the fall of Roman civilization in the light of Christian eschatology. The duty of the Christian, who is necessarily part of the earthly state, is to imbue the world with Christian principles; but the church is perfect and hence superior to the state.

St. Augustine had numerous crude imitators, of whom the most famous was Orosius. His *Seven Books of History against the Pagans* are obviously patterned after the *City of God* and may have been written at Augustine's example or urging. Orosius goes through human history recounting falls of empire in the light of Christian morality or indeed of the Christian religion, in answer to pagan claims that Rome was falling because it was turning away from the gods whose patronage had brought greatness. Although Christianity was the official religion of the state from the time of Theodosius the Great in the late fourth century, it may not have been a majority religion even then, and paganism was still very strong in the fifth century. Certainly Christianity was no more than a veneer on the totemism of the Germanic tribes.

Gregory the Great

Augustine was read only by intellectuals in the Middle Ages, and few of them understood his work. This was not a golden age of learning. The prototype of the Christian saint of early medieval Europe was not Augustine, but Pope Gregory the Great (590–604), a holy man and a practical and talented administrator of the papal territories. The first monk to become pope, he came to power in an Italy divided between Germanic invasions in the north and the state of the Byzantines, who had reconquered much of Italy in the sixth century. Gregory even raised the local militia and supervised the defense of Rome against the Lombard tribes, and warrior bishops of the Middle Ages followed his example in less compelling circumstances. Gregory furthered missions, sending monks to England in 596. Although there was a pagan reaction there after the death of King Ethelbert of Kent, whom the monks had converted, this work set the basis for the permanent conversion of the English later in the seventh century. Gregory promoted the conversion of the Visigoths in Spain from Arianism to orthodoxy. He consistently encouraged appeals from other churches to Rome and resisted all pretensions of the patriarch of Constantinople to supremacy. His *Pastoral Care,* a handbook of practical advice to bishops, was one of the most important books of the early Middle

Ages. Although he was reasonably well educated himself, Gregory considered intellectual pursuits frivolous distractions from the essential tasks of the Christian. He was a reasonably good practical theologian and wrote numerous commentaries on the Bible. The most significant was a work on Job, in which he dealt not only with the allegorical meaning of the book, but its significance for Christian living. His four books of *Dialogues* were extremely popular and encouraged the growth of monasticism. He encouraged the veneration of local saints and relics, demonology and the belief in good and evil spirits, and other religious characteristics which were far more important to the barbarous men of the early Middle Ages than the teaching of Jesus of Nazareth. St. Augustine was the theologian who most influenced medieval intellectuals and philosophers; Gregory the Great was the theologian who most influenced and typified the religion of the ordinary Christian layman and priest.

3

BYZANTIUM AND ISLAM

THE EASTERN Roman Empire, called Byzantine after the ancient Greek name Byzantium for the site of Constantinople (modern Istanbul), continued to exist after the western empire was ended by internal weakness and Germanic invasions. The eastern empire was favored by several circumstances not present in the west. It was much more politically cohesive and sophisticated. Ancient civilizations had been accustomed to government for centuries, in contrast to the barbarian regions of Gaul. While there was little native loyalty to Rome, there was scant opportunity or even desire for rebellion. The Christianizing of the empire had meant that the eastern Romans now stood as a bulwark against the pagan Persians. The barbarian invasions originating in the breakthrough on the Rhine and Danube, which had hurt the west most severely, had less effect in the east. Rather, when the eastern emperors wanted to rid themselves of Germans, they sent them to happier pastures in the west, where they might eliminate other Germans instead of Romans. Furthermore, population density was sufficiently heavy, particularly in the imperial heartlands of Greece and Asia Minor, to preserve the top-heavy bureaucracy and imperial household, both inheritances of the Roman administrative reorganization under Diocletian and Constantine. The last Roman emperors had spent more time in the east than in the west, realizing that it was much richer, better organized, and easier to govern. The eastern emperors also were abler men than their western counterparts. It is true that there was a lapse in the first half of the fifth century, and many later emperors were brutal, rapacious, incompetent, or a combi-

32

nation of these, but they compare favorably with western political figures of the time.

What the Byzantine government lacked in flexibility, it made up in comparative effectiveness until well into the Middle Ages. The bureaucracy remained totally loyal to the semisacred emperor. The domination of the Byzantine church by the emperor is an aspect of the preservation of the state, for the patriarch of Constantinople had no independent authority. The term "Caesaropapism" is used to designate this close tie, and the emperors took an active interest in theological questions. Few western princes after Charlemagne were able to do this. The Byzantine church was an important buttress of imperial absolutism, while the western church was a thorn in the side of many princes and a drain on the resources of nearly all.

Of perhaps equal importance to these considerations is the fact that Byzantium was almost totally self-sufficient economically. Abundant grain supplies were grown in northern Africa. Although the Vandals and later the Moslems deprived the Byzantines of this area, other sources of grain were available in Asia Minor and Thrace, and more still was imported from the Crimea. The Byzantines controlled ancient sources of luxury commodities, particularly spices, which were in great demand and brought good prices on the export market. The cities were thriving, and trade developed with both east and west, although eastern commerce dominated. The west had little to offer to the Byzantines in the early Middle Ages except timber and some minerals and agricultural products. Byzantine economic prosperity was due less to its export riches than to the fact that little had to be imported. Finally, until the rise of the various Moslem powers, the Byzantines had the only substantial naval force of the known world and monopolized the carrying trade in the Mediterranean and Black seas.

A fundamental strength of the Byzantine empire was that it was rarely overextended. The west was primitive, vast, and hard to govern. The east was originally immense enough. To complicate this, the emperor Justinian (527–65) attempted to reconquer the western empire. Justinian was an anachronism in a sense. He was a Latin emperor in a world which was becoming increasingly Greek. Whether he realized that the ultimate destiny of his empire was in the east is doubtful. He paid tribute to the Persians to keep them from attacking his rear while he pursued his dreams of reconquering the west from the Germans and reuniting the two halves of the empire. Certainly he encoun-

tered little opposition at first in the west. His troops quickly took northern Africa, the southern tip of Spain, and most of Italy. A western
exarchate was established at Ravenna. But these conquests were
ephemeral. As we shall see in chapter 4, the Lombards invaded Italy
and took most of it from the Greeks only three years after Justinian
died. Although the Byzantines held parts of southern Italy until Norman freebooters conquered it in the late eleventh century, they were
fighting a losing battle, for Italy was simply too far away from their
base of power. Their domination over Rome and the pope was important and helped drive the papacy into an almost exclusively western
defensive posture. But aside from this, the Byzantines were confined to
Greece, Asia Minor, and the Balkans after the Arab expansion of
the seventh century. They had some troubles even within this trun-
cated empire, for Slavic peoples were settling increasingly in the Balkans and managing periodic breakaways from imperial authority.

Byzantine government was fairly simple. Justinian's military commanders exercised civil authority and combined several provinces into
exarchates. The entire empire was organized into *themes,* which
amounted to exarchates, in the seventh century. This created very
powerful generals who were able to challenge the emperors. Dynasties
rose and fell rather rapidly from this time. External pressure also contributed to impermanence. The Persians occupied Syria, Palestine,
and Egypt, but were driven back by the emperor Heraclius (610–41).
The fighting weakened both Persia and Byzantium, however, and
there was little resistance to the Arabs in the outlying provinces. Persia
itself fell to the Moslems in 637.

A new dynasty entered the scene in the eighth century. The Isaurian
emperors (717–842) are known chiefly for precipitating the "iconoclastic" controversy. Apparently under the influence of Moslem beliefs,
which prohibited the pictorial representation of human and animal
figures, they ordered pictures and icons of Jesus and other holy persons
removed from the churches. This was absolute anathema to the entire
west and to much of the Byzantine empire as well, and the images
were eventually restored, but not before tremendous civil conflicts and
even worse than ordinary estrangement with western Europe.

The Byzantine Empire reached its height under the Macedonian
dynasty (867–1056). These rulers undertook expansion against the
Moslems in the east and against the Balkan Slavs. The Bulgarians,
who had been a problem for many years, were brought under control,

and Russia came definitely into the sphere of influence of Byzantine church and culture. Arts and letters flourished, both with and without imperial patronage. But there was a marked decline in imperial power after the death of the emperor Basil II in 1025. The empire fell on evil days and was forced to call for help from westerners, as we shall see in a later chapter. The Byzantine government was also having increasing trouble with noble usurpation of imperial authority at this time. While the stronger emperors managed to hold the landholders in check and forced them to perform local duties for the state, their independent pretensions were very burdensome on later rulers.

The final break between eastern and western churches occurred in 1054, when Cardinal Humbert, papal legate to Constantinople, deliberately provoked a quarrel, excommunicated the patriarch, and left the city. Although the disagreement was ostensibly over a minor point of liturgy, it was actually the culmination of centuries of papal power claims and Byzantine resistance of the idea of Rome's total spiritual supremacy. The break was not considered definitive, but it became so after the first Crusade, when the Byzantines were faced with often hostile armies which were allegedly helping them to recover lost territory. The loss of the rest of Byzantine Italy to the Normans at about the same time destroyed any remaining political leverage which the emperors might have had with the papacy, and the union of Christendom came to an end.

The Byzantine Greeks had less influence on the culture and civilization of the medieval west than might be supposed. There was deep suspicion between the rude westerners, with their down-to-earth warrior mentalities, and the subtle, sophisticated Greeks, who regarded the "Franks" at best as buffoons and at worst as sheep for fleecing. There was nonetheless a great deal of contact. We shall note commercial links in another chapter. Byzantium also provided the foundation of the study of law in the Middle Ages. Justinian ordered a codification of the ancient imperial edicts (the Code), a condensation of the legal opinions of the great jurisconsults of the late empire (the Digest), and the Institutes, an abbreviation for use by students. New imperial statutes, the Novels, were issued and codified periodically. Although this *Corpus Juris Civilis* (Body of the Civil Law) did not establish a totally authoritative statement of Roman law, it was a remarkable achievement for its time. The Institutes and an abridgement of some of the Novels were known in the early medieval west, but the sys-

tematic study of Roman law began only when the Digest was redis-
covered at the law schools of Bologna in 1076, with the rest of the
Corpus following soon after.

The Greeks produced little original philosophy. Their art was
unique, but it became quite stylized as time went on. Byzantium
essentially preserved and assimilated the ancient Greek and Roman
texts. Since few persons in the west could read Greek before the thirteenth century, even the little that Byzantine culture had to offer the
west was not accessible.

The Rise of Islam

Perhaps surprisingly, the Arabs had more direct cultural influence
on the west than did the Byzantines. Before the time of Mohammed,
Arabia was in a period of transition between the older nomadic culture
of desert shepherds and an increasing commercial life on the great
caravan routes centering on Mecca. There was a tremendous growth
in trading luxury commodities with both Constantinople and Persia.
This created social dislocation and greater distinctions between rich
and poor. It is significant that Mohammed was a member of a poorer
branch of the Quraish, the oldest clan of Mecca, but married a much
older woman from a wealthy family of the same clan.

Mohammed was born in 570. His early career was uneventful, but
in his middle years he became convinced that he was a divinely inspired prophet. He was noted for visions and "spells," a characteristic
which has caused suspicion that he was epileptic. His revelations were
written down in the Koran, the holy book of the Moslem faith.

Mohammed was unable to gain many followers, and he left Mecca
on July 16, 622 for Medina. This journey, the Hegira, is the beginning
of the Moslem calendar. Mohammed made his living for some years
as a bandit preying on caravans of wealthy Meccans. Finally, his religious ideas gained the support of some of the Meccan upper classes;
this, together with resentment against the older religions, allowed him
to return in triumph to his native city in 630. He died in 632 and
was succeeded by Abu-Bakr, his close friend and the father of his
favorite wife.

Much of the success of the new religion, called Islam (submission
to God), is due to its eclecticism, an absolute necessity in view of
its origin in an area full of centuries-old religions. For example, it

had a place for Christianity. Jesus was regarded as one of the prophets, and Christians thus had a fairly easy time in accepting the new faith. They were not persecuted in Moslem areas until the Turkish conquest much later, and even then the difficulties were sporadic. Christianity in the east was more ritualized and theological than in the west, but it did not have its later rigidity of doctrine, and men changed religions easily. Islam knew a stronger monotheism than trinitarian Christianity—Mohammed was the last and chief of the prophets, not a god—and this simplicity was part of its appeal.

Mohammed's religion was essentially moral. Usury, the lending of money at interest, was strongly condemned, as one would expect from a man of Mohammed's background. The use and abuse of others and their property was forbidden. Islam lacked the subtlety of Christianity, however, for it was a new religion building on an uncertain base, while Christianity was the latest accretion of a long Jewish and more recently Greek tradition. Much of the Moslem message is simplistic. It is very difficult to derive a coherent theology from the Koran, which is arranged neither topically nor chronologically, but according to chapter length. The Moslem had to live as a moral person, give alms to the poor, pray facing Mecca five times daily, and if possible make a journey to Mecca at some time during his life. Such demands were not difficult, and if the devotee performed them he would be assured of a very exotic heaven populated by harem girls to wait upon his every wish.

Religion and Empire

The religious appeal of Islam is easier to understand than the rapid political triumphs of the Arabs. They certainly were moving into a power vacuum left by the conflict of Greek and Persian. Much of Arabia was Moslem before Mohammed died, and the Persian empire, Egypt and northern Africa, Syria, and Palestine had fallen within a decade. Thereafter, there was little lasting territorial expansion. The success was accompanied by a power struggle for the succession of the Prophet. Civil war broke out in 655 between Ali, Mohammed's son-in-law, who claimed that the Prophet's descendants must furnish the Caliph (secular and ecclesiastical head of all Moslems), and the Omayyad clan, a rich merchant family of Mecca. The Omayyads won their battle in 661, but they always were faced with a rearguard action from Ali and his descendants. The Shi'ite heresy, which made this family claim, came to power in Morocco in the late eighth century, in the early ninth in Tunisia, and in the tenth in Egypt.

The Omayyad caliphate was Syrian based and made Damascus its capital. The Moslems had their greatest expansion under the Omayyads, even placing Byzantium under siege in 717–18. They developed strength on the seas and expanded to the west. A Moslem force crossed from Africa to Spain in 711 and made short work of the kingdom which the Germanic Visigoths had maintained there for two centuries. The Christians were driven into the northwestern hills, while the Moslems set up an emirate at Cordova. Despite the general success of their foreign policy, the Omayyad caliphs were overthrown in 750 by the Abassids, a Persian dynasty, under whom the capital was moved to Baghdad. The Moslem caliphs reached the height of their opulence under the Abassids, but there was a certain hardening of the arteries as the expansionary fervor died out. The caliph of Baghdad ruled Iraq and little else by the mid-tenth century, while local dynasties ruled outlying regions of the empire. The Spanish Moslems in particular were quite independent. They did not accept the revolution of 750 and were ruled by an Omayyad emir. Although they accepted the religious supremacy of the Abassids at first while rejecting their political claims, a total breakaway occurred in the tenth century. The caliphate of Cordova lasted until 1031, but thereafter fragmented. By the early eleventh century the Spanish Christian kingdoms of Navarre, Aragon, and Castile had taken the offensive.

The great effect of Islamic civilization on the west was cultural rather than political, and here the results are deceptive. The influence was particularly strong in Spain, where Christian Europeans came to learn not only the works of the Arab thinkers, but also those of the Greeks. Indeed, Moslem influence, as Byzantine, was very largely in transmission of the accomplishments of others. Since they could not portray animal forms, their art was limited to the elaborate designs and geometrical schemes that still characterize Moslem work. The Arabs taught the west the use of the zero, which makes possible systematic and complicated division and multiplication, through the abacus, a device which Gerbert of Aurillac, known in his day as a magician and as Pope Sylvester II (999–1002), may have introduced into northern Europe after his studies in Spain. Moslem medicine was far in advance of western, and unfortunately the occidentals were not ready learners. Most Moslem medical theory was derived from the Greek, and by the ninth century most of the works of Galen and Hippocrates had been rendered into Arabic. Neither Christian nor Arab could dissect bodies, and anatomical knowledge thus was minimal, but the Arabs had some familiarity with pharmaceuticals and used herbs to relieve infections. Very picturesque descriptions by Arab physicians watching French doctors perform during the crusading era show total bewilderment at the primitive westerners, whose medicine scarcely went beyond purging, bleeding, amputating, and urinalysis.

Moslem philosophy was largely derived from Greek, as was that of the west, despite the fact that so few in the early Middle Ages knew the works of Plato and Aristotle. Arabic translations of Greek material, however, were translated into Latin in the twelfth century. This involves a double distortion, of course, since no language can reproduce the nuances of another. The works of Aristotle in particular took on a peculiar cast. The Moslem philosopher Avicenna (d. 1036) modified Aristotle's teaching to include a deity lacking free will and eternally in process of becoming or in motion. Since Aristotle had not known a personal God, this was a logical derivative, but one which was unacceptable to the west. The Arabs furthermore were scientific enough to know the distinction between religious teaching and some realities of the world of matter, and Averroes (1126–98) evidently propounded a doctrine of double truth: the eternally true did not necessarily represent truth on earth. This idea was anathema to thirteenth century Europe, but is quite similar to much western thought of the fourteenth century.

In essence, however, Moslem civilization made less use of the ancient authorities than did the men of the central Middle Ages. The westerners were able to adapt the less theoretical doctrines of the ancients, particularly in law and politics, to the situations of their own day, while the Moslems continued to be imitative. Some Arab thinkers were particularly influential in the revival of significant philosophical speculation in the west, but Islamic civilization as a whole was neither a constant foe nor a serious threat to an expansionist west. The Arabs fought the Crusaders, but this was understandable. The Crusades were totally unrealistic and seem to have been regarded even by many who participated in them as political necessities inspired by mob emotion rather than sound policy. Arab and Christian had a certain meeting of the minds in the medieval west, despite the clashes in Palestine and Spain.

4

GERMANIC EUROPE TO 814

THE FIRST TRACES of the Germanic tribes which were eventually to succeed the Roman Empire are found in Scandinavia around 1000 B.C. The migration was gradual and spasmodic, and only in the last centuries B.C. did the Germans replace the Celts as the dominant ethnic group of northern Europe. They were occupying lands adjacent to the Roman Empire when Julius Caesar began his conquest of Gaul in 58 B.C.

During the centuries after the Roman occupation, Mediterranean influences began to penetrate and "civilize" the Germanic world. Trade was initiated by Roman merchants along the Rhine-Danube line. The Germans began to acquire a veneer of Roman culture and imitated Roman behavior, just as "chic" Romans of the late Empire were to play decadence games by imitating German dress and customs. During the years of quiet on the line, while movement southwest seemed permanently halted, migrations continued within the Germanic world as tribes sought better land or hunting.

The invasions were not monolithic. Numerous tribes appear in Caesar's *Gallic Wars* which were not among those entering the empire in the third century A.D. and after. Confederations were apparently formed and new names assumed easily. There never was a deliberate attempt to overthrow the Roman empire as a political entity. The Germanic wanderings into Gaul in the late Empire were simply the last stage in the gradual migration in search of better conditions which had begun toward 1000 B.C.

The Germans began moving again as early as the 160s, when the

Marcomanni and Quadi invaded northern Italy. They were pushed back, but with some effort. The Germans broke the lines again for two decades during the disastrous third century, a period which saw considerable change in the Germanic world. New tribal groupings were formed which were to last into the fifth century.

The Germanic tribes were always small. Anthropologists have compared the Franks at the time of Clovis (481–511) to the American Indians at the time of Columbus. Their forms of livelihood were so primitive that a high population density could not be sustained. Except in northern Gaul and what is now Germany west of the Rhine, the Germans were always a minority among the populations with whom they settled, a fact which explains the impermanence of many tribal kingdoms.

There was tremendous variation in economic activity, social structure, language, and religion among the tribes. Caesar and the Roman historian Tacitus, who wrote his *Germania* at the end of the first century A.D., have titillated historians' imaginations by their picturesque descriptions of blond beasts living in a primitive democratic society with all rugged virtues. This is romanticism, but the historian can learn much from these writers.

Caesar described migratory tribesmen who were basically herdsmen. Whether the Germans were practicing settled agriculture in the first century B.C. is uncertain, but they definitely were by Tacitus' time. They knew a sort of communal agrarian regime in forest clearings with common use of implements, but they also recognized private property and class distinctions. Although they were familiar with Roman coins, they used them chiefly for decoration and as a sort of wampum, not for exchange as money. Roman merchants handled all trade of the Germans with the outside world. The Germans had basically a subsistence economy based on the land, and this was to continue even after the migrations had ended. While the Germans were later to use Roman towns as fortresses, and some kings may have used them as winter quarters, Germans rarely inhabited towns as traders before the mid-seventh century. They did have some industry, but it was very utilitarian until the seventh century and consisted chiefly of pottery and weapons. Only in the seventh century did the Germans of northern Europe begin to develop artistic skills which they applied to their own tastes—more abstract and linear than the Roman—and even then much of their artisanry simply dealt with

finely ornamented weapons and jewelry. The primitive German loved
the bright and shiny and had little sense of economic value.

The Germans were very superstitious when they entered the empire,
and there is no evidence that they became less so after they adopted
Christianity. Their gods were deities of the forest. Trees were sacred
to many tribes. Frankish burial customs even from the Christian period
show much of the pagan background. The warrior was often buried
in full battle costume, with his weapons and provisions for his future
life. Even among the most orthodox and best educated there was an
almost universal belief in demons, magic, and witchcraft.

Most Germanic tribes had kings by the fifth century, usually chosen
by the great men of the tribe. Some monarchs managed to make the
position hereditary in their families, but elective kingship persisted
and was a fundamental weakness of early medieval monarchy, and
of the German monarchy throughout the Middle Ages. The presence
of a king in no way implies a well-developed concept of the state.
Certainly if the primitive Germans lacked an idea of the state, they
had borrowed one from the Romans by the time their law codes were
compiled in the late fifth, sixth, and seventh centuries, but the concept
was very rudimentary. Although these codes recognize the kindred's
right of vengeance and the fundamental duty of the culprit to pay
compensation to the injured man according to this status and degree
of damage, they did reserve a certain percentage of most fines to the
king, a fact which implies some administrative organization. Different
ethnic groups had their own law. The Visigothic king Alaric II compiled a *Breviary* of Roman law for his subjects in southwestern France
which was to be the major source of Roman legal practice known
in the west before the late 11th century. The Burgundians had two
separate laws, for themselves and for their Roman subjects. Although
the Germans tried to operate what was left of the Roman administrative and judicial system, and particularly the tax structure, they hopelessly lacked the means, and government declined into an essentially
local concern. Kingship and kingdom were regarded less as a state
than as the personal possession of the monarch, at whose death the
normal rules of inheritance would apply, with the sons dividing the
spoils equally.

The Germanic judicial system was a blend of the picturesque and
the picaresque. Local juries were used as fact-swearing boards, but
God was the judge. The *mallus,* the local assembly of the free men

of the tribe, was extremely important in some tribes, and in most
it had a judicial function. Charlemagne established a permanent body
of men who knew the law, the *scabini,* from among the free men
of each locality, but by this time there were fewer free men than
before, and tribes had become so fragmented that the *mallus* was
of little effect in government. There was no distinction between jury
and worldly judge, for the *scabini* were both. There was no concept
of trial before impartial persons who knew nothing of the deeds; these
juries knew either the law or the facts of the situation, and preferably
both. If a defendant admitted his guilt in a criminal case, he paid
the prescribed fine or underwent mutilation. If he maintained his innocence, he submitted to trial by ordeal. There were several forms
of this. A priest might bless a piece of hot iron which the defendant
would then carry for a certain distance. His burns would be certified
and bound by the priest. If his wound seemed to be healing after
a few days, he was judged innocent. Similarly, the priest might bless
a stream into which the defendant was thrown; if he sank, the waters
received him and he was considered innocent, but a guilty man floated.
Some persons, chiefly men of high social status such as priests and
aristocrats, might clear themselves by personal oath of innocence or
by the use of oath-helpers. A certain number of persons would be
required to swear to the innocence of the accused, with the number
varying according to the social status of the oath-helpers and the defendant, and the nature of the crime. Obviously those with extended
kindreds and/or personal retinues could get oath-helpers easily, while
lesser men had more trouble. Although other forms of proof gradually
were introduced as rulers began to suspect that God might need the
help of trustworthy witnesses, the ordeal ended only when the Fourth
Lateran Council forbade the clergy to participate in such proceedings
in 1215. Since supernatural sanction was the basis of the whole system,
the ordeal went out of use as a trial procedure.

Although the Germans had an embryonic idea of the state, their
society was fundamentally based upon a system of private contract
at all levels. Chief among these arrangements was the kindred. In
an age of total breakdown, everyone needed protection, and the kindred could provide at least the safety of numbers. "Kindred" meant
"extended family" and was a much more inclusive term than it is
today. When an individual was injured or killed, his kindred had
the right and duty to obtain compensation from the malefactors ac-

cording to tribal custom. They might choose instead to declare the blood feud and hunt down the culprit and his entire kindred to the death. Much of the effort of Germanic kings to keep order in their realms, insofar as they bothered about such things at all, dealt not with the limitation or abolition of the dominant role of the kindred, which remained a strong bond in criminal justice in German Europe throughout the Middle Ages, but rather with an attempt to force the injured party and/or his kindred to accept customary compensation if offered by the other side. The Germanic law codes show us not a bucolic paradise of primitive democracy, but a jungle in which there was a price on every man's head, varying with his social status. This meant essentially that a powerful man might murder whomever he pleased if he paid the man's *wergeld* (worth money), but the less powerful would think twice about the effects on their resources of the murder of a powerful man with a powerful kindred. Except among the most mighty, the kindred was only partially successful in giving protection. Hence, particularly as the tribes settled down, the band of retainers, bound by loyalty to a lord rather than by the blood tie, began to take the place of the kindred, but never did so totally. Loyalty to someone more powerful than oneself and one's kindred could provide the two essentials of the medieval existence—protection and livelihood.

Hence the war band surrounding the great men of the tribes was a fundamental social unit. The warriors were sworn to follow the lord to the death. The highest social status was reserved for the warrior who distinguished himself by service to a greater man than himself, one who could bestow lands, offices, and social distinction. A sort of prestige hierarchy developed among war bands, with the royal *comitatus* (following) at the top. But these groups fluctuated. Faithful service was rewarded by the major source of wealth of the lord—land—and when a warrior received lands he became less mobile and willing to follow his lord about at all times. Accordingly, the place of some warriors was taken by persons who could still gain by association with the king, while the older group of warriors could gain more by opposition to the king than by service to him. Service to a greater man hence did not in itself make a man without other distinction into an aristocrat, but it was a means of amassing property and dependents of his own, the signs of a life style of a great person.

Below the war bands in prestige were persons who worked the land.

The free peasant was also a warrior during the campaigning season; but since the campaigning season and the growing season were the same, military service was a burden. This group accordingly tended to sink into serfdom, giving up their freedom to persons who would protect them and do military service on their behalf. Particularly in England and Germany, however, some free peasants persisted. We shall discuss the peasant classes, free and unfree, at greater length in a subsequent chapter. The tone of Germanic society was given by warfare, within and between tribes, and the warriors hence dominated. Germanic society was highly stratified, with numerous technical gradations given in the law codes even within the general groups of free and unfree, but despite this fact it was easier to move from one class to another on the basis of strength, intelligence, or increased wealth than it became later. The blood tie was all-important with the Germans, as with all primitive peoples, but it did not necessarily affect the social status of descendants.

The Ultimate Migration

The first Germanic tribes to invade the Roman empire in force did not establish lasting political units. The most important were the Goths, who had settled around the Black Sea in the third century in two main groups, the Visigoths (Goths of the Forest) and Ostrogoths (Goths of the Beaches). They became Roman federates in 332, and during that brief alliance they were converted to Arian Christianity. The Visigoths were defeated in battle by the Huns in 375 and were forced to seek asylum within the Empire, while the Ostrogoths remained behind under a Hunnish protectorate. The Visigoths then fell out with the Romans over the exploitation of refugees. The result was the battle of Adrianople in 378, at which the Roman legions were overwhelmed and the emperor Valens was killed. The Visigoths lacked the means to conquer the Roman Empire even had they desired to do so; they simply became federates again. Then, for reasons which are uncertain, they undertook a mass migration to Italy in 401, a movement which caused tremendous economic dislocation in the Balkans and northern Italy. They sacked Rome in 410, swung back to the north, and finally settled in southern France. They again became Roman allies and established a kingdom, which reached its height under Euric, their greatest ruler. His son, Alaric II, is known chiefly for two accomplishments: ordering the compilation of the *Breviary* of "Roman law of the Visigoths" and being killed in battle in 507 by Clovis the Frank. Thereafter the Visigoths, who had been simply a warrior elite, moved part and parcel to Spain. Here they avoided their mistake in Gaul and made a thorough settlement of the land. The Visigoths formed a Spanish national monarchy until the Moslems conquered them in 711.

The Ostrogoths were more important for a time than their kinsmen, but it was a transitory significance. Pushed eventually into the eastern Empire by the Huns, they became imperial federates in 461. The presence of large numbers of Germans was a bother, and eventually the emperor Zeno sent them to the west, supposedly to recapture Italy from the Germanic bands that had deposed the emperor Romulus Augustulus in 476. The Ostrogothic king Theodoric had been raised in Constantinople and was perhaps the most highly "civilized" of the barbarian monarchs. He promptly subdued Italy, assassinated the previous barbarian king of Italy at a friendship banquet, and established an independent kingdom under only the nominal hegemony of Zeno. He continued old Roman forms and respected most prerogatives of Senate and emperor, although he behaved as an independent ruler. Despite German resistance, he worked for a merging of Roman and Ostrogoth before the law. He also tried to work out an accommodation between the Arian Ostrogoths and the orthodox Romans. His attitude changed, however, later in his reign when the Franks were converted to orthodox Christianity and a union with his Catholic subjects seemed a real or potential threat; but despite some strains, there was no persecution. His kingdom disintegrated after he died in 526. His successors were unable to resist the invasion from Byzantium undertaken by Justinian. Within a decade the Greeks controlled most of Italy, but they soon lost hegemony in all except southern Italy to the Lombards, who invaded the peninsula in 568.

The Lombards were the last and perhaps most destructive of the Germanic invaders except the Vandals. Entering an Italy torn by the struggles of Byzantine and Ostrogoth, they caused complete disarray in the last quarter of the sixth century. Roman institutions died out. The Lombards were still pastoral, spending most of their time hunting and raising pigs. They took over most of the land from what remained of the Roman aristocracy and gave inferior status to the Romans. The Lombards only began really to settle down toward the end of

Map 1. Germanic Europe and the Empire of Charlemagne

the sixth century. Roman influence was probably greater in medieval Italy than in any other region of western Europe, but it was due less to a direct survival than to a recovery of some aspects of Roman life in the seventh and eighth centuries.

Other tribes seemed similarly unpromising. Roman defenses in the north collapsed in the first decade of the fifth century. Britain was abandoned and the troops were withdrawn from the Rhine-Danube line, but the peoples of this breakthrough never had the importance of the Goths or of the tribes which were to come later. Some were spectacular. The Suevi eventually went to Spain, but were driven into the mountains by the Visigoths. The Vandals invaded Spain in 409, plundered it, then sailed for Africa in 429, where they established a brutal, despoiling regime by 442. Most barbarian chieftains took part of the land of the Romans for their men, but since so much had fallen vacant this was generally no great burden by the sixth century. In addition, however, percentages of the yield of the land, often transposed to mean percentages of the land itself, had been given by the Roman government as "hospitality" to German troops quartered on the estates of Roman citizens. The Vandals carried this to its logical conclusion and lived exclusively by plunder until the death of their chief Gaiseric in 477. Their activities included a sack of Rome in 455 which was more disastrous than the earlier seizure by the Visigoths. The Vandals established no strong roots in Africa and were easily swept away by the Byzantines in the 530s. The Burgundians also were among the tribes which broke the line in the early fifth century, establishing their kingdom first at Worms and later at Lyon in southeastern France. Although they mixed with the Romans and tried as the Ostrogoths had done to establish a binational state, they were a small tribe and their "state" was conquered by the Franks in the sixth century.

The Franks

The earliest Frankish penetration of the Roman Empire was by the unspectacular means of gradual settlement of the land of northernmost Europe. As the Romans abandoned their northern defensive line in the late third century, the Franks settled in the Low Countries. Many became Roman *laeti* (see above, p. 10), and Frankish groups also were federates of the Romans and kept their agreements until the fifth century. The Franks were the only Germanic tribe that made a permanent occupation of the land and caused alteration of the continental linguistic frontier. Although Romance-speaking peoples pushed the frontier back slightly north and east later in the Middle Ages, the modern border between Romance and Germanic tongues is quite close to the frontier of Germanic settlement in the early Middle Ages. By the time the Frankish kings had followed Frankish farmers, they had a substantial population base within the Empire. The Franks could lose battles, but they could not be dislodged from their settlements.

The great Frankish expansion came under Clovis (481–511), who began with a power base around Tournai, then extended his authority by force and duplicity over other groups of Franks. He then moved against other tribes, often on the pretext of their Arianism and his orthodoxy. Certainly Clovis' conversion to orthodox Christianity midway through his reign gave him a rapport with his Gallo-Roman subjects. The *History of the Franks* of Bishop Gregory of Tours, an educated Gallo-Roman aristocrat, shows that Clovis was a totally unregenerate savage, but he was Gregory's hero because of his godliness in furthering the church.

Clovis' kingdom was divided among his four sons, according to Germanic custom, when he died. They expanded Frankish domination south and east. Burgundy fell in 534 and became one of the subkingdoms of the Frankish realm. Between assassinations of one another and of nephews, the descendants of Clovis spent much time in fruitless campaigning in the wake of the fall of Ostrogothic Italy. The Franks even moved into Thuringia, in central Germany, but never held it solidly until the eighth century.

The Frankish realm was reunited briefly by Clothar, last surviving son of Clovis, between 557 and 561, but the kingdom was divided among his sons when he died. This division generally persisted: Austrasia, the most Germanicized of the three, consisted of western Germany, the Moselle area, the southern Low Countries, and France as far south as the Somme. Neustria, the heartland of Clovis' kingdom, took in most of central and southwestern France, while Burgundy was the old kingdom of that name in the southeast. A half century of civil war followed. Although the realm again was united in 614, the kings were controlled by the nobles, particularly those of Austrasia. The *comitatus* was becoming a territorial aristocracy. As the price of recognition as king in 614, Clothar II agreed that all royal officials should be great landholders in the territory in which they held their offices. In short, he sanctioned the growth of noble principalities at the expense of the monarchy. From this point little could be done. Although some later Merovingian kings (the dynasty was named after the half-mythical ancestor Merovech) displayed independence and initiative, the last such ruler was murdered in 675, and thereafter there was a change of dynasty in all but name. When Pope Zacharias sanctioned a new royal house in 751, to be called "Carolingian" after Charlemagne (*Carolus Magnus*) by historians, he did it on grounds that those who held power in fact should also hold it in name.

The Merovingian monarchy hence was a dismal failure. Yet to the modern mind it seemed to have much in its favor. The kings got a large share of the land which was conquered, although Germanic tradition demanded that much of the spoils of battle also go to the warriors. The practice of division among rulers was not important, for no Merovingian could have ruled the entire kingdom without a good system of communications or administration. The personal excesses of the kings are no explanation, for they were no worse than the princes who were controlling them.

The explanation for the Merovingian failure is a combination of piety and largesse. The Merovingians endowed churches and particularly monasteries very heavily. They had to buy the loyalty of their retainers with land. Once given, this land could be recovered only with difficulty, although much of it was given in technically revocable or non-hereditary tenure. A good master has to distinguish himself by generosity in all primitive societies. The lord must give even more than required by custom. The Merovingians thus used up their capital in gold and silver, and particularly land, by the early seventh century. They had nothing more to give out, and political emphasis shifts to the alliances among the territorial princes and how certain of them became powerful through conquest and the use of the fruits of conquest to obtain loyal followers. The king kept a certain prestige, but he had little material power. As the nobles ruled the realm, so the most important of them were those who dominated the king, in particular the so-called mayors of the palace, who were general masters of the royal household. They could use royal resources, in addition to their own, to buy retainers. The most important and powerful were the Arnulfings, the Austrasian mayors of the palace and leaders of the Austrasian aristocracy. Pepin of Heristal defeated the Neustrian mayor of the palace in battle in 687 and in fact reunited the Frankish kingdom. A new period of expansion began, particularly in south-western France, the area farthest from the center of royal power. As he reconquered land from persons who had been disloyal to the king, the mayor of the palace developed tremendous personal authority.

The successful prince of the early Middle Ages ruled from the saddle. Charlemagne was great not only because of his force of personality, but because he campaigned constantly. He made almost annual campaigns to conquer new territories or to bring disloyal subjects into line or confiscate their property and give it to another favorite. Following the campaigns of his ancestors in the southwest, Charlemagne expanded into Germany and northern Italy. The extensive military activity increased the need for soldiers and burdened the free peasant who had to fight. It also created new lands to be granted to the soldier-aristocrats. After Charlemagne, the conquests stopped and campaigning slowed down, but the great men still had to be bought. Eventually the Carolingians, just as the Merovingians before them, used up their landed capital. When this happened, a long period of weakness followed, and finally another change of dynasty.

Early England

The Romans left less trace of their occupation in Britain than on the continent. Their civilization had been merely a merchant and military aristocracy, and the administrative structure collapsed when the legions left in the early fifth century. Scarcely any written material has survived from Britain for the next two centuries, and the historian is forced to use the evidence of place names and archaeology. The continental origin of the tribes which conquered Britain is uncertain. The Angles evidently came chiefly from Frisia, in northernmost Germany and the Netherlands, although some may have lived elsewhere; certainly the local institutions of Frisia and East Anglia show a striking similarity. The Saxons came from northern Germany. Although there are distinctions between their artifacts and those of the Angles, the two groups became almost merged in the minds of contemporaries. The Jutes are hardest to explain, for there is no evidence that they came from Jutland. Settling chiefly in Kent, they established institutions which suggest that they may have been Franks.

The Germanic conquest of Britain from the Celts was slow and gradual and involved a thorough occupation of the land, although the Celts were not exterminated completely, as once was thought. The fact that Wales and southwestern England remained Celtic is due less to Celtic flight than to the fact that large numbers of Germans did not get that far west. They did, however, enslave the Celts when they took over their lands. The Germanic settlement was chiefly along major river valleys, the most fertile and accessible lands.

Whatever their institutions may have been when they migrated, the Germans of Britain soon developed kingships. There were seven kingdoms—Sussex, Essex, Wessex, Mercia, Northumbria, East Anglia, and Kent—and numerous subordinate jurisdictions. One of the seven kings was usually considered to be *bretwalda* (ruler of Britain), with a loose suzerainty over the others. The earliest *bretwalda* was King Ethelbert of Kent in the early seventh century. Predominance passed to Northumbria in the late seventh century and early eighth, to Mercia in the late eighth century, and finally to the kings of Wessex. King Alfred the Great of Wessex (871–99) and his successors founded the English national monarchy during the Viking invasions of the ninth and tenth centuries. There was nothing particularly remarkable about the institutions of these kingdoms, but they were in regular commercial contact with the continent by the eighth century at the latest, and probably before.

Intellectual Life

German literary endeavor was miniscule. Most works of Frankish Gaul and Visigothic Spain were written by such Gallo-Romans as Gregory of Tours, whose *History of the Franks* gives a mine of information to the historian about barbarian morals and mores. But a native Germanic intellectual life is readily discernible in the seventh and eighth centuries, and the monastic side of this revival was to have a significant effect on Frankish royal policy.

The intellectual leaders of early medieval Europe were the Irish, then later the English. Ireland had never been Romanized, but had evidently been Christianized by missionaries from the continent, particularly St. Patrick in the mid-fifth century. Irish Christianity had peculiarities of usage which had to be reconciled with the Roman, particularly in the intensely personal and mystical nature of Irish monasticism, its loose organization, and the Irish date of celebrating Easter. The synod of Whitby settled these differences in favor of the Roman custom in 664, and from this time Irish intellectual life began to decline in favor of the English. The Irish had amassed the greatest libraries of the day, and only in Ireland and Italy was Greek known in the early medieval west.

Irish monks crossed to the island of Iona in 565 under St. Columba and began to convert the English. England thus was converted from two directions, as later missionaries came from Rome in the time of Gregory the Great and through the seventh century. Although English culture borrowed much from the Irish, particularly in art work, the great expansion of Anglo-Saxon culture came from the continental influence of Theodore of Tarsus, sent by the pope as Archbishop of Canterbury after the synod of Whitby. He established several monasteries and schools and strengthened ecclesiastical organization. The abbey of Jarrow was founded in Yorkshire later in the seventh century. Bede (d. 735), the greatest of Anglo-Saxon scholars, was a product of Jarrow and spent his life there.

Bede was a theologian, although in keeping with the tenor of his age he was uninterested in philosophical speculation. Building upon a suggestion of Isidore of Seville, he popularized the system of chronology from the incarnation of Jesus. He composed several scriptural commentaries, but his greatest work was his *Ecclesiastical History of the English People*. The basic thesis of this work is the decisive role of the Roman church in the foundation of English civilization, but it has great historical value in spite of its apologetical nature. Bede repeated miracle tales, but he had a sense of criticism and was careful of his sources. He even sent a messenger to search the papal archives for the letters of Gregory the Great regarding England. Astonishingly, perhaps the most learned man of his age never left his Northumbrian monastery.

Irish and later English missionary work was to have strong influences on the continent. A body of Irish monks led by Columban went to Burgundy around 590 and founded several abbeys. They continued Irish observances, and this, combined with their severe asceticism and condemnation of the barbarism of the Frankish court, led to their expulsion. Columban moved to northern Italy and founded the abbey

of Bobbio in 614. This monastery kept close contact with the Irish
foundations of the north and was instrumental in Christianizing the
Lombards.

The English began to evangelize from the mid-seventh century,
particularly among their Frisian kinsmen in North Holland. These
monks maintained close ties with Rome, and a new see of Utrecht
was established in 695 under the English St. Willibrord. But the most
eminent English missionary on the continent was Wynfrith, known
to history as St. Boniface. He spent his first forty years as a monk
in Wessex, but went to Frisia in 716. He left quickly, having no taste
for the barbarous Frisians, but after a trip to Rome in 718 he was
empowered by the pope to do missionary work among the heathen
in Germany. He spent the rest of his life proselytizing in central Germany and organizing the church there. He was responsible for the
creation of several bishoprics and himself became archbishop. He built
a coherent ecclesiastical organization under the direct authority of
Rome. Indeed, although the Frankish mayor of the palace, Charles
Martel, had furthered Boniface's work and placed him under royal
protection as early as 723, the Frankish church still had no strong
tie with Rome. But Boniface's work increased after Charles' death
in 741, when his son Carloman began taking more interest in the
moral reform of the Frankish clergy. Boniface himself returned to
his original scene of embarrassment, Frisia, where he was martyred
in 754. Through his work the ecclesiastical organization of the lands
east of the Rhine had been brought close to that of the Franks. As
agrarian settlement had preceded the Merovingian kings into northern
France, so religious conversion preceded the Carolingian kings into
Germany. The entire nature of church-state relations began to change.

Charlemagne

Charles Martel created the position of power from which Charlemagne eventually was to rule. Although his defeat of a Moslem raiding
force at Poitiers in 732 in no sense saved western Europe for Christianity, his frequent campaigns against Moslem raiders in southern
France did aid his prestige and helped increase his private domains.
His authority was divided between his sons, Pepin and Carloman,
when he died in 741, but Carloman retired to a monastery in 747
and left his brother sole ruler.

The pope meanwhile was having problems in Italy. Although the Lombards had been Christianized, they continued to move south into lands which the pope wished to dominate. The Byzantine emperor, the nominal overlord of Rome, was of little help, and in addition had pretensions of domination over the church which the pope found burdensome. Accordingly, the pope appealed to Pepin for help against the Lombards, and as quid pro quo crowned him king of the Franks in 751. Pepin kept his part of the bargain and limited Lombard aggression against the papacy. He confirmed secular lordship of central Italy to the papacy in the so-called "Donation of Pepin."

But the pope had merely exchanged one ruler for another, although he continued to try to play off the new Frankish royal house against the Byzantine emperors. Pepin himself was evidently nearing a reconciliation with the Lombards after years of fighting in Italy when he died in 768, leaving two sons.

The two brothers were about to fight for sole domination—a thread that runs through European royal history until primogeniture became normal in the eleventh and twelfth centuries—when the younger died in 771. His brother, known as Charles the Great, or Charlemagne, created an empire.

Charlemagne tried to consolidate the work of his father and grandfather in southwestern France, but his success was minimal. Aquitaine remained virtually ungovernable throughout the Middle Ages. An area of mountains and uneven topography, it was well suited to the petty baron who placed his castle on a hilltop and defied the world. Charlemagne generally left his eldest son in Aquitaine as viceroy in the last years of his reign and busied himself elsewhere.

Most of Charlemagne's important work was done in Germany. He subdued Saxony, perhaps the least civilized part of Germany, and Christianized it at sword's point. After the Saxons revolted against his domination in 782, he returned and perpetrated fearful slaughter, supposedly massacring 4500 men. He forced the duke of the Bavarians to become his vassal. His Italian policy followed the same lines. The Lombards again were threatening the pope, and Charlemagne disliked his Lombard queen. For these reasons, evidently equally important to Charlemagne, he entered Italy when the Lombards threatened to move south, and assumed the "Iron Crown of Lombardy" himself in 774. He confirmed the Donation of Pepin, but soon was limiting the pope's freedom of action, for he regarded himself as God's vicar upon earth and the pope merely as his chief priest, whose job was to pray for the success of the emperor's Christianizing ventures. Accordingly, in the 780s one of the most famous forgeries of the Middle Ages was done in the papal entourage. According to this "Donation of Constantine," the emperor had given Pope Sylvester I temporal dominion not only in the "papal states" of Italy, but in the entire western world, while the emperor was to rule in the east. This forgery was to be a basic authority used by the popes in their battles with kings and emperors.

Charlemagne interfered readily in church affairs, particularly as he became old and concerned with his place in the next world. He was a concrete realist, in keeping with the temper of his age. Although he held some opinions which later would be declared heretical, Charlemagne supported a totally orthodox position involving the veneration of the images of holy persons, but not their worship. In this, he seems to have been somewhat ahead of Pope Hadrian I (772–95), who took an extreme position in favor of the worship of images. Charlemagne, however, regarded himself as the final arbiter of doctrine.

Charlemagne's ecclesiastical policy led to his coronation as emperor of the Romans by the pope on Christmas Day, 800. Lengthy controversy has raged over whether he expected to be crowned or was surprised by the pope. Charlemagne was in Italy at the time to rescue the pope from his political opponents. In view of this, it seems unlikely, although possible, that Pope Leo III would have perpetrated such a coup. The affair had some unpleasant implications. At the time of the coronation Charlemagne was negotiating with the Byzantines for a diplomatic marriage to the empress Irene, and the Byzantines could hardly have cared for the elevation of a new western emperor in defiance of their universal claims. Coronation by the pope left the implication to this symbol-conscious age that the pope could take it away and that the emperor owed his power to the pope. Charlemagne evidently saw it that way and never returned to Italy. He made several divisions of his empire among his sons in his last years; only one was to survive the father's death in 814, and Charlemagne crowned him with his own hands at Aachen, his favorite hunting lodge. The son, Louis, later accepted coronation in Rome by the pope, thus setting a precedent which was considered binding on later emperors.

In contrast to many of his successors, Charlemagne never lost sight of the fact that his real power came not from his position as emperor, but from the kingship of the Franks and the tribes they conquered. His conquests took in everything which the Romans had held in western Europe except Spain, Britain, and southern Italy, and he penetrated much farther into Germany than they and set up an administration.

But how did he administer this enormous empire? His realm was held together by the force of his personality and by the fact that he had plenty of land with which to buy the loyalty of his great men. Such conditions could not continue in an age in which there were no new worlds to conquer, when monarchs were lesser men, and when Europe was suffering from new invasions that the kings were unable to prevent.

We have noted Charlemagne's innovation in establishing a permanent board of assessors at the county courts. He limited the sessions of the courts to three general trial days a year. This form of judicial organization was preserved in some areas, with modifications, into the modern period. He also formalized the idea of the "jury of present-ment" or grand jury, a body which testified from supposed knowledge of the facts. Charlemagne did not originate county subdivisions in Europe, but he did unify his administration on the basis of a more regular county organization. His counts were the most important men of their localities, and they were often the focal point around which new territorial principalities developed as Charlemagne's empire frag-mented. The duchy was a larger unit than the county, often on the frontiers of the empire.

The Carolingian empire had perhaps 250 to 300 counties. The king urged the counts and dukes to keep notaries and clerks on hand, but it is very doubtful that in vicariates and hundreds, local subdivi-sions of the county, literate personnel were available. Indeed, the fact that the king repeated his injunctions so often shows that there was lack of compliance, probably more from lack of personnel than inclina-tion. Even if each county court had a person who could read and write, there may have been as many as 2000 to 3000 persons in the entire bureaucracy of the vast empire, including the counts and dukes and their entourages, the local courts, and the royal palace court, and few of these were literate. Communications were poor enough, with roads bad and dangerous. The king's orders to local populations had to be promulgated orally, for use of the written instrument might stop with the count's secretary. The student can easily comprehend this chaotic situation if he tries to imagine a city government today, let alone a national or regional government, trying to rule on the basis of oral orders, but in the absence of radio, television, telephone, and other forms of modern mass communication.

Hence Charlemagne's empire was doomed to destruction. Characteristically, he ordered all free men of the realm to swear oaths to him as king and supreme ruler several times during the first quarter-century of his reign, but in 802 he changed this to an oath in which all free men would act toward the king as a good vassal should toward his overlord. The most significant governmental innovation of the Carolingian period, the growth of feudal relationships, which fragmented the empire but may have preserved some measure of local order, will be discussed in another chapter.

Intellectual Life

Charlemagne demonstrated some interest in the life of the mind. He ordered churches to maintain schools to educate the local populations. He maintained a school in his own palace and took some interest in the curriculum. But this was not a thorough educational reform. The palace school was for the sons of nobles, while the local schools were designed expressly to educate clergy to the point where they could perform the divine services correctly. This meant some reading and writing and study of the classics, but little else. Charlemagne's intellectual interests, as his political and ecclesiastical policies, show him to have been simply a barbarian tribesman of foresight and exceptionally strong personality. He maintained himself by force, not by his changes in the institutional structure or the foundation of anything which could be permanent. His biographer, Einhard, has left an interesting portrayal of Charles the man and of the palace school. Charlemagne could read but not write. His court "intellectuals," notably the Englishman Alcuin, and he adopted pet names for one another from the Bible or the classics. There was no philosophical or theological speculation worthy of the name at Charlemagne's court, although the king presided over a synod in 794 which declared Adoptionism (the belief that God the Father had adopted Jesus as his son) a heresy.

The achievement of the Carolingian intellectuals took more mundane forms. We have noted Alcuin's definitive edition of the Vulgate Bible. Monastic writing offices were very active during this period.

Most texts of ancient authors known in the early Middle Ages come to us in Carolingian copies. The "Carolingian Renaissance" also saw the creation of an easily legible handwriting, Caroline minuscule, which replaced the various provincial Merovingian scrawls. Although Carolingian script remained standard in western Europe until the spread of Gothic in the late twelfth and thirteenth centuries, a more angular version of Caroline was used by the men of the Italian Renaissance and is the direct ancestor of the modern printed page. But the literary aspect of the Carolingian Renaissance is known chiefly for its lack of originality, its all-encompassing reverence for the past, and its desire to reproduce past work and style as literally as possible.

The age of political breakdown and economic dislocation that followed Charlemagne's death witnessed greater intellectual endeavors. While Charles' educational activity had centered on the bishoprics, the most significant effort after his death was again in the monasteries. Stimulated in part by Charlemagne's interest in theological questions and the iconoclastic controversy, patristic studies and theology were reviving by the mid-ninth century. The scholars at the court of Charles the Bald (840–77), grandson of Charlemagne, were proficient and prolific. The monks Radbertus and Ratramnus argued there over the nature of the Eucharist; Ratramnus held that the bread and wine were only symbols, and his view was condemned. The Anglo-Saxon monk Gottschalk carried St. Augustine's views on predestination to a length otherwise unheard of before John Calvin, claiming that all were predestined to salvation or damnation from the beginning of time.

The most original thinker of the early Middle Ages, the Irishman John Scotus Erigena, lived at the court of Charles the Bald. Indeed, he was so original that no one understood his work, and only much later was it realized that his writings were heretical. He propounded a mystical, neoplatonic theology with strong overtones of pantheism.

Some decent historical writing was done. Einhard's biography of Charlemagne is of great historical value, despite the fact that some descriptive passages of it are taken verbatim from Suetonius' life of Augustus Caesar. The *Annales Regni Francorum* (Annals of the Realm of the Franks), apparently a semi-official compilation, date from the early Carolingian age. But history was transcending annals, works arranged by year rather than topic. The best work of the period was the *History of the Sons of Louis the Pious* by Nithard, Charlemagne's grandson, in which the political developments of the mid-ninth century are detailed.

The Carolingian achievement was tremendous. From a semi-nomadic group of barbarians who settled in Gaul in the late fifth century, the Franks had developed considerable accoutrements of civilization and culture by the early ninth. We must not make the mistake, however, of downgrading this very real achievement by suggesting that for a brief moment government was regularized and centralized and literature and learning suddenly took on great new horizons.

5

THE GROWTH OF FEUDAL
RELATIONSHIPS

Feudal relationships and ties of servile peasant dependence evolved from a common root: the desire of nearly everyone to obtain the protection of a person more powerful than himself in the violent Germanic society of the early Middle Ages. The Romans knew a similar relationship called clientage, but this tended to develop into servile dependence in the Middle Ages. The Germanic war band was much more important in the development of feudal vassalage.

Most important warriors had their entourages, not only for protection but for the prestige which such large groups of followers gave to the primitive chieftain. The members of these groups had various designations, such as "the faithful" and "the king's boys." The lord's prestige and one's own position within the band determined social station, and a hierarchical aristocracy of service thus was formed. Although kinship ties were important, the Germans did not have a juridical class of nobles bound by the blood relationship. The warriors might notice an ordinary fighting man who performed good service and make him a trusted advisor. The entire system was very loose.

Social status could be elevated particularly through service to the king, the greatest man of the tribe. The concept of ennoblement through service spread more rapidly among tribes which had contact with the Romans than among those remaining in Germany. The development of the word "vassal" shows this clearly. The term originally meant a servile person who performed personal services, often, but

61

not always, military. Although it kept its servile connotation for centuries in Germany, it came to mean exclusively a military retainer in France by the Carolingian period. The west had inherited from the Romans ideas of service to the state by all persons, whether servile or free, and joined this with the Germanic custom of dependence by free and unfree upon persons of more elevated social status. Accordingly, there was less reluctance in the west even among the great to become vassals of other persons. Germany remained true to the primitive concept of lordship, the relationship of one free man to another without the servile hint of vassalage, and Charlemagne had some trouble in forcing German princes to become his vassals.

Hence the vassal was a person quite similar in the beginning to the later *ministerialis,* a man of low social standing who sought to elevate it through service to the powerful. Accordingly, there was little distinction between the lower levels of Merovingian vassalage and the upper reaches of the peasantry. Both had "commended" themselves to someone more powerful and hence with a higher social rank. Commendation is the simplest form of entering a binding tie of loyalty to another and becoming his "man." As persons who were vassals became wealthy and powerful in their own right, vassalage spread as a concept to the point where an aristocrat might become a vassal without demeaning himself. The distinction between free and servile commendation in the beginning was in the nature of obligations incurred by the contracting parties. The Merovingian vassal incurred chiefly military duties. He would fight for his lord whenever summoned, while the peasant did farm work in return for protection. The distinction is also between honorable and dishonorable services: fighting was honorable to the primitive German, but plowing was not. This is the essential point of differentiation between feudalism and seigneurialism or manorialism. As the Germans settled down and social groupings became more fixed, the distinction generally included rank. Free men became vassals, "free men in relationships of dependence" in the language of contemporary documents, while others, perhaps also free in the beginning, lost the practical expression of their freedom. In the early Merovingian period, however, ability and personal or military prowess determined how far one might rise.

The lord's obligation was to protect his vassal or his peasant. This was the extent of his responsibility to his free and unfree dependents alike in the Merovingian age. Later he assumed more positive obligations toward his vassals, although not toward his peasants. He agreed not to harm his vassal's property or dignity in any way and to provide him with sufficient means of performing his military duty. This was no great problem, and in the Merovingian period most war bands lived in a bunkhouse in the lord's household and were provided with food, drink, and arms. The arrangement was simple, for most fighting was done on foot (although cavalry was known), and armament was simple. The household knight or vassal continued to exist much later in the Middle Ages than is ordinarily thought; he was not in a feudal relationship with his lord, however, for this requires the juridical union of vassalage with the holding of a fief or benefice.

Such direct maintenance was clumsy, however, and it became harder to keep up as money passed out of circulation. Furthermore, since social respectability came from obtaining a piece of land and surrounding oneself with one's own retainers, the vassals wanted land. Chieftains had to buy loyalty on their retainers' terms; just as they gave land to the church to insure their souls' salvation, they gave land to their followers to insure loyalty. Land gave independent power to the retainers, for they could use it as they wished. As one group of retainers got land, the king sought new warriors from the lower classes, and they in their turn would become a new aristocracy of service and subsequently obtain land. Under strong kings the landed retainers would appear with their own followers at the March (later May) Field for the year's campaign, but they ignored this duty when the king was weak. The very clumsiness of the land benefice weighted the arrangement in the vassal's favor. Theoretically it was given for a lifetime or term of years. It was not hereditary and could be recovered by the lord when the vassal failed to perform his obligation or harmed the lord's interest in any way. But it was easier to pronounce a vassal contumacious than to take his land away from him, and the tendency for benefices to become hereditary was especially clear under weak monarchs.

A complicated ceremonial concerning feudal ties had been developed by the Carolingian age which was to characterize feudal relationships for the rest of the medieval period. Homage was an elaborate form of free commendation. The vassal placed his hands between the lord's and promised loyalty and fidelity. His lord in turn promised to protect his vassal. The vassal strengthened his bond with an oath of fealty to the lord, who then invested him with the benefice (later called fief) by placing a rod or similar symbol in his hand. Other ceremonials were added later, but this remained the basic procedure.

Hence the fief, lordship, and vassalage were known by the late Merovingian period. Some scholars have maintained that vassalage and fiefholding were normally united juridically in the Carolingian period but only exceptionally under the Merovingians, and accordingly that the Merovingian period was not "feudal." This is a needless quibble over technicalities. The word "feudal" is an invention of the seventeenth century. It had no meaning in the Middle Ages, although certain forms of tenure and obligation were designated by terms which may be translated "feudal." But the "system" was very fluid in the Merovingian and Carolingian ages and indeed was never rigid. There is simply no statistical information from this period which can show the date at which a situation ceased to be exceptional and became normal.

Many have seen changes in military technology and tactics affecting governmental relationships in the eighth century. The Franks allegedly were forced to change their military tactics from infantry to cavalry to fight the mounted Moslem invaders. This necessitated the breeding of larger war horses which could carry heavy armament. The process was facilitated by the introduction of the stirrup from the east, a device which allowed a rider to sit more easily in the saddle and throw a spear. This theory has been thoroughly discredited. The Franks often fought on horseback before the eighth century and on foot thereafter, and the stirrup, while known, was not part of the equipment of most Frankish warriors. Chain mail furthermore was no monopoly of the horseman, for the foot soldier also needed such protection.

This hypothesis also argues that the decline of the Germanic free peasant into serfdom was due largely to the higher costs of soldiering. The peasants could not afford horses and chain mail and hence lost their importance to the state. It is true that military service was becoming increasingly burdensome. Charlemagne decreed that each group of 12 manses (farms which could support one peasant household) should furnish one fully armed horseman for the royal host; this meant that mounted military service was exacted only from the great landholders and large groups of free peasants. Each group of 4 manses furnished a foot soldier. More peasants were free in Germany and England, where infantry remained in vogue longer, than in France. But an absolute correlation cannot be made. Frankish armies never were large enough to take in the entire free population, and the fact that they were becoming more exclusive cannot have affected many persons.

However misleading rigid hypotheses may be, however, we must note a tendency in the Carolingian period for cavalry to spread at the expense of infantry and for peasants to sink into serfdom, although for essentially nonmilitary reasons. The formal development of feudalism dates basically from the ninth century, but usage was becoming regularized under Charlemagne. We have noted his ultimate command that his subjects behave toward him as toward their overlords. This change away from a state-subject concept is very significant. Charlemagne realized that his realm was ungovernable. Accordingly, he forced his counts and dukes, who held their offices from him as head of the state, to reinforce their obedience to him with an act of homage, tying themselves to him as vassals to lord. The personal relationship was much more real to the Germans than the more abstract tie of subject to state. The king urged his officials also to create a series of descending relationships by receiving the homage of the leading men of their localities, who in turn would proceed one step further down the social ladder, and so on. The king would theoretically have no control over rear vassals (vassals of his vassals), but could deal with them only through their overlords. In this way Charlemagne created the beginning of the territorial principality. This arrangement did not work as well in practice as in theory, but the system of private legal ties among free men, which in effect replaced the state in France, created some degree of order on the local level. The leading theme of the political history of early medieval France is the development of the principality, not the monarchy.

Vassals ordinarily owed military service to their lords, and the lords were expected to give them fiefs, so that they could provide their quotas of soldiers with the income of the lands. Charlemagne was a conqueror king and had plenty of land to grant. His ancestors had enfeoffed their followers with church lands, theoretically allowing the land to remain church property but in practice granting the territories in perpetuity to secular lords. Charlemagne continued this practice, although he pacified the church's complaints. But problems arose when the ruler's strong hand was removed. Vassals began to make their fiefs hereditary. The Capitulary of Quierzy of 877, in which Charles the Bald promised to enfeoff the sons of his counts who would die on the forthcoming Italian campaign with their fathers' fiefs, merely confirmed existing practice. Multiple vassalage also sapped the vitality of the personal tie, the essential element of the feudal relationship. The first recorded case of a vassal doing homage to more than one lord occurred in 895, but this certainly means that the practice was known earlier. As long as the two lords of the same vassal were at peace with each other, there was no problem, but often they were not.

The Broadening of Feudalism

Problems of heredity led to the expansion of the concepts of vassalage and fiefholding. Feudalism remained basically a means of raising troops, but it took on governmental overtones, for the obligation incurred in return for a fief by a person who was simultaneously a royal officeholder could easily become merged with the office. Hence we find, for example, a count holding a royal office and acting as royal vassal on another more personal level. As the king's vassal, he received fiefs, usually in the area of his comital jurisdiction. As royal authority weakened, the increasingly hereditary right to these fiefs was confused with an increasingly hereditary right to the office. Office and fief became merged in the mind of the beholder and shortly thereafter in law. When the office is held in fief, we have the territorial principality held in hereditary and inalienable tenure. Although there was a tendency for this to occur even before Charlemagne's death, most territorial principalities came into existence during the period of the Viking invasions in the late ninth and early tenth centuries, as powerful local lords took over local defense from the weak monarchs.

This development was not as haphazard as it might seem. The battles which elevated the Carolingians to the Frankish throne reduced the power of the Merovingian aristocracy. Charlemagne's great officeholders came from approximately 100 to 125 Frankish families, most of them related to one another. The genealogical base of the European nobility thus was quite narrow, as cousins entrenched themselves in different parts of Europe. Secondly, although the principalities were probably at their height in the tenth and early eleventh centuries, they began to face the same sort of internal fragmentation which they had imposed earlier on the monarchy. Some warded off these dangers, while others did not. The network of territorial principalities which characterizes the late Middle Ages and to some extent the modern period took form very largely in the eleventh century.

The church also became involved in feudal relationships. Ecclesiastics did homage and swore fealty to temporal princes and were invested by them with the lands and properties attached to their churches. Local princes in the west and the kings in Germany normally appointed prelates to church office in the early Middle Ages, and the tradition of the proprietary church remained strong even after the Investiture Contest of the late eleventh century. The problem was particularly severe in southern and central France, where secular princes had an unusual degree of control over the church and abused it. Most of their appointees were unworthy of their offices, and we encounter warrior bishops entering battle swinging their maces, since canon law forbade them to shed blood.

Advantage in the feudal relationship was always with the stronger party, and this was usually the vassal in the early Middle Ages. Yet even before the fiscalization of feudalism in the central Middle Ages, the lords developed rights over fiefs which stood them in good stead later when they were able to enforce them. Although most fiefs were hereditary, the land would escheat to the lord if there was no heir of the immediate family. Lords often regranted the land to more distant relatives and even to women who could do no military service on their own behalf, but they were under no obligation to do this except in Germany after the twelfth century. Sons usually inherited rear fiefs from the ninth century in the regions between the Loire and Rhine rivers, the heartland of classic Carolingian feudalism, but even here it became an ironclad rule only in the eleventh century. Although this custom was known in Germany from the eleventh century, it only became the rule there and in southern France in the twelfth.

The vassal furthermore could subinfeudate or divide his tenure only with the lord's consent, for the lord kept legal title to the land. The vassal could sell it or give it away, but only if the lord authorized it and took homage and fealty from the person acquiring the fief. But as time went on, feudalism everywhere acquired a characteristic which it always had in Germany and Italy: the personal tie came to be considered secondary to the proprietary. The intent of the feudal relationship became less to reward vassals for faithful service, especially as lords began using mercenaries to build up most of their armies, and more to help vassals accumulate properties by amassing fiefs held of different lords. Multiple vassalage gave a new economic and political potential to vassals, and the most fundamental characteristic of all human society, the survival of the strongest and/or the shrewdest, was given free play.

The vassal had positive obligations to his lord, although whether the lord could compel him to perform them is another matter. The mutual oaths taken in 858 by Charles the Bald and his vassals enunciated the standard obligations of aid and counsel. The vassal had to attend his lord's court whenever requested and give him advice (counsel). The lord's court judged offenses committed by other vassals, who were entitled to trial by their social peers, and cases coming to the lord as a public functionary, for public and feudal were virtually (although not quite) the same in France and the courts thus overlapped. The vassal might be asked for advice on matters ranging from high policy to the treatment of a recalcitrant mistress. The court met regularly once or twice a year, usually on a great church holiday, and was an occasion of general merriment. Christmas and Easter were favorite times. Since prominent vassals did not work, and the weather usually prevented military campaigns except between May and early October, the meetings of the court offered plenty of off-season feasting, drinking, wenching, and other noble pleasures. Hence the vassals were fond of their assemblies, although they often involved troublesome or dangerous journeys, and the lords continued to consider the presence of their numerous vassals as a mark of social prestige. Only in the eleventh century did royal vassals in France get out of the habit of coming to the royal court, and the custom persisted longer elsewhere.

Aid was both financial and military. Although the "feudal aids" were only regularized in the twelfth century as payments owed when the lord knighted his eldest son, gave his eldest daughter in marriage, or was captured and had to be ransomed, vassals always owed vague assistance to their lords, usually on the basis of individual arrangement based upon the vassal's ability to pay. The military service owed by vassals always depended upon their fortune. In the beginning they owed service on horseback for an entire campaigning season, but this was restricted in many areas to forty days annually in the eleventh century. As principalities fragmented, the camaraderie of the extended family which had marked many early feudal relationships diminished, and younger sons in particular stayed home and carved out little lordships of their own, from which they could scarcely be dislodged. The focal point of local order and government by the late tenth and eleventh centuries was the castellany, the territory under the military and political control of the lord of the castle. The petty lord of a manor or two could build a castle, have it guarded even by his serfs, and rule the known world between the west road and the east stream.

The Geographical Diffusion of Feudal Relationships

The heartland of feudal relationships was between the Loire and Rhine rivers. This was the royal stronghold, where the nobles also had extensive territories and, as we shall see, a large subject peasantry on the fruits of whose labors the lords could feed. But the classic picture of feudalism gradually engulfing western Europe must be nuanced. England knew both vassalage and the benefice before the Norman conquest of 1066, but supposedly not in juridical union except in a minority of cases. This quibble need not detain us. The English monarchy before 1000 was strong enough to keep the great lords from obtaining excessive governmental authority even on the local level, but the aristocrats' powers grew tremendously in the eleventh century.

Feudalism never spread significantly to southern France except on the upper levels of society, where the great princes were vassals of the king. The inheritance of Roman law here preserved a concept of the state to which all were subject. The ordinary freemen accordingly owed services and taxes to the state. The dukes and counts were representatives of the state, not feudal overlords. Italy also presents a divergent picture. There was no early feudalism in southern Italy or the region of Venice, the lands controlled by Byzantium. Although there were principalities, immunities (territories held under a princely grant which excluded the prince's functionaries from jurisdiction within the immunity), and seigneuries in these regions, they were held as simple property. Homage and the oath of fealty were unknown. When the Normans conquered this area in the eleventh century, they imposed a feudal regime, as they had in England; English feudalism shows striking similarities to that of southern Italy. Similarly, the papal states of central Italy knew no feudalism in the sense of the union of vassalage with fiefholding. Personal ties of subordination often involved tenure of land for one or more lifetimes, but it was not hereditary. The Lombard duchies of central Italy, Salerno, Benevento, and Capua were not under the strict control of the Lombard monarchy, and political power fragmented in the eighth and ninth centuries without being bound into a feudal network. Feudalism was known in northern Italy, evidently brought by the Carolingian conquest, although the area had numerous allods (lands held as absolute property under no feudal or seigneurial tie). Charlemagne employed Franks to govern northern Italy, and his officials had enfeoffed their own vassals by the ninth century. Heritability of fiefs and public functions took the same course as in France in the ninth and tenth centuries, although it only spread to rear fiefs in the eleventh. The custom of investiture with the fief before the ceremonies of vassalage was peculiar to Italian feudalism, and indeed much of the elaborate feudal ceremonial of the north did not penetrate Italy.

German Feudalism

Germany also was incompletely feudalized. Military operations were based largely on infantry, and there were many allods and a large free peasantry. There was tremendous regional variation. Bavaria and German Burgundy, which had entered the Frankish sphere of influence at an early date, and Lotharingia, the region between Germany and France, knew feudal relationships, but although ties of subordination gradually developed in the rest of Germany, the degree of feudalization remained incomplete.

German society and feudal structure have often been called "archaic" in comparison to those of France, for they resembled models of Charlemagne's period, rather than of the politically confused ninth century. Accordingly, territorial fragmentation came much later to Germany than to France. When it appeared, it was under peculiar forms which hindered monarchical centralization, while the French kings, as we shall see, were able to use partly feudal means to unify France in the twelfth and thirteenth centuries. Germany kept a clear distinction until the twelfth century between the office and the lands or fiefs appertaining to it, while these were merged in France. In further contrast to France, the concept of public law survived in Germany.

German feudalism also was very attached to ceremonial peculiarities; the upper aristocracy disliked anything which might have servile connotations. Accordingly, while the oath of fealty was quite common, since it implied only a freely given performance of duties, homage only became general in the twelfth century, for subordination can be implied in one person becoming the "man" of another.

Germany was a land of lordship or vassalage, rather than feudalism, before the twelfth and thirteenth centuries. Old Germanic conceptions of the king and his war band remained strong. Although princes were independent, subordination was implied to the state, but not to the person of the king. The political problem of Germany in the central Middle Ages is similar to that found in Aquitaine somewhat earlier. When princes did come to hold offices in fief, even though feudal relationships had not penetrated deeply into the lower levels of society, subjects who held allods came to owe primary allegiance to the local prince, not to the absent king. The German princes became lords of allodial territories, tied to the state through public law and to the king only through a late and peculiarly stratified form of feudal law, as we shall see. They could be dislodged from such a position only if the king was the embodiment of the state, and from the late eleventh century he was not.

The Fragmentation of the Carolingian Empire

Much of the development of western feudalism occurred during the breakup of the Carolingian empire after 814. Charlemagne had realized that his source of authority was basically in northern Europe, but his son Louis (814–40) lost sight of this. The popes of the middle and late ninth century viewed the emperor as the man who was called by God to rescue them from their political difficulties in Italy, while they were ordained to save the emperor from his personal sins, whatever the political cost. Louis "the Pious" was ahead of his time in many ways, but he lacked the strong personality needed to control the centrifugal forces within his kingdom. He tried to favor his son Charles, offspring of his second marriage, over Louis and Lothair, his older sons. Revolts and counterrevolts weakened the power of the monarchy, and in 829 Louis had to consent to severe limitations on his power. Invasions from Scandinavia made matters worse, and territorial princes became increasingly independent. When he died in 840, his squabbling progeny succeeded him, with Lothair, the eldest, keeping the imperial title, which he had held with his father since 817. They plotted against one another; in 842 at Strasbourg Louis swore fidelity to Charles in the Romance vernacular of west Francia, while Charles swore to Louis in the Germanic vernacular. These oaths, preserved in the chronicle of Nithard, provide the first written example of French from the Middle Ages.

A final settlement was imposed on Lothair in 843. Louis was given Germany and most of the Netherlands to the Rhine. Charles' northeastern border was the Scheldt, upper Moselle, and the Rhône. Lothair received everything between these two, the so-called "Middle Kingdom," including most of Belgium, Burgundy, Provence, Alsace, Italy, and the western Rhineland, a territory totally lacking natural unity and cohesion which accordingly fractionalized within a generation of Lothair's death in 855.

The Vikings

The Viking invasions were the most important political feature of the ninth century. We know little of why the Northmen left Scandinavia and Denmark. There was evidently some overpopulation, in view of the primitive hunting and fishing economy, and the increased power of the kings in the eighth and ninth centuries may have left too little room for venturesome spirits. Insofar as Viking institutions are known, they were similar to those of the Germans of the period of the great migrations, and indeed their very invasions should be seen as part of the continuing movement of Germanic peoples.

The terror of the Vikings was twofold. As heathen, they were objects of horror and repulsion, and they compounded this by striking at churches and seizing their shiny gold and silver ornaments. This has given them a very bad press, for most writers of history in this age were ecclesiastics, and they almost certainly have given an exaggerated picture of Viking destructiveness. Second, the Vikings were sailors, and western Europeans had few nautical skills. Coming up the numerous navigable rivers of northern continental Europe and England, they raided, moved inland, and departed.

The Swedes, moved largely by geographical considerations, concentrated their activities in Russia and the Baltic and Black Sea areas. Swedish pirates who settled along the Dnieper in the late ninth century were the first persons called Rhos (Russians or Varangians) by the Byzantines, and in a sense they were the founders of medieval Russia. Most damage to the west was done by Norwegians and Danes. The Norwegians expanded far to the west and settled Iceland, Greenland, and briefly around 1000 the northeastern coast of North America. The

Illustration 1. Viking technology:
a ninth-century cart from Oseberg

Illustration 2. Early medieval church architecture: the church of
St. John the Evangelist at Escomb, County Durham, England

Danes made extensive conquests in England. Although King Alfred of Wessex was again expanding against them after a low point in the 870s, he ceded much of northeastern England to the Danes in 886. This area, known as the Danelaw, was distinguished by peculiar social and political features, including an unusually free peasantry, even after Alfred's descendants recovered it in the tenth century. On the continent, the Northmen settled in Normandy (hence the name) in western France in the early tenth century, allegedly taking it in fief from the Carolingian king Charles the Simple, but they created a coherent political unit there only many years later.

The Northmen hence began to settle during the very late ninth and tenth centuries, although they were again to invade England in the late tenth. But the problems of Charlemagne's successors were compounded by the appearance of the Magyars from Asia. Forced by disturbances in their homelands to move west, they were in the region of the Danube by the late ninth century and moved through Bavaria, Venetia, and Lombardy, leaving destruction in their wake. Some then turned into central Germany, and isolated bands got as far west as Burgundy. Only in 955 were the Magyars finally defeated at the Lechfield by the German king Otto the Great and forced to retire into what is now Hungary, where they settled permanently.

Invasion thus complicated political unrest. A peculiar coincidence of deaths briefly reunited the Carolingian empire under King Charles the Fat (884–7), a son of Louis the German and great-grandson of Charlemagne. When it became obvious that he could not defend his empire from the invaders, he was deposed. He was replaced in the west by Odo, count of Paris, who defended central France against the Vikings. His dynasty, known as Capetian after Hugh Capet, who dethroned the last Carolingian in 987, vied with the descendants of Charlemagne for a century before finally ousting them. The eastern Frankish kingdom went to Arnulf (887–99), a bastard grandson of Louis the German, who was noted as a fighter. He was succeeded by his son, Louis, known as the Child, whose premature death in 911 ended the Carolingian monarchy in the east and led to the establishment of a more firmly founded German kingship. The old "middle kingdom" became fragmented, as the kings of France and Germany fought each other and lesser princes for it. The imperial title itself was given to a series of minor south European potentates, and finally lapsed for lack of anyone who wanted it in 924.

6

AGRARIAN EUROPE FROM THE SIXTH THROUGH THE NINTH CENTURIES

THE PERCENTAGE of the population of the Roman Empire which lived in towns during the second century was surprisingly large, in view of the primitive technology, communications, and transport facilities of the day. This had changed completely by the mid-fifth century. The towns had shrunk terribly even in Italy, and in the outlying regions of the empire, notably Gaul, we can no longer speak of "urban" life, although some population still lived within the town walls. Europe had entered an almost totally agrarian period of its history, with an economy based on subsistence rather than production for sale, and would emerge from it only in the late tenth century.

Roman agriculture during the Christian era was based upon the great estate. The Italian free peasants had been forced into dependence upon great landlords during the period of Rome's expansion. Most paid rentals and were tenant farmers, not independent proprietors. The great estates were worked with slave labor, but the supply of slaves died out as the Romans ceased to expand. To make up the labor shortage, the Roman lords often imposed labor services on their rent-paying tenants, especially as money became scarcer after the third century. Clientage and commendation, discussed in chapter 4, played their role in the decline of the independent freeman. During the confusion of the third century, many peasants in northern Europe gave up their freedom in return for the physical protection which a great landlord could provide. Peasants thus made dependent were called colons. Their position was frozen by Constantine in 332, and they could not leave the land. Hence the most common form of Roman agriculture by the early fourth century was similar to the medieval manor: peasant tenants performed labor services on lands reserved for the lord's use and usually paid rents in money or kind (produce), and in return received plots which they farmed for themselves. These plots were often pieces of the lord's land enlarged by what the peasant himself had held earlier but had now given up to the lord.

But the medieval manor did not evolve directly from the Gallo-Roman *latifundia*. There is little evidence of physical continuity. The great estates generally fell vacant for a generation or so after the Romans withdrew. When they were repopulated, the new medieval estates were not on precisely the same site as the Roman. There is furthermore no direct continuity of the peasant classes. Particularly in southern Europe, where the Roman peasantry was most numerous, the farmers used the confusion of the invasions to flee and regain their freedom. Not surprisingly, this was a region of many allods in the Middle Ages. While the Germans had dependent peasant laborers in addition to the free proprietor, the laborers usually did not live on tenures of their own, but were maintained directly in the lord's household. The colons found on northern European estates in the ninth century were not descendants of Roman peasants, but rather were Germans with an economic and juridical status similar to that of the Roman colons.

Much good agricultural land returned to forest during the Germanic invasions. Except in northernmost Gaul, the Germans began to settle down in significant numbers only in the sixth century in the north and in the seventh in Italy. There is considerable evidence that previously existing estates were being expanded and new ones created in the late Merovingian age. Peasants who were anxious to get land of their own cleared it for their lords and in return agreed to hold it for labor services, since money was scarce. Such an arrangement was not particularly exploitative: there was little money for rentals, and payments in kind were clumsy, although they were used. Money rentals became much more common in the Carolingian period, although they were still much less important than labor duties and payments in kind, for Charlemagne instituted a silver coinage which replaced the Roman gold coinage. Silver is of much less intrinsic value than gold and was better suited to the small transactions of the Frankish period. The use of money increased accordingly.

As land under cultivation increased from the seventh century, there was a corresponding increase in population and a primitive division of the land. The word "manse" originated in the seventh century as a tenure which could support one household. The size varied according to the fertility of the land and the size of the household originally occupying it. Some were designated free, others servile, according to the juridical status of the holders. It is impossible to generalize about the size of the manse, but it was always smaller than the English hide of roughly 120 acres in the east and 40 in the south and west; indeed, the English hide was rarely held by one peasant family, and the virgate, of 30 acres or one-fourth hide, was a common household unit by the late eleventh century. The smaller Merovingian manses were soon subdivided. By the age of the great Carolingian polyptyques (surveys of lands, peasant dependents, and assets in rentals and judicial rights conducted by several great monastic houses, perhaps as part of a general program promoted by Charlemagne), quarter and half manses were common. Some manses were inhabited by more than one family, giving further evidence of population increase even to the margin of subsistence.

Merovingian agriculture was extremely primitive. Iron implements were unusual even on the cutting edges of plows. Most plows, hoes, and the like were made totally of wood, and accordingly it was impossible to plow very deeply. Cross-plowing, involving the return of the plow at right angles in a second operation, deepened the furrow but took twice the labor. Seed yields even in the late Middle Ages, from which statistics have survived, were around one-fourth the modern in most regions, and they were much lower in the Merovingian period. Hence an immense amount of land was needed to sustain the peasant household. Although the late Merovingian period was generally an age of rising productivity and extension of the arable, famines were frequent. The only source of poor relief in time of trouble was the church, which received tithes in kind from its parishioners and hence was always well stocked. Marks on teeth in Merovingian graves indicate that some humans were reduced to eating grass in time of famine.

The legal status of the peasant was probably declining in the late

Merovingian period, despite the increased productivity of the land. A laborer working for wages could move about, although he would not do so unless he had somewhere to go, but the landed peasant lacked this mobility. As both free and unfree got land during the expansion of the arable, distinctions between the two were obliterated. The peasants holding land, whether free or servile, were virtually an aristocracy. The sources distort the human reality, for most deal with land conveyance. Peasants who held no land are rarely mentioned. Scattered hints, however, show that household serfs without land were still numerous. The total labor services of the tenant farmers listed in the Carolingian polyptyques could farm only a small part of the land reserved for the lord's demesne. The landless peasant often was a slave or only slightly above this status.

The expansion of the late Merovingian period did not move at the same rate in all regions. The great abbeys were scientific landlords and good managers, and in north central France between the Loire and Rhine they had created a "prototype" of the early medieval manor by the ninth century. Several characteristics of these great farms strike us. Practically all peasant tenures—not the peasants themselves—owed labor services on the lord's land, the demesne. The demesne might consist of strips in the various fields of the estate or of a single block of territory, entirely or partially enclosed. The great estates were made up of numerous farms or villas. The villa often, but not invariably, coincided in territory with a peasant village, but the village could be the property of several lords. This is particularly characteristic of the English villa after 1066, which was as much an administrative and governmental unit as economic. The "nucleated village" had peasant shacks of crude construction around some central point, usually the parish church, a path, or a building belonging to the lord. The fields were on the outskirts. Most manors were of this settlement type; "hamlets," in which dwellings and fields were dispersed, characterize regions of less stringent control by landlords and less intensive agriculture. Depending upon the topography, the land in the arable fields might be arranged in strips or in more coherent blocks. There was usually a forest on the outskirts of the village which provided the timber supply and pannage for pigs. The lord's demesne normally contained vineyard, woodland, meadow, and even wasteland in addition to arable. Peasant manses were chiefly of arable, although they often held some vineyard and meadow as well. While some cultivation of large fields was done in common, since the peasant who was rich enough to own an entire team of plow oxen was rare, many peasants worked specific pieces of demense on an individual basis. The peasant's labor services on the demesne might be a number of days each week in addition to or instead of "piece work," consisting of fixed tasks. Women owed household tasks, such as providing the lord with a quantity of flax. The peasants owed "quitrents of recognition"—as recognition of servile status or nonservile dependence—to their lords. These payments were in kind and did not tend to be economically onerous—a few chickens or eggs, for example. An exception was the animal, usually a horse or pig, that many peasants had to furnish each year to the lord. Lords later acquired *banalités* on their estates. These were rights to force peasants to grind their grain at the lord's mill, use his brewery, and the like, but they are not in evidence on Carolingian manors. Similarly, the various duties which peasants owed on inheriting the tenement, marriage outside the manor, and other marks of servile status developed somewhat later, as lords fiscalized their interests in return for giving the peasants a formal statement of what they owed.

Most farming was done in either a two- or three-field system. The area under cultivation would take in one of two fields or two of three, with the last field lying fallow. The old generalization that the two field system predominated in southern Europe and the three field in the north is true for the most part, but there are many regional variations. There is little evidence that two fields were expanded into three as arable was extended; the existing fields were simply enlarged or new villas were created. Conditions of local topography and soil fertility determined patterns of agricultural exploitation more than a desire to practice more scientific agriculture, although the three field systems would average a one-third higher yield annually than the two. Some soils, and particularly the thin, sandy soils of the Mediterranean basin, simply could not sustain cultivation for two-thirds of the time. Furthermore, the climate of southern Europe did not permit a three-field system. There were no summer rains which could nourish a crop planted in the spring. Hence there could only be one planting and harvest a year in the south, while two were possible in northern Europe. Perhaps for this reason, even the primitive Germans had developed three field agriculture in the early Christian era.

The primitive technology of the early Middle Ages contributed to low soil productivity. Manure was the only fertilizer known. Grass planting in vacant fields and other expedients to enrich the soil rather than simply allowing it to lie fallow developed only later. The topsoil was exhausted easily. Three-field agriculture could be practiced effectively only in areas of high fertility of soil, reasonable technical development, particularly involving the use of some iron implements (for the soil of northern Europe, although richer than that of the south, is thicker and harder to turn), efficient agricultural administration and to a certain extent specialization, and large open spaces which might be used for extended fields.

The crops grown were almost exclusively grains. The winter sowing included wheat and rye, while oats, barley, and legumes were grown in the spring. The diet of all but the most elevated classes of the countryside consisted largely of grains until the very late Middle Ages, interspersed with a few dairy products, chickens, and such meat as was killed when the animals could not be fed over the winter. Abundant meat was the chief variant from this pattern for the upper classes, for whom hunting was a way of life. Fruits and vegetables were not grown in significant quantity. The peasant population of the Middle Ages suffered from chronic malnutrition. Furthermore, since milk did not preserve well and much water was contaminated, particularly in the cities but to a degree in the rural villages as well, there was a much higher per capita consumption of cheap alcohol, particularly beer and mead, than today. These dietary considerations obviously made farmers and townsmen alike extremely susceptible to disease, contributed to a very low life expectancy, and helped to create the peculiarly violent changes of mood and feeling which we associate with persons of most primitive cultures, not least among them those of the European early Middle Ages.

Society

Social classes were carefully graded on the large manors, but there was blurring of distinctions as groups intermarried. No society is absolutely static. Statutes reflect a desired condition, not reality. By the early ninth century we find numerous free men holding servile manses, serfs holding free manses, and the like. The mixture was of little advantage to anyone, for a serf remained a serf, while a free peasant was felt to become more if not totally servile by virtue of his possession of a servile manse. Especially in the ninth and tenth centuries, as lords became less mindful of peasant rights than they had been in

an age when their power was limited by the comparatively strong
monarchy of Charlemagne, the various free and semifree classes characterizing early Germanic society tended to merge into an all-encompassing serfdom. The children were sometimes considered to follow
the status of the lower parent in cases of mixed marriage, but matri-
lineal inheritance of rank was also common. Although to the modern
mind the manorial serf seems oppressed, he at least had a reasonably
secure livelihood on the great estates, while the independent proprietors could suffer the vicissitudes of nature.

Peasants holding substantial tenements, however, were a minority.
Most held only a tiny cottage (if that) with a small plot of ground
for a garden. Wives and children cultivated these plots, while the
head of the household worked for a wage or other reward on the
demesne. Yet one must introduce a caveat here. The gardens of the
cottagers could not have sustained them throughout the year. The
only answer to the question of where they got their food was the
local village market. The peasants holding manses either were producing a surplus or were selling some of what they needed to get other
goods or money. Commercial relations existed even on the most "self-
sufficient" of manors.

Landless peasants might also serve as domestics in the lord's household. Such persons came to the master's attention more easily than
did the most capable of field workers. They were given important
duties, such as messenger service or even military duty in defense of
the estates. They thus were not bound to land, and as such had more
mobility than the landholding peasants. Many such persons later were
merchants, while others administered estates on the lord's behalf and
often carved out little properties of their own.

Landholding peasants could also rise in the social hierarchy. Most
large estates had peasant overseers, usually holding larger amounts
of land than their fellows and performing less onerous labor services.
The priest of the local church was usually drawn from a peasant
household. If servile, he had to be freed to enter holy orders. Most
churches were quite prosperous through endowment with peasant
tithes, and the priests lived well. Particularly significant are holders
of "cultures," the large blocks into which the lord's demesne was divided on the great estates. Persons in charge of these properties were
hard to keep under control by the slipshod administration of the day.
Especially in time of disorder, they behaved as if the property were

their own, and eventually they perpetrated large-scale usurpation of demesne lands from both secular and temporal lords.

Non-manorial Agriculture

The manor of the early Middle Ages, usually containing hundreds or even thousands of acres, involved a number of preconditions not found everywhere in Europe. Although most areas had some large estates, this form of exploitation was the rule only in comparatively flat areas with open and elongated fields, a large servile peasantry, powerful lords who could own such domains, and a high population density, so that a large area could be cleared and cultivated for large farms. Some estates of the abbey of Saint-Germain-des-Prés, near Paris, reached a population in the ninth century which they were not again to attain until the modern age! Hence there were two heartlands of the manor: France and western Germany between the Loire and the Rhine; and later, after the Norman conquest of England, the "champion" country of the English midlands. Most of our documents come from manors, but they were an exceptional form of agriculture, even in the early period.

There were large farms in the Low Countries, for example, but the tenants simply paid rents rather than doing labor services. Later, as more land was drained and made into arable, the independent peasant proprietor dominated the coastal regions. Extended fields were totally impossible in the rocky regions of Brittany and western Normandy. These areas had small, enclosed (usually by hedges or rocks) fields and free peasant proprietors. Similarly, there were nonmanorial forms in the mountainous, wooded areas of central France. There were some large estates on which peasants paid rents, but especially in the comparatively flat but barren or wooded territories, there were enclosures and small homesteads. In the mountains and least fertile areas, such as the southeast of France and parts of Switzerland, farmers practiced "burning and paring," cultivation of land for a few years until it played out, then burning everything on it and abandoning it. Another generation of settlers might cultivate it again later, when the soil had regained some fertility.

The manor existed in southern France, but it was less important than in the Loire-Rhine areas. The lighter soils of the south required only a simple scratch plow, in contrast to the heavier wheeled plow

Illustration 3.   The open fields: Braunton, Devon (England)

often used in the north even by the Carolingian period. This meant that the peasants did not have to band together to the extent of their northern counterparts to possess farm implements and animals. Since the two-field system had smaller yields than the three, large scale farming was less profitable than in the north, and individuals farming their own plots were more common than the manor. In addition, the Romans had a heritage of a semifree peasantry. Principles of Roman law survived in southern France, with the individual considered subordinate to the state. As a result, lords had more trouble here than in the north in tying peasants to a Roman style colonate once they had escaped this form of servitude during the confusion of the invasions.

Italy was too mountainous for large estates. There were great lords, but most simply leased to peasants for rentals. Until the townsmen began to subjugate the countryside and invest in rural land in the central Middle Ages, Italy was a land of the small peasant proprietor eking out a precarious existence from marginal soils. Only in southern

Italy did some manors develop, and there only under the influence
of the Norman freebooters who carved out a kingdom in the late
eleventh century.

There was considerable diversity in German agricultural practice.
The Rhineland and Bavaria north of the Alps were heavily manorialized, but Saxony, Thuringia, and central Germany were not. These
areas were brought into contact with the neo-Roman agricultural
forms practiced by the Franks much later than the western lands,
and kept a substantial free peasant population even after the Frankish
conquest. Serfdom was unknown in Thuringia and unusual in Saxony.
The great region of the German manor was eventually to be the flat
grassland area of the north and east, conquered from the Slavs in
the central Middle Ages.

Early medieval England was generally a land of the small proprietor. The southeast and north were never heavily manorialized, and
the "classic" manor only appears in the country after 1066, particularly in the flat and fertile midlands. When it came, it amounted
to a throwback to the Carolingian prototype, not to forms of exploitation more ordinary on the continent by the eleventh century. Anglo-
Saxon society had numerous categories of free peasants, as did German, and distinctions between them are often hard to make. Most
Anglo-Saxon free peasants were called ceorls. The ceorl was a substantial landholder in the beginning, but the Norman conquest later turned
him into a serf. The Anglo-Saxons also had a class of geburs, unfree
dependents who were much more numerous than the ceorls. The ceorls
kept their freedom in large measure because they still were of value
to the royal infantry. Yet here, as with the German free peasantry,
we must note that the only man who could afford to go on military
campaigns during the growing season was someone rich enough to
hire others to work his land for him. The status of the ceorl thus
was declining in the eleventh century, as Anglo-Saxon society became
dominated by great magnates.

Peasant Society in the Early Middle Ages: a Balance

The social history of the early medieval peasant classes is complex.
Certainly there is no necessary correlation between economic prosperity and freedom. There were poor freemen, who tended to become
more impoverished as the Carolingian period wore on, and prosperous

serfs. The Germans held slaves, who had absolutely no rights, worked at the lord's will, could be sold away from their families, and could hold no property. Slavery was particularly common in Italy and in Germany east of the Rhine, where slaves were probably the majority of the labor force on the great estates. This, indeed, may have been involved in the comparatively slow decline of the German free peasant into servitude. Both free and slave were becoming assimilated to the new serf class, involving a decline of the one and a rise of the other. The serfdom of the Middle Ages gave the peasant a piece of land, technically only for his use and with title remaining with the lord, but actually a hereditary tenement passed from generation to generation of serfs almost as a piece of property. The serf could own property, ordinarily could not be separated from his land, and in some cases had freedom of movement. He could sell the produce of his land, a right which meant comparatively little before 1000 but later would be very important as town markets developed. Insofar as public courts still existed in 900, the serf had access to them. Since he was technically not unfree, he might have to perform military service. German serfs in particular served in the infantry and performed castle guard. The amount of work which the serf performed for his lord was limited by manorial custom or by the agreement by which the serf or his ancestors became dependents of the master. As time went on, many of these arrangements were written down.

The various rural social groups lived close to nature, with little hope of material improvement. Most had only huts of wood or even of straw or mud. Even the nobles lived in drafty blockhouses with dirt floors and no conveniences. Plumbing and cleanliness were unknown, and noble and peasant families alike often lived in a single room, with personal privacy unheard of. The peasants had the most primitive of farm implements, and seemed to resist technological improvement as contrary to "the way we have always done things." But there were ambiguities in the social and legal situation of most peasants which they could exploit in a more peaceful and prosperous age than the Carolingian period and the ninth century.

Trade and Commerce in the Early Middle Ages

Mercantile activity and the growth of towns must be seen in the light of the all-encompassing rurality of this period. The confusion of the great Germanic migrations ended town life north of the Alps. Only in the sixth century did a few places begin to be repopulated. Even then, the new settlements were not always those which had been important Roman depots. While Roman centers inevitably developed some commercial activity stimulated by the garrisons or governmental functionaries, they were not primarily geared or situated with a view toward trade.

Most medieval towns were very different. After the Germans began settling down, the towns began to grow once again, at first with a returning Gallo-Roman population, then later with Germans. In the sixth century such settlements often clustered around a parish church built inside the old Roman walls, or in a corner of a Roman fortification. The entire area of the Roman fortification, which had often been overextended, was rarely repopulated. Much farming was done inside the old city walls. Most important Roman towns which remained inhabited in northern Europe were episcopal cities, in which the bishop and his retinue used the old city as an administrative center of the diocese.

But we are not dealing with genuine towns (settlements which are distinguished legally, economically, and topographically from the surrounding countryside) in the early Middle Ages, but rather with "pre-urban nuclei," settlements which might be separated from the rural areas surrounding them in one of these ways, but not in all.

Town Origins and the Problem of Long-Distance Trade

Trade over considerable distances, and particularly between eastern and western Christendom, virtually collapsed in the fifth and early sixth centuries. By the mid-sixth century commercial contacts were reviving, but they were isolated. Most commodities were of a luxury nature, such as wine, olive oil, spices, papyrus, and fine cloth, although there was some interregional trade in salt and a thriving international slave market, centering on Verdun in the west. Except salt and slaves, this trade involved small items which were usually transported by individual peddlers from the east, mostly Syrians and Jews. Some writers have concluded on the basis of references in the history of Gregory of Tours, written in the 590s, that a thriving eastern trade persisted across the period of the Germanic invasions. Yet in all the written sources of the Merovingian age, including Gregory, there are only six references to Syrian and Jewish traders, and in all cases luxury commodities were being exchanged. There is no chronicle surviving from the seventh century of the same historical interest as Gregory's history, and this absence of sources has misled many into thinking that long-distance trade actually fell off in the seventh century. But archaeological finds, coin hordes, and toponymic and topographical evidence show conclusively that the preurban nuclei were expanding in population and in distant contacts in the seventh century after a low point in the sixth. Long-distance trade need not be with the East to be significant. The charter of 629 establishing the fair of St.-Denis near Paris provided a four-week period each year in which traders from Lombardy, Spain, Provence, England, and those from the Merovingian royal domain in northern France might come to exchange and sell their wares. There is fragmentary evidence of Merovingian trade among the Slavs of central Europe in the seventh century. Interior trade routes were developing. The Rhône and Saône valleys were significant until the eighth century as arteries for European trade with Italy and then Byzantium, but the disorders of Charles Martel's expeditions against the Arabs led to their decline. England rejoined the continental trading network in the seventh century, and the Loire thus became an important link between Britain and the Rhône. The Meuse was extremely important in the seventh century in providing a water link almost without overland transfers between England and the Rhône.

Increasing commercial contacts revitalized the towns along the trade routes. The commercial importance of Spain was minimal, but that of Lombard Italy was growing by the seventh century. Texts of the early eighth century show a large class of professional merchants. Some monasteries in northern Italy maintained depots in the towns by this time to sell their surplus produce on the urban market. Italian merchants were in regular contact with the Byzantines. Even more than Lombard Italy, the coastal regions, under the nominal control of Byzantium, were important for trade in the eastern Mediterranean. Venice had emerged as an important commercial center by 800 at the latest. Located on the lagoons off the mainland, the city was virtually unassailable by land. Its location and nominal Byzantine overlordship directed its interests toward the east. By the early ninth century Venice was the leading port for reconsignment of the goods of

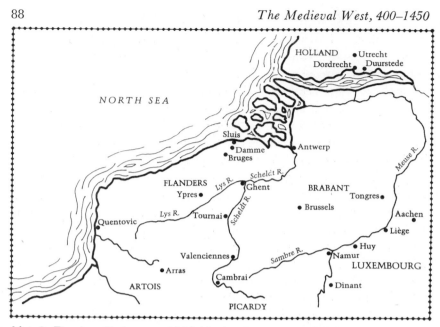

Map 2. Flanders, Brabant, and Neighboring Regions in the Middle Ages

northern Europe to Constantinople; only in the next century was there competition from Pisa and Genoa.

Towns in northern Europe did not have the spectacular early growth of Venice, but many centers were evolving along the rivers. The Roman towns often gave place to new settlements or to places inhabited only as small forts by the Romans, such as the Meuse towns of Dinant, Huy, Namur, and particularly Verdun. Overland routes were dangerous, and were used chiefly for local trade in bulk commodities. Accordingly, such Roman towns as Tongres, located away from the rivers, declined precipitately, while coastal settlements not inhabited by the Romans were important for trade with England.

This bloom of preurban life involved comparatively few persons and only a small commodity value, but it continued under the early Carolingians. There was an essential continuity in economic life between Merovingians and Carolingians. The general economic upturn so visible in the seventh century, as arable was expanded and trading settlements grew, continued at least until the mid-eighth century in the Mediterranean regions of southern France and until the ninth in the north. New settlements are found in places never occupied by the Romans, particularly along the Scheldt. The coastal emporia of Quentovic and Duurstede, later to be destroyed by the Vikings, were flourishing. Charlemagne placed merchants under his personal protection (however effective or ineffective that may have been) and ordered his officials in the newly conquered eastern territories to protect traders among the Saxons, Slavs, and Avars. The great invasions and political instability of the ninth century brought some decline—the number of charters given to markets had been rising tremendously in the early Carolingian period, but fell off markedly in the ninth century—but the great and continuous growth of the medieval town began as the invasions ceased in the tenth century.

Our picture of Carolingian economic life differs sharply from that of the great Belgian historian Henri Pirenne (1862–1935), whose interpretations are still current in many medieval history texts. Pirenne claimed that the Arabs closed the Mediterranean to Christian traders in the seventh century and forced a reversal to an almost totally agrarian, subsistence economy. Yet goods from Moslem lands continued to appear in western Europe long after the seventh century, and the Arabs did not control the Mediterranean long enough to have ended commerce. Most Arab trading was conducted by overland caravans, and the Moslems usually permitted traders in conquered territories to follow their older patterns. Most Arab goods reached the west through Constantinople, and indeed it has been argued that the decline in east-west trade which certainly occurred in the early ninth century resulted from a Byzantine attempt to cut off all trade with the Moslems. It is true that the Arabs conquered Sicily and obtained naval supremacy in the western Mediterranean in the early ninth century, and their pirate nests (the last of which was only eliminated in 972) were a severe hindrance to the commerce of the towns of southern France. Yet the Moslems did not blockade Christian commerce, but were trading actively with the Italians all the while.

Indeed, the entire question of long-distance trade in the economy and town formation of early medieval Europe seems malposed. While it was increasing in the seventh and eighth centuries after a low point in the sixth, there is precious little evidence of it in the total body of documents of the period. Numerous tolls hindered the development of long-distance trade. Although there was some problem of gold drain to the east, it has been overemphasized. The west had little to offer to the east except timber, hides, and some minerals. The total amount of luxury cloth and spices which east sent to west was not large, for only great princes could afford such things, and the crude Germanic warriors lacked the taste for these refinements. Hoarding and melting down of gold and silver into church plate was much more important than a drain to the east in the decline of the monetary reserves of western Europe.

Local Commerce

Most commerce was conducted locally, either within the preurban nuclei or on manors. While the agrarian economy of the early Middle Ages was designed chiefly to support those who were growing the food, there were good years and bad years. The towns had prosperous grain markets by the late sixth century. Gregory of Tours tells of several magnates who tried to corner a grain supply during the famine of 585 and sell it expensively. Charlemagne issued several edicts attempting to regulate grain prices during the famine in the 790s.

Indeed, some trading, even without the evidence of larger markets, was absolutely essential. Within the same region one estate was certain to have need of grain, some animal, or the like which was found in surplus on another. The great ecclesiastical landlords actually furthered the volume of interregional trade, for their estates were so dispersed that they could act as transfer agents. Most agrarian villages had little markets, held once a week or even less often. The local parish church was frequently a focal point for trade and barter, in addition to being a general social center of the entire village. Markets were often held on Sundays or saints' festival days, despite the attempt of the clergy to preserve the spiritual purity of the holy places. Marketplaces in the early towns often developed in front of the church.

The estates also had industrial operations which could further commerce, such as metallurgy and ironmongering. For example, several estates in eastern Belgium of the German abbey of Prüm had salt pans. Salt was the chief means of preserving food in the Middle Ages and hence was valuable in trade. To get the salt processed, the abbots gave more favorable conditions of tenure to the local peasants than to those living on estates whose economy was based chiefly on the exploitation of arable and vineyard. Small preurban nuclei grew up around the salt pans, and although no large town ever developed there, local exchange operations of this sort were an important aspect of social mobility and a significant force in breaking Europe out of the post-Carolingian economic stagnation.

There is other evidence of an essentially agrarian orientation of most early medieval town life. When the old Roman settlement was repopulated in some Rhineland towns, the marketplace and major lines of settlement developed not on the Rhine, where interregional trade was conducted, but rather on land routes running into the Rhine and leading to a prosperous agrarian hinterland which would furnish

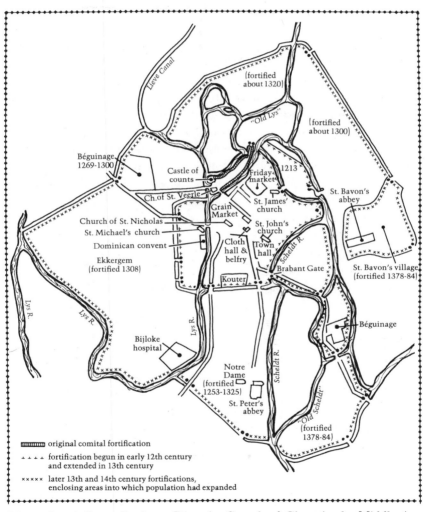

Illustration 4. From Castle to City: the Growth of Ghent in the Middle Ages

the town with food. Security of the food supply was absolutely essential to every early medieval commercial settlement, even those which had some long-distance trade.

Long-distance traders were wanderers, since business had to be conducted personally. These men tended to settle outside princely redoubts, Roman ruins, bishoprics, or even monasteries in a single-street formation which later expanded. Numerous *Wike,* settlements along either a land route or a waterway, and *portus,* usually along rivers, developed in Frankish Gaul and Germany. But although these wanderers were eventually to be the richest men of many towns, they were not the essential population base, and indeed their markets in the early period often were less important than those inside the fortification. Since the preurban nuclei continued to be inhabited while the long-distance traders were away, a permanent settlement remained behind. These persons farmed, tended the docks, provided hospitality to passing merchants, and above all provided a market for local farm products. Exchange operations hence furthered peasant mobility and aided the prosperity of the embryonic towns. When the hinterland produced some commodity which had an industrial use, the prospects for an eventual great city in the area were very bright. Ghent, for example, was settled by the eighth century at the junction of the Lys and Scheldt rivers, and thus had easy access to the growing river commerce of the Carolingian period. Studies of personal and place names suggest that the earliest settlers were farmers, but they began to expand their interests as the obvious commercial advantages of their community became clear. Ghent became and always remained an important center of the grain trade, at first because the city was in an area with a substantial grain production, and later because the Scheldt and Lys gave access to the grain of Picardy and Artois. The Ghent region was also important for grazing sheep, and the city soon began to develop weaving. It was to become one of the great textile centers of medieval Europe.

The merchant hence was often merely a transposed farmer. He always remained essentially rural in his social orientation except to a certain extent in Italy, although in the early period this was imposed on him by the total dominance in economy and society of the countryside classes. Laws of the Lombard and Anglo-Saxon kings considered merchants of a certain wealth to be the social and political equivalent of persons holding a certain amount of land. The medieval city had agrarian beginnings. The later development of substantial long-distance trade must not cause us to forget the process of history.

Conclusion: Town and Countryside

Hence, in reconstructing an economic curve of the early Middle Ages, we find that the low point both of commercial development and agricultural productivity in northern Gaul came with the Germanic invasions in the fifth and early sixth centuries. The process was retarded by approximately a century in Italy. The Germans disliked towns. No town developed from a pre-Carolingian Germanic settlement; all were either resuscitations of Roman towns or were creations of the Carolingian age and after. Although the Lombard invasions delayed Italian economic development briefly, a substantial class of local merchants had arisen by the eighth century in local trade and in dealings with Constantinople. Fairs and markets were growing in the north as centers of essentially regional or local exchange by the seventh century. Even the manors had some commercial activity. Preurban nuclei were developing on the great rivers, and population was increasing. The peasantry was sinking toward serfdom for essentially political and social, rather than economic reasons, but it is doubtful whether serfdom as opposed to freedom made a great difference to the individual in terms of life and bread.

The economic revival was slowed somewhat by the growth of Moslem power in southern Europe and the Mediterranean in the mid-eighth century, and severely by the confusion of the ninth. Agricultural productivity and population declined, and the tendency of the peasants to fall into serfdom was accelerated. Trade diminished in volume as the invaders harassed, looted, and burned, and as princes were unable to keep order among even themselves, let alone impose it on outsiders. The ninth century shares with the fifth the dubious distinction of being one of the darkest periods of medieval economic and social development.

Part II

EUROPE IN REVIVAL: THE CENTRAL MIDDLE AGES

7

GOVERNMENT AND POLITICS: EMPERORS AND CRUSADERS

POLITICAL AUTHORITY on all levels, often even the local, was fragmented in the Middle Ages. Only in England did a national monarchy manage to establish reasonably effective government, and the exception had little to do with talent. England was much smaller than the continental kingdoms, and the kings only ruled effectively in the south, east, and to a certain extent the midlands. In France, the kings began from a virtually nonexistent power base, but managed to build a kingdom with a facade of unity at the top. The German kings began with considerable power, but lost much of it in the late eleventh and twelfth centuries; their realm splintered beyond hope of repair in the thirteenth century. Italy was in the sphere of influence of the German kings; it was ungovernable, and the Germans wasted precious resources in attempting the impossible. Monarchies under reasonably coherent administrations were being created as Christian reconquered the Iberian peninsula from Moslem.

Lotharingia

The "Middle Kingdom" of 843 did not remain a kingdom long. Most of the petty princes there owed formal allegiance to the kings of Germany in the tenth and eleventh centuries, a few to the kings of France, but in practice most were independent. This is sometimes

97

called the land of "feudal anarchy" par excellence, but when we use this term we must remember that there was nothing necessarily feudal about anarchy in the Middle Ages; it was merely the normal state of affairs. Most of these principalities were not very well organized internally. Petty lords fought one another, holdings were split, and loyalties were divided as families subdivided. Such fragmentation continued to characterize Lotharingian political life in the late Middle Ages. The "War of the Cow of Ciney" of 1275–78 is a classic example of Lotharingian high politics and low comedy. It received its name from contemporaries who thought that it was caused by an official of the bishop of Liège who stole a cow; the matter was actually more substantial—the burning of the manor of Goesnes in the principality of Liège as the result of a quarrel over a vassal's right to alienate a fief without his lord's permission. Although several greater Low Country princes were drawn into the fray, it was characterized by sporadic violence and pillage rather than battles. Such local feuds usually had less repercussion in the outside world, for they were so common that few except the participants and the victims of depradation really considered them extraordinary.

Germany

On the surface, Germany was the best governed large monarchy in Europe in the tenth century, but there were serious internal weaknesses. The German monarchy was always elective, rather than hereditary. Although a son (not necessarily the eldest) of the late ruler was usually chosen before the twelfth century, the kings were insufficiently prolific, and Germany had four ruling houses between 919 and 1197. Furthermore, the German monarchy lacked a firm territorial base, although the kings consistently tried to obtain one despite the opposition of their barons. The Carolingian line had died out in Germany in 911, and the barons elected Duke Conrad of Franconia as king. The duke of Saxony succeeded him in 919 as Henry I, but in accordance with German tradition he gave up his dukedom. Although he kept his own family property within Saxony, the duchy itself was never assimilated into the royal domain. Franconia escheated to the monarchy in default of heirs in the 930s, and this gave the kings some power base in central Germany which succeeding rulers tried, with limited success, to join to their own household lands.

Map 3. Germany and Eastern Europe

Under Otto I, the Great (936–73), the German monarchy attained tremendous authority and prestige. Otto put down a civil war upon becoming king. This was endemic in the German situation, as disappointed brothers made trouble for their successful siblings. Particularly when the dynasty changed, a new king could count on spending two or three years subduing rebellion. As long as it was a family affair, no one was particularly bothered by it, and the loser usually received substantial territories and offices. A baron who picked the wrong side could witness his lands confiscated. Otto then ended the Magyar threat to Germany in 955 at the battle of the Lechfeld; the Magyars retreated into what is now Hungary.

To Otto, however, is due a disastrous intervention in Italian affairs which ultimately was to cost Germany its chance of national unity in the Middle Ages. In retrospect, it is hard to see what else he could have done. The imperial title of Charlemagne had lapsed in 924, after being batted about by various Italian potentates since 899. The tenth-century popes were degenerate and needed some help from the outside in maintaining their position, but no one thought them worth helping. The German king's hand was forced, however, when the Lombard kingship in northern Italy fell vacant. Otto's brother and son, dukes of Bavaria and Swabia respectively (for Otto had managed to appoint members of his own family to key positions throughout the realm in an ultimately unsuccessful attempt to weaken the great barons), went to Italy to carve out their fortune. Otto could not allow either of his powerful relations to create a territory combining northern Italy and southern Germany which would rival his own strength in northern Germany. Accordingly, he intervened in 951, married the widowed daughter-in-law of the last Lombard king, and had himself crowned king of the Lombards. Since he thus became the leading prince of Italy, he was the logical person to whom Pope John XII would turn when he next had trouble. Otto I was crowned emperor by the pope in Rome on February 1, 962.

Otto I never lost sight of the fact that his essential power base was in Germany and spent most of his time there, but his successors became extremely involved in Italy. Otto II (973–83) suffered a disastrous defeat at the hands of the Arabs in southern Italy and died soon after. His death was the signal for the Slavic princes into whose areas the Germans had been expanding in the northeast to revolt, and it took years for the Saxons to reestablish their authority there. Otto's heir, Otto III, was an infant with a Byzantine mother, for the Greeks had hoped to renew ties with a renascent western imperial power. Otto III was an impressionable young man and was much taken with Byzantine ideas of "renewal" of the Roman Empire, but he did not sacrifice German policy to Italy. Otto, or the persons controlling him, tried to install German officials across northern Italy and make it an administrative unit with Germany. He died at 21 in 1002, and much of his work was undone in the following years. Henry II (1002–24), last of the Saxon line and chosen from a collateral branch of the family, busied himself chiefly with Germany and generally allowed the popes to have their way in Italy.

With Conrad II (1024–39), first of the Salian dynasty, we enter a new chapter in the German involvement in Italy. A territorial concept of imperial power was replacing the mere personal union under the emperor which had characterized previous reigns. Conrad also allied with the Italian lesser nobility against their lords and allowed them free heritability of fiefs. In an effort to weaken the great bishops, Conrad tacitly allied with the Italian towns. He furthermore enlarged the imperial base of power in Germany. Several important princes died without heirs during his reign, and he gave their lands to his son and heir, Henry III (1039–56). German domination of the papacy perhaps reached its height under this devout churchman, who deposed two unworthy popes and installed a third of his choice at the synod of Sutri in 1046. Significantly, Henry thought of the church as a department of state, which indeed it had been in Germany since the time of Otto I.

The German involvement in Italy thus had been in no way disastrous as late as 1056, when Henry III died leaving a six-year-old son. During the minority of Henry IV (1056–1106) and the "investiture struggle," however, many weaknesses inherent in the imperial constitution became painfully apparent.

Germany was still essentially nonfeudal. Relations of lordship or vassalage not involving fiefholding prevailed through the lower levels of German society. Most land was held under public, rather than feudal, law, for Germany had preserved this distinction which had been virtually lost in France. It is true that the German barons held their lands in fief and rendered homage and fealty to the king, but only their lands, not their offices, were held in feudal tenure, and the kings could make new appointments to countships and dukedoms if they had the power. But the kings had trouble with small allodial landholders. If there were no feudal bond, there was little that the king could do, for he could not unilaterally confiscate territory held in public law. Such lands were controlled by the king's representatives, the counts and dukes, who were the same great princes whose power the monarch had to keep in check if he were to govern effectively. When a count or duke held allods in addition to his fiefs, furthermore, it was hard to dislodge him if he had been disloyal. Early German feudalism had known some of the feudal "incidents," rights such as wardship over minor heirs of vassals, the right to marry an heiress to a loyal man who would perform the services owed from the fief, and particularly escheat, in which the fief of a vassal who died without

heirs would revert to the lord. But Germany did not know relief, a
duty paid when the heir succeeded to the fief, and the other incidents
were being challenged as early as the eleventh century. This meant that
the fiscalization of feudalism which western princes were to find so
profitable, particularly from the twelfth century, was of little use to
the German kings.

The German kings used *ministeriales,* serfs from their domains who
were totally dependent upon imperial favor for social rise, to govern
their territories and defend their castles. In this way they hoped to
undercut the great magnates. While the kings of the western lands
would enfeoff a baron or local lord with territories which they could
not govern themselves, the German kings entrusted such lands to their
serfs and hence kept control. Eventually, of course, as the German
kingship weakened, the *ministeriales* merely kept the lands and powers
which they held in delegation of the king and exercised them independently, but this was a century and a half in the future when Henry
III died.

The Investiture Contest

Had the German kings not quarreled with the popes, however, there
is no reason to assume that the monarchy would have experienced
all the worst possible implications of German feudalism and society.
For the disorder which papal involvement had brought to German
politics and the repeated papal excommunications of the emperor had
weakened royal authority beyond hope of recovery perhaps even as
early as the beginning of the twelfth century.

The nature of the German state church was of fundamental importance in the Investiture Contest. The popes were latecomers to a general reform movement which had seized western Christendom. The
foundation of the monastery of Cluny in Burgundy in 910, directly
under papal control and free from external interference by temporal
powers, is often cited as the beginning, but actually the reformist
monasteries in Lorraine, such as Brogne, had more direct influence
on the popes. The reformers found a totally degraded church, particularly in Italy and France. The principle of secular control of local
benefices and even bishoprics and abbeys was established by Charlemagne, if not earlier, and no one questioned it until the papacy became dominated by monastic ideals in the eleventh century. The ex-

treme reformers urged total withdrawal of the church from the world while paradoxically arguing that the church should control the world.

The French church was impossibly corrupt. Although Pope Gregory VII seemed to hold King Philip I (1060–1108) personally responsible, the monarch had so little power that he could have done little had he been so inclined (he was not). But the German clergy was probably the most morally upright in Europe. It was affected by the reform movements at an early stage, and its activity in converting the Slavs had preserved its missionary zeal. It was common in Germany as in the west for leading churchmen to serve in princely bureaucracies, for there were few literate laymen. It was comparatively unusual, however, for things to be carried quite as far toward official state control of the church as in Germany. The kings appointed bishops and abbots and only went through the form of canonical election by clergy and "people" of the diocese or by the monks. The kings then invested the churchmen with the ring (symbolizing marriage to Christ) and the staff (symbolizing the shepherd of his flock), the two symbols of ecclesiastical office, as well as with the lance, which symbolized the temporal possessions of the see.

The decision to use the German clergy systematically in secular government was made by Otto I, who had trouble with lay administrators. The kings usually appointed worthy churchmen, and since monarchs were anointed (in contrast to other temporal princes), they were thought to have powers of anointing others. Most German churchmen supported the king as the natural ruler of the church at the beginning of the quarrel with Gregory VII, and only changed sides when the pope spread the idea that all laymen were to be excluded from participation in church affairs.

The *ministeriales* were the main secular bureaucrats at the king's disposal, and use of them was extraordinary before the eleventh century. The kings thus governed through the ecclesiastical immunity. An immunity is territory subtracted from the power of the ordinary civil authorities and placed under the control of its holder. The counts and dukes, whose powers were feared by the king, were thus excluded from considerable land as the king extended these immunities. The churches had to have secular patrons, or advocates, to direct their affairs with the outside world. In France the advocate was usually the most powerful potentate of the immediate neighborhood, who in effect was the proprietor of the church, but in Germany he was the king. In this way the monarch controlled territory that he had with-drawn from the control of the great princes. The immunities were to haunt the kings later, for the bishops ceased to choose advocates and governed their immunities through their own *ministeriales,* and the kings could not recover the land. The great churches had territorial ambitions, and perhaps paradoxically the German churchmen became more worldly as they escaped royal control and became independent powers.

As the reform movement tried to exclude lay interference in church affairs, however, the church developed an almost morbid preoccupa-tion with simony, the buying of church office. The concept was ex-tended to include any act of dealing with a secular power to obtain church office, whether money were involved or not.

The movement of papal independence and reform began under Pope Leo IX (1049–54) and continued during the minority of King Henry IV. The papacy became increasingly sure of itself. In 1054 the papal legate at Constantinople precipitated the definitive separa-tion of eastern and western Christendom over a minor point of liturgy. As part of this policy, the popes allied openly in 1059 with the Norman bandits who were conquering southern Italy from the Byzantines. The popes recognized the legitimacy of their conquests in return for homage and fealty. Finally, a synod of 1059 made the election of the pope the province of the college of cardinals (the bishops and priests of the major churches in and around Rome), thereby excluding imperial nomination.

The emperor in turn found these actions contrary to his preroga-tives, and he showed himself unwilling to truckle to the pope when he began to rule on his own in 1066. The German barons also had become accustomed to a much looser control during his regency than before, and when he tried to reassert his rights he trampled on theirs. In 1073, Hildebrand, who had dominated papal councils in the late 1050s and 1060s, became pope himself as Gregory VII. He imme-diately encouraged the barons of Saxony to revolt against Henry IV. The uprising was over by 1075, but the monarchy had used many of its slender resources.

Matters came to a head in 1075 when Gregory VII formally for-bade lay investiture of the clergy with ring and staff. This meant in effect that the emperor could no longer control the appointment of his most important bureaucrats, and his answer was defiant.

Gregory was in open alliance with the German nobles and excommunicated Henry IV. The barons scheduled an assembly for February, 1077 to depose the king unless he received prior absolution from the pope. Henry travelled to northern Italy and intercepted the pope, who was en route to attend the synod, at Canossa in January, 1077 and asked forgiveness. Gregory knew that the repentance was insincere, but he could not refuse absolution to a sinner. By relieving Henry IV from excommunication, he cut the ground from under the German barons. They elected a new king anyway, and Gregory VII claimed the right to decide between the two rulers. He finally opted for the antiking Rudolf in 1080, shortly before Henry IV killed Rudolf in battle. The king resumed control of the German church, returned to Italy, and expelled the pope from Rome. Gregory VII died soon after in exile with his Norman allies.

The contest was by no means over, for the position of the monarchy had been shaken by the revolts. The clergy began to switch to the papal side. The pope was spiritual arbiter of Christendom, and kings were subject to him for their souls' salvation. Propaganda literature circulated over the issues of the controversy, and the emperor was generally considered to have lost his sacramental position; rather, he received the imperial designation (although not his rights as king of Germany) not directly from God, but from the pope, who crowned him. The German princes continued to exploit the king's troubles with the pope and the Italians to consolidate their own position. Finally, Henry's own son, Henry V (1106–25), revolted against the aging monarch in an attempt to force an accommodation with the pope to save Germany from disintegration. Henry IV died soon after, and the new king then became less subservient to the pope than he seemed at first. Matters dragged on, and the issue was finally resolved by the Concordat of Worms (1122), a solution similar to that reached in 1107 regarding clerical investiture in England. Lay investiture with ring and staff was forbidden, but in Germany the king might be present at episcopal elections, decide disagreements between candidates, and withhold investiture with the temporal possessions of the see if he wished. This in effect gave him a veto power over German episcopal elections. In Italy and Burgundy, however, he could not be present at the election and had to invest a bishop with the temporalities within six months of his election. This settlement shows clearly the essentially temporal nature of the popes' ambitions: the

German church might remain under royal control, but the emperor had to yield to the pope in southern Europe.

Indeed, it is hard to avoid the impression that the ferocious pursuit of Henry IV by popes who only mildly troubled the kings of France and England is a reflection of the position of the German king in Italy, which the pope wanted to rule. The papacy had been dominated totally by the local Italian nobles in the tenth and early eleventh centuries, and the series of unworthy pontiffs was ended only by the emperor Henry III. Precisely at the time when the popes became genuinely interested in spiritual reform, moreover, they were presented with a magnificent opportunity to create a state in central Italy which could exclude all temporal powers, German and Italian alike, from their decisions and policymaking.

The ruler of Tuscany (the area around Florence and Siena), Countess Matilda, was the widow of the duke of Lorraine. Her husband's ecclesiastics had imbued her with reformist ideas, and indeed the Lotharingian reformers were controlling the papacy in the mid-eleventh century, in alliance, in the beginning at least, with Henry III. Matilda had no children, and her inheritance ordinarily would have escheated to the emperor as lord of northern Italy. But she was a personal friend of Hildebrand and wanted to will Tuscany to the papacy. Such a bequest would give the popes a state consisting of the papal territories of the Donation of Pepin with Tuscany adjoining them on the north as a bastion against imperial Lombardy. Pope and emperor quarreled over this issue for nearly half a century. When Matilda finally died in 1115, the vastly weakened imperial posture enabled her to leave her territory to the papacy. Resistance within Tuscany to all forms of outside control, however, prevented the popes from using the inheritance as they had hoped.

The Investiture Contest supposedly ended in 1122. The monarchy had been weakened to the point where the king no longer could govern through public law in Germany. He had to use coalitions of princes, attempting to build up feudal ties at a late date. This, of course, could only succeed if the king were strong, but the Salian line died out in 1125 and the princes began using their rights of election to choose candidates who would give them no trouble. Hence Lothar von Supplinburg, duke of Saxony, was chosen in 1125, but his son-in-law and logical successor, Henry the Proud, duke of Bavaria, was passed over in 1138 in favor of Conrad III, the first of the Hohenstaufen line and a very weak man. The son of Henry the Proud, Henry the Lion, inherited Bavaria and Saxony, while the kingship was given to the nephew of Conrad III, Frederick I Barbarossa, in 1152. The rivalry of Hohenstaufen and Welf (the line of Henry the Proud) was to dominate German imperial politics for many years, and the Welf power base in Germany was indeed larger than the imperial, which was confined largely to Swabia.

If the Investiture Contest ruined the empire, it also had important consequences for the popes. An aspect of the papal program of which sight is often lost is the claim to govern the church directly, as well as the empire. Gregory VII's position is summarized in the *Dictatus Papae,* a memorandum which he inserted in the papal register of 1075. Some of its claims were political. He claimed the right to depose and excommunicate emperors, absolve subjects from their fealty to unworthy princes, have sole right to use the imperial insignia, and hear cases appealed from secular courts. While the pope continued to make such claims, few princes took them seriously, and papal domination over the secular power remained ideal rather than practice even in Italy. But Gregory also disputed the traditional rights of local synods and bishops. He claimed the right to depose bishops without hearings, send his legates anywhere with preeminence over local ecclesiastical authorities, make total disposition over local administration, and pass on the validity of provisions of canon law. He claimed that the Roman church was infallible. The support given originally to Henry IV by the German church is not surprising in view of this, for Gregory's program was totally revolutionary, but it was adopted to a striking degree in the western church in the twelfth and thirteenth centuries.

Dispute has raged over the character and aims of Gregory VII, but he had a tremendous influence. He was more adept at propounding claims than at enforcing them, but Pope Urban II (1088–99), who is most famous for calling the first Crusade, is extremely important in the development of an ecclesiastical bureaucracy. He reformed the papal central offices into a coherent *curia,* a term meaning court in a very extended sense and having functions beyond the purely judicial. The papal chamberlain (head of the chamber in the household) became head of the financial arm, and the judiciary received a tentative organization. Much of this is on the same principle that we shall observe more closely with princely administrations, save only that the papal *curia* was dominated by cardinals, rather than by feudal tenants-in-chief. The pope's judicial business was so extensive by the mid-twelfth century that he and the cardinals spent considerable time in hearing appeals, a development which took the church toward legalism and away from spiritual functions. As the monks had dominated the reform papacy of the eleventh century, so canon lawyers dominated during the twelfth. Papal legalism may have reached its climax in the time of Alexander III (1159–81), the great opponent of Frederick Barbarossa, but it was only in the mid-thirteenth century that the *Rota Romana* was organized as a sort of papal supreme court, replacing the use of commissions set up as the need arose.

The Reign of Frederick Barbarossa (1152–90)

Frederick I and Alexander III were a classic case of irresistible force meeting immovable object. Frederick was determined to reinvigorate imperial rule in both Italy and Germany. This could be done in Germany by increasing still further the use of *ministeriales*, who by now were very powerful despite their technically servile status, and by forcing the princes to recognize the king as supreme feudal overlord. Frederick made this work for a generation, although at a great price; but such a restitution of imperial authority was impossible in Italy. Imperial control there had been weak for half a century, and towns had grown tremendously. The emperor's "regalian rights" to market tolls, excises, appointments, and the like had long been exercised by the towns as part of their self-government. They now considered these privileges theirs by established custom, while the emperor was determined to reinstitute a German-controlled government.

Frederick I began a long Hohenstaufen tradition of total misunderstanding of the movement for town liberty which had become so strong in the central Middle Ages, although he did favor some German towns for political purposes. Basically, however, he tried to govern through princely coalition and regalian right, viewing most towns in Italy and Germany alike as contumacious upstarts. The king could not have ruled Italy by feudal practice anyway, for such ties were ill-developed in the Mediterranean world save in the Norman south. Finally, Frederick faced a series of strong popes. He encountered the opposition of Pope Hadrian IV, the only Englishman ever to occupy the see of St. Peter, as early as the imperial coronation in 1154. The pope demanded that Frederick lead the papal mule as a sign of subjection to the papacy, a demand to which Frederick acceded only when assured that no slight to imperial privilege was intended. Of perhaps greater significance was an incident earlier in 1154, when the papal legate met the king at Besançon, conveyed the pope's best wishes, and offered "even greater *beneficia*" if the emperor cooperated with the Holy Father. The word "beneficium" still meant fief in Germany at this time, and the pope knew it. When the emperor refused to accept this claim of papal overlordship for the empire, Hadrian replied that he had intended *beneficium* in the older sense of "kindness," but he could have used other words if this had been the case. The papal legate at Besançon, whom only the personal intervention of the king saved from assassination by German nobles standing nearby, was the later Pope Alexander III.

The pretensions of the towns of Lombardy were openly supported by the new pope, and Frederick replied by installing a series of anti-popes and declaring open warfare. The quarrel was only to end in 1183 in total disaster for Frederick. Although he destroyed Milan, leading town of the "Lombard League," and ravaged Lombardy repeatedly, the towns always came back to the fray and finally inflicted a crushing defeat upon him at Legnano in 1176. He made a separate peace with Alexander III in 1177, recognizing the *status quo ante* 1159. Matters with the towns dragged on until 1183, when the Peace of Constance generally recognized the cities' claims with only a nominal imperial overlordship.

While Frederick I was busy in Italy, matters drifted in Germany as the great princes built up estates more powerful than the Hohenstaufen. Henry the Lion was a particularly far-sighted ruler, colonizing the lands on his eastern frontier and establishing new towns. The emperor's hands were tied in a sense, for he had to control Lombardy with Swabia to rival Welf power in Bavaria and Saxony. As the quarrel with the Lombard towns sputtered out, Frederick was able to deal with the threat of Henry the Lion, but only by granting concessions to the other German barons.

As a great prince, Henry had to be tried by his peers. The emperor could not allow the tremendous loss of face of failing to win his case (although he actually was able to do so because Henry failed to answer the summons to trial), and accordingly had to make concessions to fix the jury. German society was more stratified than that of the west.

The compromise of Frederick with the barons, formalized in thirteenth-century legal texts, gave the king no direct control over rear vassals. He could deal directly only with the great princes, who were made a distinct order of society. The stratification became statutory. Henry the Lion was declared a contumacious vassal for refusing to help Frederick in Italy in 1180 and accordingly lost his duchies and lands held by feudal law, although not his allods. He went into exile in England, and his lands were divided among several baronial families. Frederick confirmed the status of the "East Mark" (Österreich or Austria), already separated from Bavaria in 1156. He may have agreed to give up the feudal incident of escheat and regrant vacant fiefs within a year and a day, although this is uncertain. Thirteenth-century emperors did not exercise this right, but often did grant vacant lands to their own relatives. The royal domain thus could be extended only with difficulty.

Frederick I was faced with a challenge to his power which could not be overlooked. In combatting it, he mortgaged the German policy of his successors. Only a strong king could hold such a system together. Seven years after Barbarossa's death, the heir to the Hohenstaufen claim to Germany was three years old.

Although Frederick I never lost sight of his German background and always seems to have had in mind a German domination of Italy, he spent most of his time in the south except after 1183. Finally, he went on Crusade and was drowned in 1190. He was succeeded by his second and ablest son, Henry VI (1190–97), under whom the Hohenstaufen monarchy reached its height.

Norman and German

Tancred d'Hauteville was a petty baron of Normandy with twelve sons. Since there was no place for the boys in Normandy, many went to Italy. Other Norman freebooters had preceded them there, and they led lives of banditry in Calabria and Apulia in southern Italy. Spreading from this modest position under Robert, called Guiscard ("the cunning"), they had conquered Byzantine Italy and Moslem Sicily by 1091. Although the conquered lands were ruled at first by separate branches of the house, the new territory was united under Roger II, called the Great (1101–54). Through Roger's support of Pope Innocent II in the divided papal election of 1130, he obtained papal recognition of his territory as a kingdom. The "Kingdom of the Two Sicilies" as it was called later was well administered, basically on an Arabo-Byzantine model, with Latin, Arabic, and Greek as official languages. It was based on sea power, although there was some rivalry with the north Italian cities. Religious toleration was decreed. Roger ruled in the personal style of an oriental despot.

The Normans had allied with the pope against the German kings in the eleventh century, but as they consolidated their power in the south they became as much a threat to papal independence as the Germans. In 1186 Frederick I arranged a diplomatic marriage between the future Henry VI and Constance, aunt and heiress of King William II of Sicily. The pope countenanced this arrangement, since although William was childless, he was still young and might produce an heir, but the king died in 1189. The threat of encirclement by a child of Constance and Henry VI might have been temporary, for the two cordially loathed each other, but to the surprise of everyone they produced an heir in late 1194, the future Frederick II (1212–50). Resolution of this dilemma was to occupy much papal attention in the thirteenth century.

The Crusades

The Crusades were a peculiar mixture of the secular and the religious, but with a decided preponderance of the former. There was much more to the political expansion of Europe than fights with Moslems in Palestine. German kings and princes had expanded their eastern frontiers against the Slavs from the tenth century, and conversion to Christianity quickly followed. This movement was making vast strides in the northeast by the twelfth century. Crusading activity against the Moslems had been going on for centuries in Spain, and the concept of the Holy War in a Christian context may have originated in Iberia. Although there were several Christian principalities of note, they were gradually uniting into three: Portugal, on the western coast; Castile, the largest of the three, in the interior; and Aragon, the richest and most heavily urbanized, on the eastern coast and north, created by the union of the earlier kingdoms of Aragon and Catalonia in 1140. The Moslem Caliphate of Cordova had fallen on evil days in the early eleventh century, and in 1085 the kings of Castile conquered Toledo, the great center of the caliphate. There was a renewed Moslem offensive in the twelfth century, but their remaining strongholds were reduced in the thirteenth century, particularly by the Castilians and Portuguese. After the fall of Cordova in 1236 and Seville in 1248, only the tiny coastal kingdom of Granada remained to the Moslems. Since the Christians celebrated their victory over the Moslems by two centuries of fighting one another, Granada held out until 1492.

The crusading movement to Palestine originated with the defeat of a Byzantine army at Manzikert in 1071 by the Turks. The Greeks appealed to the pope for aid in recovering the lost provinces of the empire. They apparently expected a few companies of knights, but what they got was rather different. Pope Urban II saw it as an opportunity to regain the holy places in Palestine for the Christians. Accordingly, he preached the crusade in 1095 and promised plenary remission of sins for all who died for the faith. A massive outpouring of religious sentiment followed. Hordes of impoverished and unarmed enthusiasts, led by such persons as Peter the Hermit and Walter the Penniless, presented themselves at the gates of Constantinople. Uncertain of what to make of the whole affair, the emperor offered them free transportation to Syria, where the Turks immediately cut them down. The main force of crusaders arrived in 1097. There were numerous lesser princes of northern Europe who were being cut out of family inheritances by older siblings and wanted to conquer lands in the east, several dukes and counts, but no kings.

There were immediate problems with the Greeks, who intended for the crusaders to reconquer territory for themselves, and the supposed perfidy of the Byzantines throughout the military engagements of the following years is a recurrent theme. Actually, we are simply dealing with two cultures which were as two lines which never meet in space. The Byzantines did refuse help at times, but they also saw no sense in offering themselves to be slaughtered. They helped the crusaders get to Asia Minor, but did not accompany them to Palestine. City after city fell to the Christians. Jerusalem was taken in 1099 in a bloodbath immortalized by the chronicler Fulcher of Chartres. Fulcher intended to glorify the deeds of the Christians for subsequent generations; he portrays quite innocently a group of primitive and bloodthirsty defenders of the prince of peace, rude and vicious "knights in shining armor" whose mores and standards were a source of amazement to all Moslems who had contact with them.

The history of the Latin Kingdom of Jerusalem is a story of disaster and near disaster. The Latins were cut off from their homeland, although they did conquer a reasonably large area. Much of their contact with Europe was provided by Italians, particularly Genoese and Pisans, who had resident commercial colonies in the major cities as early as 1098 and generally monopolized the trade in luxury items which the crusader kingdoms might provide for the west. The Venetians also entered the picture after 1100 and were given rights to have colonies, markets, and tax immunities. They had already obtained a virtual monopoly of Byzantine trade with the west in 1080 in return for helping the emperors against the Normans in southern Italy. The opening of greater eastern trade created the fortunes of the Italian coastal cities.

The new kingdom had various dynastic troubles. Although the Christians intermarried with the local populations, they never settled the land thoroughly. A resurgent Turkish force took Edessa in 1144, calling forth the second crusade under the personal sponsorship of St. Bernard of Clairvaux. The kings of France and Germany took part this time, but the crusade accomplished nothing except increase the distrust of the Byzantines.

Moslem power continued to grow under the great leader Saladin, and the third crusade (1189–92) was led by the kings of France, Germany, and England against him, but it accomplished little. The Christians reconquered Acre and the coastal areas and got visitation rights in Jerusalem, which Saladin had conquered in 1187. The cooperation of the western kings did not last, and Philip II of France left early to ravage the lands of Richard I of England, who stayed longer in the Holy Land. Richard himself seems to have gotten along better with Saladin than with his fellow Christian princes.

Moslem unity was ended after Saladin's death, and various proposals for a crusade under imperial auspices were considered. The premature death of Henry VI hindered this, but a new crusade was expected shortly thereafter. This crusade, however, was the beginning of the end of the crusading ideal. There had been a palace revolution at Byzantium, and the loser eventually appealed to the Venetians, who as we have seen had important interests in Constantinople. The crusaders were to meet at Venice and had arranged for transport and supply with the Venetians. They were unable to pay the price agreed upon, however, and in compensation they agreed to conquer Zara, a city in modern Yugoslavia claimed by Venice. After this was accomplished, the Venetians diverted the crusade to Constantinople, which was taken and sacked in 1204 in a scene recalling the plundering of Jerusalem in 1099. Many Greek treasures and manuscripts were stolen and eventually came to the west. A Latin Empire of Constantinople was set up and the Greeks withdrew. They continued to fight, however, and in 1261 they established a new empire which was to last until 1453, but it was a shadow of its former greatness. The west could no longer be protected by the Byzantines from incursions from the east.

The crusading ideal was dragged through the mud by the popes later in the century. Frederick II had promised to go on crusade, but was delayed and finally became sick just as he was about to leave. He was excommunicated for failing to go on crusade. When he recovered his health, he did go, and the excommunication was renewed since he went before being released from the first condemnation. He compounded his error in 1229 by obtaining Jerusalem and becoming its king, and that by the most unknightly means of negotiation with his opponents. His success came despite the open attempts of agents of Pope Gregory IX (1227–41) to foment trouble for the emperor among the Moslems.

Jerusalem was recaptured by the Moslems in 1244. Inspired by this, King Louis IX of France took the cross, the major preoccupation of his last years. The center of Turkish power was now northern Africa, which Louis invaded. He was captured and held for ransom during a six year crusade, but repeated his folly in 1270, dying in Tunisia. The Latin mainland kingdom was ended when Acre fell to the Moslems in 1291. Periodic crusades against the infidel were called in the fourteenth and fifteenth centuries, but without real hope of territorial conquest.

The Crusades have been overemphasized in the history of medieval Europe. Certainly they represent an expansion of economy and of horizons, but the economy was already prospering when the Crusades began. There was increased trading with Arab and Greek during the crusading era, but such avenues were being opened by the Italians even before the Crusades, and the warfare probably hurt commercial contacts. The Arabs and Greeks showed eagerness to trade with Venetians and Genoese even as they defeated Christian armies in battle. The crusades were a waste of manpower in the interest of the religious enthusiasm of many and the imperial dreams of a few.

8

GOVERNMENT AND POLITICS: ENGLAND AND FRANCE

After promising beginnings, the German kings had lost their chance to unify Germany by 1200. In contrast, the French monarchy saw its period of greatest degradation in the eleventh century, but by the early thirteenth the kings were the obvious great powers of the future. England was scarcely in the same category. It was always relatively well governed, in part because of its small size, and even the English involvement in continental affairs under the Norman and Angevin dynasties did not hinder English constitutional development.

Anglo-Saxon England

The England of the tenth and early eleventh centuries has had an extremely bad press as a result of the Norman conquest. Historians of Norman inclination have attempted to credit the Normans with various institutional developments which in fact they merely borrowed from the conquered English. Certainly the Anglo-Saxon monarchy was the most powerful state of its day in the regions where it was operative, the south and the Midlands. Marcher (frontier) barons under a merely nominal overlordship to the kings dominated the northern and western frontiers, and the Norman conquest changed nothing of this. Social forms in Anglo-Saxon England were similar to the German in having numerous gradations and a comparatively large free population. Neither Germany nor England had a substantial Roman heritage, and both developed a strong vernacular culture in the early Middle Ages. England, as Germany, was incompletely feudalized. Although cavalry was known, the military was largely infantry. The free peasants had to fight in the general levy, the "great fyrd," in defense of the homeland. This usually meant defending the local neighborhood or county against marauders, for only a core of highly trained warriors did constant service even during the campaigning season. This "select fyrd" was recruited on a basis similar to the Carolingian: every five hides (roughly 600 acres) owed the mounted military service of one man. This meant that the "thegns" and other great men owed cavalry duty but through their obligation to the state, not through a feudal tie to the king. Some were vassals of the king, but they did not hold fiefs in return for military service. Most fighting was done by this select fyrd as time went on, and the general levy became less important.

The kings had a good system of local administration. England was divided into 39 shires (counties), each under a shire-reeve (sheriff). This man was the king's deputy, roughly the equivalent of many continental counts, but with a stronger tie to the monarch. He collected tolls, court fines, and the like which were owed to the king and led the local militia. Under him were hundredmen, local officials in charge of the "hundreds." This term had a variety of meanings, but usually indicated a territory of 100 hides within the shire. The kings also had a strong borough (town) organization. Towns developed early as the English traded with the continent, and especially with northern Europe, Scandinavia, and Flanders. The kings maintained a bureaucracy, and concentrated mints chiefly in the coastal ports. Since royal power was strongest in the southeast, where most of the towns were located, royal control over trade was much stronger from the beginning in England than in most continental principalities.

England had been united under the royal house of Wessex in the ninth century, but the kings had been forced to allow the Danes to settle in the northeast. The successors of Alfred the Great reconquered the "Danelaw" in the early tenth century, but the Scandinavians had made a substantial settlement. Renewed Danish invasions struck England in the late tenth century, although not the continent, perhaps because of dissatisfaction among the English Danes, perhaps because the English king, Ethelred I (978–1016) was extremely weak. In 991

Map 4. England in the Middle Ages

the Danes forced him to pay tribute to keep them away. This so-called Danegeld was the first national tax on land; it was to be continued by the later Danish and Norman kings of England, although hardly to buy off the Danes! The very fact that Ethelred could levy and collect such a tax shows the strength of royal institutions, even as the personal position of the king was weakening. Ethelred helped matters not at all by personal cruelty, such as his attempted massacre of all Danes in England in 1002.

The Saxon line was finally replaced in 1016 by Cnut, who later became king of Denmark and Norway as well. Under him England was drawn even more into a northern European orbit, as trade with Scandinavia flourished. Cnut's successors were unworthy, however, and the son of Ethelred, Edward, known as the Confessor, became king in 1042. His mother, who had married Cnut after Ethelred died, was Norman, and Edward had been raised in Normandy and had Norman sympathies. Edward was married to an English lady, but concern for his personal sanctity prevented his consummation of the marriage, and a succession quarrel was inevitable. The strong Norman influence at Edward's court prompted fears that the duke of Normandy might become King of England, and the English barons revolted in 1051 under the greatest of their number, Earl Godwin. This was suppressed, but the desire of Duke William of Normandy for the throne was public. In 1062 Harold, son of Godwin, was shipwrecked off the Norman coast, and William forced him to promise that he would support the Norman claim to the English throne when Edward died. Released from captivity, Harold repudiated this promise, and himself succeeded Edward the Confessor in January 1066. The allegation of broken promise gave ecclesiastical sanction to the conquest of England the following October by Duke William.

The political confusion of the eleventh century increased the power of the great lords. Barons combined several shires under their control and in effect neutralized the sheriffs' value to the king. The growth of great lordships tended to depress the condition of the free peasantry even more than the normal state of affairs in the Middle Ages tended to do. The best land, along the major river valleys, had been inhabited for many centuries and was no longer available for settlement, and this in turn forced farmers to turn to more powerful lords. Disorder and private warfare in the countryside were so rampant that Cnut, the one strong king of eleventh century England aside from William "the Conqueror" (although Harold had obvious promise, he reigned only ten months), ordered all free men in the kingdom to choose lords and follow them. The free population was divided into tithings (groups of ten persons) under Cnut, and each man was considered responsible for the behavior of the other nine.

Despite the troubles of the eleventh century, however, the England of 1066 was a land of comparatively strong monarchy, a high degree of social mobility, a substantial free peasantry, and an only moderately powerful aristocracy. The aristocracy could always be penetrated from below by anyone who had enough money to hold five hides of land or make three trips abroad as a merchant. If members of his family held this position of wealth for three generations, they became thegns (landed aristocrats). Despite the changes of the early eleventh century, the Normans built their state, the most centralized and effective of the Middle Ages, to a great degree merely by imposing a feudal superstructure upon strong Anglo-Saxon royal and local institutions.

Capetian France in the Eleventh Century

The early Capetians were kings in name, petty barons in fact. When the direct Carolingian line died out in 987, leaving only a collateral branch, the French barons chose Hugh Capet, whose lands were centered in a narrow belt of territory between Paris and Orléans, as king. Since he was unable to threaten the barons, his elevation to the monarchy was a result of his weakness, rather than strength. The French kings spent increasingly less time in the outlying areas of France controlled by their great vassals. Royal inactivity reached a low point with King Henry I (1031–60), and the kings of France were much less powerful than their great vassals: the counts of Anjou, Flanders, and Champagne and the dukes of Normandy and Aquitaine. Most of the princes owed a formal allegiance to the king, but paid little attention to it unless they needed help in time of trouble.

The early Capetians did, however, have the virtues of inertia. While they have been criticized for not going on Crusade, they obviously knew that their weak position would be made much worse if they left France. Similarly, King Philip I (1060–1108) made no attempt to keep Duke William of Normandy from conquering England in 1066 and increasing his own power tremendously, but he would have failed if he had tried. The early Capetians, in short, knew their own limitations and gave no one cause for taking away their slender resources.

The French monarch had a sacred position through anointment and was thought to have supernatural powers, in particular the ability to cure scrofula (this ideological buttress was later borrowed by the kings of England). But the kings derived less advantage in the beginning from the sacerdotal aspect of monarchy than from making the French monarch hereditary. They were lucky in having one, and only one son to succeed them until 1226, and hence were spared the succession quarrels which plagued other dynasties. Before a trip to Aquitaine,

Hugh Capet had the barons choose his son Robert as king. With the anointment, Robert succeeded him without question in 996. Subsequent kings repeated this practice, and the Capetians thus established a precedent that the king's son would be king after him. There was always something vaguely illegitimate about the origin of Capetian power, and the kings of the twelfth century accordingly were careful to call themselves successors of Charlemagne. It is significant that Philip II (1180–1226), son of a Carolingian mother and husband of a Carolingian heiress, was the first Capetian who did not have his son crowned during his own lifetime.

Changing Forms of Government

Only in the central Middle Ages does the history of the monarchies become significant for either national or institutional development, for before this the power of kings and great princes was personal and minimal. The power of the lord of the local castle over his peasants, free and unfree, was always very great. There were ecclesiastical immunities, territories of local usurpers of varying origins, and the like. Government throughout the Middle Ages was characterized chiefly by its venality. Lacking an effective bureaucracy, princes and towns farmed out their revenues and rights to private entrepreneurs, who paid a lump sum in return for rights of collection. Offices could be bought and sold, and exemption from taxation could be purchased or might be the prerogative of a given social group.

Nonetheless, the monarchies were making progress against the dictatorships of local potentates. Much of this must be understood as the result of changes in feudal relationships. Many sons were surviving noble fathers and had to be provided for. Land which could be given out in fief was limited, and we find increased fractionalizing of noble properties and impoverishment of lesser noble families, particularly in southern France. The result was that some nobles were driven into the towns, others into the peasantry, and still others into royal service.

The essential aspect of primitive Germanic feudalism was vassalage, the tie of man to man in an honorable relationship, but this was changing by the central Middle Ages. Investiture with the fief often preceded homage and fealty, particularly in Germany and Italy. Multiple homage and lordship gave the vassal the upper hand against his lord. Feudalism had originated through the desire of lords to obtain vassals who would perform military service for them, but it continued through the desire of vassals to obtain territories over which their lords would have little control. The fief was a private possession for all practical purposes, and it was the primary aspect of the feudal relationship by the eleventh century. As the feudal tie became essentially fiscal rather than personal, the lord's rights over fiefs were limited chiefly to the feudal aids and incidents in England and France.

An important part of this fiscalization which was rendering the personal element of feudalism an empty form by the mid-twelfth century was the money fief. The land fief was a clumsy relic of an earlier age, and lords were running out of land to give in fief. Land fiefs could not provide enough soldiers for armies even in the post-Carolingian period, and lords used mercenaries. But in the central Middle Ages it was not yet socially acceptable to hire another prince as one's mercenary. Furthermore, the money fief allowed lords to build diplomatic alliances in areas where they had no fiefs to give; for example, the English kings used money fiefs to obtain vassals in the Low Countries against the kings of France. The money fief had most of the characteristics of the land fief, except that it was rarely hereditary. Lords gave annual sums of money to vassals in return for homage, fealty, and some form of honorable service, usually military, but occasionally political or diplomatic. The money fief was usually granted for a lifetime or a term of years, and the flow of funds could easily be cut off in case of the disloyalty of the vassal. Money fiefs worked to the advantage of both lord and vassal.

The growing fiscality of the feudal tie is reflected also in measures taken to avoid the military service characteristic of primitive vassalage. The nobles of the twelfth century were much more sophisticated than their forebears and had some cultural interests. Accordingly, the term which a lord might demand of his vassal in the field was limited in most areas (a 40 day period was most common); if longer service was demanded, the lord had to pay. The idea also spread that an unpaid feudal host could be required to fight only in defense of the homeland—the characteristic of the old general levy incumbent on all free persons—and not in foreign wars. The English barons resisted being sent to fight in France after they had lost their French possessions in 1204–5. Many vassals also preferrred to pay rather than fight. In both England and France the custom developed exacting a fee, called scutage (shield money) in England, which would release the vassal from his military obligation. The taking of scutage began as an option of the lord, but the vassals soon came to consider it their right to offer scutage if they wished. The payment eventually became annual, and the nobles did increasingly less personal military service, preferring instead to play-act in tournaments, which were rather rough entertainments with high fatality rates despite their artificial character. Lords hired mercenaries and gave money fiefs with the revenue received from scutage, generally to petty lords who still held the fighter ethos of the older feudal nobility.

England under the Normans and Angevins

Hence tremendous changes were to occur in the western national monarchies in the late eleventh and twelfth centuries. The defeat of King Harold by William "the Conqueror" in 1066 was made possible only by a Danish invasion which struck England at the same time and forced Harold to fight at Hastings with exhausted troops. William's position in Normandy had only recently been secured. This principality had been extremely turbulent, and William's accession to the dukedom as a minor and bastard made his situation doubly difficult, for illegitimate children normally were not considered heirs. He clawed his way to the top by raising a nobility of *nouveaux* to whom he gave the lands of older families which fell into disloyalty. These men were loyal, for they owed their position totally to William, and with them, together with Flemish mercenaries, he conquered England. The Norman barons quickly replaced the native Anglo-Saxon nobility, which was driven out during the civil wars after 1066. A group of French landholders ruled England.

The Normans kept the essentials of the strong Anglo-Saxon local government, except that after William I (1066–87) the kings lost much direct control over shire and hundred courts as they enfeoffed them to their great men. The changes introduced by the Normans were chiefly in the central administration, and even here the age of great modification was the Angevin period after 1154. The conquest strengthened the personal situation of the king immeasurably, but it may actually have weakened his institutional position.

"Institutions," however, were of no great concern to anyone until the mid-twelfth century. The essential fact of medieval kingship was brute force and personal charisma. Philip Augustus of France was

Illustration 5. The knightly repast

Illustration 6. The battle of Hastings

the rare weak man who succeeded as a king, and his triumphs were due to mediocre opposition and a combination of his judicious treaty-breaking and his ability to reward his followers with lands, as we shall see. This was an age when government, insofar as the term is not an anachronism, was done by personal contact. The kings were itinerant. The Norman dukes preferred Normandy and spent most of their time there, and the later Angevins were French rather than English in orientation, even after they lost most of their French territories. Governments were only beginning to develop resident offices, and there was nothing to bind a monarch to one place. Vassals owed their lords "hospitality," meaning that the lord could come to the estates which he had given the vassal in fief whenever he desired, and was to be fed and entertained as long as he wanted to stay. This right was limited later, and most early kings preferred to migrate between demesne estates rather than to the farms of their vassals, but the monarchs of England and Germany began settling down only in the thirteenth century. Paris became a capital under the early Capetians, since the French kings had less territory in which to roam, but even the Capetians continued to move about in the late Middle Ages. Communications were poor. Even in the fourteenth century, when conditions were vastly improved over the twelfth, a messenger on horseback could cover only 50 miles a day in summer, and a royal convoy of course moved much more slowly. Accordingly, all kings had to rely to a degree on controlled decentralization, and only the real or potential fear of the king's wrath was sufficient to force attention to be paid to the royal will.

Travel thus was necessary for every medieval monarch. As they ate their way across the kingdom, demolishing the stores of estates which they maintained directly and those of their vassals, the kings maintained personal contact and inspected. Aside from this, however, their only necessary contact with the great men of the realm was at meetings of the royal council, at which every vassal owed attendance. The conquest had placed the barons in a direct feudal relationship with the king, owing knight service to him in return for the great domains which they subinfeudated to individual knights. The "knight's fee," the basic unit needed to support one mounted soldier in the force, was quite small. The domains of most Anglo-Saxon nobles were scattered throughout England, and Norman barons took over these territories directly as the native nobility was annihilated; scattering of baronial domains to keep the great men from having concrete blocks of territory as a power base was not a Norman innovation, as has been argued. Although some local governmental structures were feudalized, particularly as local sheriffs made their positions hereditary, William I showed toward the end of his reign that he comprehended an essential feature of the Anglo-Saxon achievement: the preservation of public law and of allegiance to the state. At Salisbury plain in 1086 he forced "all free men" (i.e. all great men) to swear primary allegiance to him as king and not necessarily as supreme feudal overlord. By this "reservation of fealty" to the king, conflict of loyalties was avoided as subinfeudation was carried out, and vassals' first loyalty was to the king and the state, not to their overlords. The Capetian kings of France were able to attempt such a measure only in 1209, and it was never effective. Public law in France was a revival of the

Roman legal tradition, not a spontaneous development from Germanic roots.

The king governed through his feudal council, as did most princes of Europe. This body was basically advisory. The king did not have to call it, and it had no legislative function at this time. But the king could not afford to alienate his great barons or govern in direct contravention of their wishes in this brutal society with such a personal government, and some consultation was probably the rule before important measures were promulgated. Some kings tried to defy their barons, but only the strongest, such as Henry II (1154–89) got away with it, and they faced open opposition.

The Great Council was the entire assemblage of the tenants-in-chief, together with the few bureaucrats who were necessary for the continuous operation of royal government. The Small Council consisted of the few great men who were the king's particular favorites, for whose advice he often asked and who were in constant attendance on him. This was a fluctuating body, depending on where the king was, whose wit he appreciated in a given mood, and the like. Members of the royal household were also in the Small Council.

Day-to-day governmental operations in the Norman period, and to a lesser extent under the Angevins (the house of Anjou acceded to the English throne in 1154, as we shall see), were less the sphere of the Great Council, whose members were no more professional about government than about managing their own estates, than of the royal household. The household was just that, and organizations similar to the English are found throughout Europe.

Most major offices of the household emanated from the royal chamber. The chamberlain managed the king's daily affairs and provided for the royal table. Since the king's private treasure was kept in a chest under his bed, the chamberlain had financial prerogatives as well. The chamber eventually "went out of court" as it became an administrative department with offices, unable to follow the king about. Its place as an office directly under the king and answerable to him alone was taken by the wardrobe, an office emanating from the chamber, which was extremely important in the late Middle Ages.

As early as the 1050s the Anglo-Saxons had a permanent treasury at Winchester, from which funds were disbursed as the king travelled about. It was basically a storehouse of funds which the king obtained from his sources of revenue: his own estates, court fines, customs and market duties, the Danegeld, and later the feudal aids and incidents. The Exchequer, in contrast, is a Norman innovation of the time of Henry I (1100–1135). It was an accounting department and developed its own court for handling financial questions and cases which grew out of disputes over the king's revenue. The Norman and Angevin sheriff was in effect a tax farmer, and the Exchequer's chief business at first was auditing the accounts of the sheriffs for the king's local revenues. The department received its name from the checkerboard shape of the floor on which money was placed after being weighed. The head of the Exchequer, its chancellor, was at first an official of the royal chancery who was sent to observe proceedings, but he soon became a permanent fixture.

The chancery was the royal writing office, originating in the royal chancel, a division of the palace church in which those ecclesiastics who could write (few laymen could) were maintained. The chancellor was perhaps the most important figure of twelfth-century government, often acting as the king's deputy. The chancery certified royal acts, and later could make its wishes known in opposition to those of the king if it felt that he was being misled. The king would eventually adopt other devices, including secret and private seals, to circumvent the chancery as it fell under baronial control.

The justiciar was the viceroy left in charge of England while the king was on the continent. The first of them, Ranulf Flambard, was a grasping Norman squire who was later appointed bishop of Durham for his services, but the office subsequently took on considerable power. It went out of existence when the kings were confined largely to England in the thirteenth century.

William the Conqueror was succeeded in England by his second son, William Rufus (1087–1100), in Normandy by his amiably incompetent eldest, Robert. William II has received a bad name from historians due to church-state conflicts during his reign. Relations with the church had been unnaturally rosy under William I. Although he rejected the suggestion of Gregory VII that he hold England as a papal fief, he separated church courts from lay and gave a broad sphere of jurisdiction to the church in all cases involving crimes imputed to the clergy. His archbishop of Canterbury, the chief primate of the realm, was Lanfranc, a decent man but essentially a royal servant. William Rufus left the archbishopric vacant when Lanfranc died in 1089 and had taken the revenues of the see as a regalian right, but in 1093, when William II thought that he was dying, he appointed as the new archbishop the saintly Anselm, prior of Bec in Normandy. Anselm brought the Investiture Contest to England, refusing to receive investiture with the temporalities of Canterbury from the king and insisting that he go to Rome to receive spiritual investiture. Rufus objected, adding that no one might leave England for the purpose of appealing to a foreign jurisdiction, and was supported by a church synod. Matters dragged on until a compromise was reached in 1107.

William II died in a very suspicious hunting "accident" in 1100 and was succeeded by his younger brother, Henry I (1100–1135). After consolidating his position in England and issuing a charter confirming his subjects' liberties—such charters from a new king became a tradition, although the content of the liberties was a subject of debate—he relieved his elder brother of Normandy and reunited the inheritance. Little is known of the details of his reign, although he was obviously a strong king. Henry had numerous bastards, but only two children who reached maturity: a son who drowned after a drinking bout while crossing the English channel, and Matilda, married first to the emperor Henry V and later to count Geoffrey of Anjou. Matilda was certainly one of the less endearing figures of English history. A thoroughly unpleasant, although intelligent woman, who was to be a trusted advisor of her son when he became king, she was to be the focal point of rebellion in the next generation.

Henry I was succeeded in a coup d'état by Stephen of Blois, son of the daughter of William I. Stephen happened to be in England when Henry died; he marched on the treasury and took it, and so personal and possessory was monarchy in the twelfth century that little could be done about him thereafter. Matilda, however, fought for her inheritance for nearly two decades. The civil war witnessed a great proliferation of private castles in England, a tendency which the earlier Normans had been able to control, and the great barons generally increased their power.

When Geoffrey of Anjou died in 1151, his son by Matilda, Henry, inherited Anjou and Maine, which his father had conquered during his lifetime. The English settlement of 1153 allowed Stephen to remain king for life, but provided for Henry's succession; as it happened, Stephen died the next year. The young Henry had already enlarged his inheritance tremendously by marrying Eleanor of Aquitaine in

1152. This lady, some eleven years Henry's senior, had been the wife of King Louis VII of France, who had divorced her on alleged grounds of consanguinity, on real grounds of being a bit too much for the saintly monarch to handle. Eleanor's relationship with the lively Henry was pleasant at first, but became stormy in the 1160s, and he kept her in prison from 1173 for inciting their sons to rebellion.

Henry II was a powerful personality. He was short, stocky, red-haired, had a ferocious temper and quick intelligence, and was good in the manly arts of hunting, fighting, and fornicating—the very sort who might keep a turbulent baronage under control. He managed the barons, but had more trouble with his sons, who were given lands to rule when the reached maturity. Each of the four boys except John (who was aged 7 at the time) aided his mother and the barons in a ferocious revolt in 1173 which took two years to extinguish. Two predeceased the father, and when Henry II died in 1189 his two surviving sons, Richard and John, were in open rebellion against him.

Although Henry spent more time in England than some of his predecessors, he in effect used England to pay for his continental empire, which with his marriage took in most of western and southern France. England and Normandy were the only parts of his immense empire which could be administered and taxed effectively, and accordingly it is there that we find his great reforms.

In 1166 Henry sent inquisitors to ask how many knights had been enfeoffed by his barons in the time of Henry I and how many were enfeoffed presently. Then, significantly, he took scutage on the difference, since he had no desire to get a few more knights for the royal host. The barons had subdivided the knight's fee drastically in building up armies of private retainers, and many lesser knights had fiefs too small to support them in military regalia. Some sank into the peasantry; the king was capitalizing in effect on the economic distress of the lower aristocracy. Henry also fired all sheriffs and reviewed their activities. Many were not rehired, and the decline of the sheriff as a local lord and royal official dates from this period.

The "common law" courts (so called because they promulgated law which was common to all Englishmen) began their systematic development under Henry II. The king sent itinerant justices from the great council on circuit throughout the realm to hear cases which the king might have power to judge: those involving free men, justiciable in courts which had not been leased or feudalized, who had bought the documents necessary to get a case transferred from a seig-neurial court into a royal. Before this time petitioners had to follow the king wherever he went, and this could be expensive and time-consum-ing. A permanent delegation of these councillors, mostly barons but with a few professional lawyers, soon began staying at Westminster. This formal session was the origin of the court of King's Bench.

Other judicial reforms of Henry II were of a similar character. His famous quarrel with Thomas Becket was fundamentally judicial. Becket was a Londoner who became the king's boon companion. Thinking him a safe candidate, Henry had Becket chosen archbishop of Canterbury. At this moment Becket had a sudden change of heart, or perhaps reintegration of power urge, and began opposing the royal will at every turn. The king had ruled in 1164 that clerics who were judged guilty of crime in a church court were to be handed over to a royal court for punishment. Since the church could not administer corporal punishment, but merely degraded the guilty party from cleri-cal status, a clerk was entitled in effect to one free homicide; only with the second crime, following degrading, could corporal punishment fit that of the soul. Becket claimed that the royal ordinance constituted double jeopardy. He was murdered in 1170 after a royal outburst which inspired four knights to action. The public outcry forced the king to revoke the ordinance of 1164 and made a saint of a very worldly figure. From this time church courts in England were an even greater nuisance for the kings than were French ecclesiastical courts to the kings of France.

The great judicial reforms of Henry II had a threefold aim: curbing the private baronial courts, of limited competence but with growing powers in the period of Stephen; reduction of the nobles' power; and primarily money. Justice was for sale, for one bought the privilege of using the new procedures. An "assize" ("sitting," determination of a judicial principle supposedly in a session of king and council, or an order directed to a sheriff or a local court holder) or a writ (short charter giving an order) could be bought by those who could afford them, and this action would transfer the case into a royal court. This was not the right of all free men, but only of those who could and would pay.

The great assizes of Henry II covered several points, including the relations of church and state over property questions. Most important were the "possessory" assizes, which determined possession without reference to right. The most characteristic of these was the assize "novel disseisin" (recent dispossession): a jury was to be empaneled from the locality and asked whether the man who bought the writ had been recently dispossessed. Whether he had been dispossessed legally was not the issue: if his property had been taken away, it was restored to him. A more complicated possessory assize was "mort d'ancestor" (ancestor's death): the heir was to receive possession even if another man had a better right to the land, such as from sale by the father.

Injustice could obviously be perpetrated in a system in which possession was quite literally nine points of the law. Accordingly, one might buy a writ of right, in which a baron was ordered to "do justice" in his court. If he refused to do what the plaintiff considered justice, another writ might be bought which would take the case to the royal court. The barons even more detested the writ "Praecipe," in which the king ordered the sheriff to "order" the local lord to restore a free tenement or answer for refusal in the royal court. This writ was abolished by *Magna Carta* in 1215, and the other assizes were limited to hearings within the county in which the action originated.

We must also note the beginning of a jury system. The Anglo-Saxons apparently knew the jury of "presentment," a body of men who knew what happened and swore to their knowledge, but the systematic use of such juries in England began with the Assize of Clarendon of 1166. Henry II ordered 12 men from every hundred and 4 from each village to come before the sheriffs and royal itinerant justices and state under oath the names of persons whom they believed to be murderers, thieves, or their accomplices. This is a forerunner of the grand jury, which brings indictments but does not decide guilt or innocence. When the accusation had been made, the accused would be tried before the proper justices, with the ordeal as the method of proof. The list of crimes was gradually extended.

The use of the trial jury, which is presumed not to know the facts and will judge impartially, began with the "Grand Assize" of 1179. The defendant in civil cases in any court, franchisal or royal, could decline trial by battle (a form of proof introduced by the Normans into England for free persons) and have the question settled by a jury in the royal court. The normal use of the trial jury in criminal cases only began in 1215, when the Fourth Lateran Council forbade the clergy to officiate at ordeals and thus deprived the ordeal of its divine force. Pressure, including torture, thus was put on defendants to accept jury trial, for no other form of proof was possible. Many refused, since as free men they were entitled to trial by ordeal, and if they died under torture their families would inherit their property, while they would lose it if the defendant lost his case in court before a jury. Trial by a jury of one's peers (social equals or above) was not the unmixed blessing in the central Middle Ages that later proponents of constitutional liberties have found it. It was a burden and a novelty, particularly because the trial and grand jury were not always distinct and the men who brought the indictment might sit on the jury which decided guilt or innocence.

In short, we still find a very primitive judicial system, and accompanying it a rudimentary government by household, under Henry II. Only under his much maligned son John (1199–1216) and John's son Henry III (1216–72) were these beginnings extended into something approaching a modern legal system and administration. Household government was much modified as departments went out of court and subdivided. We find the beginnings of a genuine bureaucracy. Most of the great series of English government records have survived beginning with John's reign, giving one the impression, historical accident or not, that systematic record keeping may have begun around this time. The great courts were becoming professionalized in the thirteenth century as lawyers came to dominate them, without however supplanting the feudal tenants-in-chief.

But the English government at the end of the twelfth century was so effective for its day that it was able to function under the justiciars during the reign of Richard I (1189–99), who spent only six months of a ten year reign in England. England was a century ahead of the continent in government and administration. The peculiar nature of English "feudalism," culminating so absolutely at the top, deprived feudalism of much of its original content. Yet there are elements of the feudal relationship which would be important for later constitutional development. It involved a contractual and mutual obligation between free men. Consent to the extraordinary was implied in the great council routine, and certainly consent had to be obtained for either lord or vassal to do anything affecting the other which was not covered in the original bond, such as levying extraordinary aids or taxes.

By 1189 the Anglo-Norman barons were grumbling over what they considered royal usurpations, carried out by virtue of the king's very un-Norman and very Anglo-Saxon position in public law against their prerogatives as feudal princes. Government was too efficient for the barons, who were a reactionary element, but law and custom tended to justify their position. The real problem began, however, not with Richard I, but when John lost Normandy and Poitou, forcing the barons to choose either their Norman estates or their English. Even more the issue, however, was the succession of Henry II, the great administrator, and Richard I, the great warrior, by John and Henry III, two kings who were feared by no one, however excellent an administrator John may have been and however decent a man Henry III may have been. The result was a clash of feudal custom, monarchical weakness, a strong public legal tradition, strong local government, and baronial self-interest. It produced some of the most fruitful constitutional experiments of European history in the thirteenth and fourteenth centuries.

Capetian France in the Twelfth Century

The Capetian kingdom presented a very different picture from the English. It was a land of principalities greater than the monarchy. Philip I (1060–1108) was something less than a chivalrous figure, but he did add some small territories in central France to the royal domain, the first such additions in a century. The royal domain was consolidated under Louis VI, the Fat (1108–37) and Louis VII (1137–80). Louis VI made his home territory in the Ile-de-France around Paris safe from robber barons in the first years of his reign. Louis' interference—on the losing side—in a succession dispute in Flanders in 1127 was the first such meddling of the crown in the internal affairs of a great principality since the beginning of the dynasty. Louis' prestige was such that the Duke of Aquitaine, ruler of the largest crown fief, made him the guardian of his daughter Eleanor; the king married her to his son, the future Louis VII. We have noted the results of this union. When Eleanor offended her second husband, he imprisoned her; Louis VII allowed her to marry his most powerful opponent and subtract the rich Aquitainian inheritance from royal control. Louis VII has undergone a certain rehabilitation in recent years, but he still was a weak figure. He made only one significant addition to the royal domain, and was forced to spend

Map 5. Medieval France

most of his time in the field against the expansionist pretensions of the Angevins, whose Norman possessions came to the very edge of the Paris basin. Louis did acquire a certain reputation as a judge. Crown vassals came increasingly to the royal court, which now became a court in fact as well as name.

Philip II Augustus (1180–1223) was the real founder of the French monarchy, apparently institutionally as well as territorially, but there is no evidence that his personal ability had much to do with it. His great advantage was in facing John, rather than Henry II or Richard. There was little loyalty in France to the Angevin house, although the dynasty was French rather than English. The "people" simply did not matter, for government concerned only ruling elites until, at the very earliest, the mid-thirteenth century. The "people" of the Angevin domains cared little for either Angevin or Capetian. Philip used physical force as well as persuasion. He placed Burgundy in the royal orbit in the late twelfth century by naming one of his relatives as duke. He allied with the towns outside (but not inside) the royal domain and encouraged their separatist tendencies. One of the most incredibly double-dealing princes of the entire medieval period, he in a sense created modern France in one fell swoop when he declared King John of England a contumacious vassal for failing to answer a summons to the royal court and confiscated his French fiefs. Declaration and enforcement are not the same, and Philip's power was no match for the Angevin; yet John simply stayed in Normandy and did nothing while Philip conquered his entire continental empire except Aquitaine, which was so hard to govern that it was to be a severe drain on English resources in the late Middle Ages.

It is often said, largely on the basis of the confiscation of the Angevin territories, that the French kings used feudalism and the fact that France was so thoroughly feudal to unify their kingdom. Yet this is only partially true, and it is largely the case only in the thirteenth century and after. The territorial principalities were held theoretically in fief of the king, and there was thus considerable value in some of the feudal aids and incidents. Escheat was sometimes difficult to bring about, for heiresses could get in the way. The heiress of the Champagne was first married to a king in the thirteenth century, but the land later reverted to a collateral branch of the comital family and only fell to the monarchy in the mid-fourteenth century. The right of the lord to marry an heiress to a loyal man was important. Louis VII brought about the most important and largest pre-thirteenth century annexation to the royal domain in 1180 by marrying the future Philip II to the heiress of Artois. Rights of wardship over minors might mean that a youngster was raised at the royal court and became friendly with the princes. Reliefs were quite large when principalities changed hands.

Capetian administration was basically a more primitive version of the Anglo-Norman, but there were differences. The Capetians did not develop permanent administrative departments until the mid-thirteenth century. There was little to govern until the annexations of the Angevin domains in 1204–5, and it could be handled by a very simple administration. The royal domain was originally governed by tax farmers and local administrators called provosts, but bailiffs make their appearance under Philip Augustus. They are first mentioned in a text of 1190, when Philip disposed of his property in the event of his death on crusade and provided administrative continuity. The bailiffs were officials of the *curia regis* (king's court, or the great council) and performed both judicial and tax-collecting functions for the king; they combined the duties of the English sheriffs and itinerant justices. Eventually they made their local authority too great and abuses crept in. Under Louis IX (1226–70), "inquisitors" were sent out to check on them, but the same thing eventually happened to the inquisitors. The bailiffs' powers were limited to judicial actions in the late thirteenth century, but they had performed an important function of consolidating local administration.

When the Capetians annexed the Angevin territories, they found an administration far in advance of their own. Accordingly, they simply maintained local custom while sending in officials at the top. The fact that the great principalities had been independent for so long meant that they had developed local organs of government and traditions of particularism, and the Capetians never really united France institutionally. Some areas were similar to the royal domain administration, but others were quite different. Unity was made more difficult in addition by the practice common from the time of Louis VIII (1223–26) of giving *apanages,* separate territories, to younger sons, who could govern them independently of the king while still maintaining loyalty to him. Accordingly, adminstrations overlapped. Some parts of France had no royal officials and some had several sets competing with one another in fleecing the populace. The annexation of much of southern France in 1270, when the county of Toulouse fell to the monarchy, only compounded the problem.

Royal administration, in short, was very rudimentary, but was specializing in the thirteenth century without streamlining. As an example, when Philip II lost his baggage train in a battle with Richard of England in 1194, he lost his entire chancery with it. As a result, our knowledge of Capetian history before 1194 comes almost entirely from documents found in the chanceries of princes, of which one copy went to the recipient and one to the king. The household officers and financial organization of Philip Augustus were probably no better than those of England under Henry I, and were of the same organizational type. The *curia regis* was becoming more important, but the great professionalization was the work of Louis IX and Philip IV.

9

ECONOMY AND SOCIETY

Europe entered a period of economic expansion and social change in the tenth century which was to last until the late thirteenth in most regions. Certainly the political changes which we have been describing would have been inconceivable under a Carolingian-type economy. As we shall see, however, economic expansion outstripped man's capacity to adjust his social relationships and some hardship and dislocation resulted.

Various explanations have been given for the economic revival, most of them having a grain of truth but by no means accounting for the whole picture. Probably the most important force for prosperity was the return of comparative peace. The Vikings had been particularly destructive of the commercial settlements located on the rivers of northern Europe, but they were settling down by 900. The towns began to grow again soon after. As the Magyar and Arab menaces were ended later in the tenth century, there was new opportunity for expansion of the towns of Germany and the Mediterranean basin.

Despite the increased fragmentation of the territorial principality, we find the growth of a "peace movement" in the late tenth and eleventh centuries. All public and private personalities except serfs and slaves had a "peace." The king's peace could be extended to a particular place or individual, and offenses against such persons or on such places were considered offenses against the king. Merchants were collectively under the king's peace. Towns later were to develop the capacity of sworn peace associations. An offense against one mem-

ber of the group was an offense against all, who would avenge wrongs
collectively.

The churches also formulated a "peace and truce of God." The
peace of God applied to noncombatants, peasant dependents of warriors, women, and children. The peace of God also extended to the
churches, for violence within or immediately outside churches or holy
sanctuaries was considered sacrilege; indeed, the safety which this religious consideration evidently involved contributed to the growth
of settlements around many churches. Somewhat later, in the eleventh
century, the truce of God was elaborated. It extended at first from
Friday evening until Monday morning, and included Lent, Easter,
Christmas, Whitsuntide, and various other church festivals and holy
days. Fighting was forbidden during these times.

Such an otherworldly movement obviously could not work without
cooperation from the temporal princes who had powers of enforcement. Many, particularly in the eleventh century, were quite willing
to use the peace movement and the threat of ecclesiastical sanctions—
which were often disregarded, but which nonetheless were some de-
terrent to violence—as a means of furthering order and disposing of
recalcitrant subjects and vassals. The dukes of Normandy are excellent
examples of princes who furthered the peace movement and with it
territorial unification. In their turn, the churches benefited from peace
and contributed to the ideological armament of many princes by furnishing elaborate justifications of state power which was being exercised in the service of God.

The eleventh century was certainly no golden age of nonviolence,
but it was infinitely more peaceful than the previous period. This
made possible more substantial harvests and a population expansion.
Peasants were less likely to be killed during raids than before, and
they could be more certain of harvesting a crop once sown. As the
arable was extended, more farmers grew a surplus for market. As
roads and streams became safer, the volume of trade and commerce
expanded.

Changes in the Agrarian Economy

In any economy as overwhelmingly agricultural as that of medieval
Europe, change had to begin in the agrarian sector. We have noted
the three-field system of exploitation, but largely because of conditions

Illustration 7. A wheeled plow

of climate, there is little evidence that two-field systems were changed into three, although this could mean an increase in yield of 33 percent, even from the same total acreage. The great clearance movements of the central Middle Ages occurred chiefly in areas of three-field agriculture, as new territories were cleared from forest and existing fields were extended. Indeed, as population pressure became intense, some poor areas developed three-field agriculture and contributed to a growing problem of soil exhaustion by the mid-thirteenth century.

Controversy over field systems has given rise to a sort of technological determinism of social relationships. A scratch plow was used in southern Europe which only lightly turned the thin, often sandy topsoil. In the north we more often find the wheeled plow, with a moldboard to turn the soil thoroughly and a cutting edge, often of iron, heavier than that of the scratch plow. The wheeled plow almost invariably was drawn by a team of oxen, or later horses. It has been claimed that use of this plow, which permitted much more intensive cultivation than the scratch plow and as such a higher population density, contributed to communal agriculture, since few peasants could afford a team of eight oxen to pull the plow. Furthermore, the shape of the furrow created by this plow was conducive to the open, elongated fields characteristic of the manor, and as a result this plow tended to be used in areas with a large servile peasantry. These generalizations are often true, but there are many exceptions; in particular, medieval miniatures often show fewer than eight animals pulling a wheeled plow, despite its heaviness.

Certainly there were tremendous improvements in agricultural technology in the central Middle Ages. Although peasants seemed reluctant to move toward the "new-fangled" even then, despite obvious advantages which could be derived from changes, there was a greater diffusion of iron implements in the period after Charlemagne. Hoes and axes more often had iron cutting edges. It was admittedly rather poor iron; medieval industrial technology was quite simple, particularly in the countryside, and one does not get very good iron from smelting with wood fires. The use of the wheeled plow became more common throughout Europe. The horseshoe was invented in the post-Carolingian period, but it was of little immediate importance for agriculture in view of the general preference for oxen over horses as draft animals until the late Middle Ages. Of greater importance was the horse collar, with a principle which could be applied to oxen as well. Draft animals in the early Middle Ages were harnessed by a simple thong around the neck. When a heavy load was pulled for a long period, the animal's wind was cut off, and hard work became impossible. With the collar, a plank was thrown across the beast's shoulders, with a cord run through his mouth to the ends of the plank and thence to the plow and driver. The weight of the plow was thus shifted to the animal's shoulder and back, and the result was a tremendous increase in the productivity of horses and oxen.

Other changes affected both agricultural and industrial technology. The watermill was known in the Carolingian period, but it only became common in the following age. Domesday Book, the great land survey undertaken by William the Conqueror in 1086, records several thousand watermills in late eleventh-century England. Water power once harnessed could be used for grinding grain and for industrial operations. The windmill was used by the twelfth century and became very important for drainage operations as more land was cleared, but it could also have some of the same uses as the watermill. Hands were released for field work as machines began doing the work of men and animals.

For a combination of reasons, then, largely the return of comparative peace and improvements in agricultural technology, productive capacity was increased. While all evidence suggests that a tremendous

Illustration 8. Miller and windmill

amount of land was necessary to maintain an average household in the Merovingian period, this amount dropped in the ninth and tenth centuries until the *quartier* (one-fourth manse, the equivalent of the English virgate of 25 to 30 acres) became the "normal" unit for a landholding household—this, of course, merely meant that most persons held less than this, if indeed they had land at all, and had to supplement their income by other means.

The decline in size of the household unit may not have indicated rising productivity as much as population pressure. Although statistics are scarce, they show that after a brief period of stabilization or even decline in the wake of the invasions, population again increased and was to continue to grow until the middle or late thirteenth century. In terms of the means of subsistence, some areas were overpopulated even as early as 900. Technological improvement alone could not suffice, and more land had to be brought under cultivation. The new inventions of the ninth through early twelfth centuries were not followed by further advances in the late twelfth and thirteenth, and the result was a population pressure which had reached crisis proportions by 1250.

The Expansion of the Arable

The economic growth came in various ways. Particularly in the early period, lords were uninterested, for they had little sense of scientific estate management; they were too busy with the noble social prerogatives to worry overly about such mundane concerns as their revenues. Accordingly, most pre-twelfth century clearance movements were the work of peasant entrepreneurs who simply obtained the consent of the lord of the land that they wished to cultivate. Fields already in existence were thus extended into the ever-present forest, and new fields were created. The coastal areas were drained and put under the plow, and indeed peasant specialists in drainage circulated in the Low Countries and the North Sea regions, making farmland for themselves at advantageous terms. For the clearance of new land gave tremendous opportunities to both lord and peasant. The vacant land had brought the lord no income, but he could get rights to judicial fines, land rentals, and the like from new arable, in addition to exacting a fee for permission to clear or drain.

Such an expansion could not but affect the relationship of lord and peasant tenant. In the Carolingian age, geared essentially toward a subsistence economy, tenures were usually hereditary and held for fixed services or quitrents. There was tremendous inflation of the coinage in the central Middle Ages. Labor injects value into a commodity not inherent in the raw material. Borrowing increased, making possible large-scale business enterprises through accumulation of capital from numerous sources. The interest on these loans, open or concealed, created "fiduciary" (based on trust, and hence not real) money which inflated the coinage, even apart from the question of debasement by princes. In other words, if a businessman borrowed £100 and agreed to pay 20 percent interest, a not uncommon figure, he had to get £120 from some source, either by injecting his own labor into the value of the commodity involved or through the desires of others to use his services in a manner profitable to him. As inflation proceeded, lords were losing money on the clumsy system of fixed payments and forced labor services.

Furthermore, there were loopholes in the manorial structure. The exact nature of peasant services was being specified in the central Middle Ages, curbing the arbitrary power of lords. Peasants were often bound to work only for part of the day. Although slaves were totally at the lord's disposal, slavery was quite unusual in Europe by the eleventh century and would only reappear in the late Middle Ages. Serfs rendered services which were assessed on the lands which they occupied. Hence if a virgate owed a certain demesne service to the lord, its holder might send a son to do it while he and the other children farmed their tenement. Furthermore, no one works as well at enforced duties as for himself, and malingering was a persistent problem.

Some lords solved the problem by exacting cash payments from their serfs in lieu of labor services and using the extra money to hire labor for the demesne. Persons who could not support themselves on the available land might go to a town. There were limits to this, however, since few migrated over a great distance to a city, for the towns drew most of their population from the immediately surrounding territory until very late in the Middle Ages. The landless peasants worked cheaply, since there was little else that they could do to make a living. The wage-earning peasant was more efficient than the landholder, for in the classic manorial regime the peasant tenants had worked certain days throughout the year on the lord's demesne, and this meant that extra peasants were hanging around the demesne at times when they were not needed. Despite these advantages, however, the great use of laborers to cultivate the demesnes comes only in the thirteenth century. There was such a surplus population on the land by this time that it was usually quite easy to obtain the lord's permission to leave the estate and go to a town or to another estate in search of work.

In most areas, however, the reason for lords' commuting of labor services was somewhat more elemental: they needed ready money. As the real value of their properties decreased, they allowed their local officials to take advantage of them, even to the extent of carving out little lordships of their own. These *maires* were charged with minding the lord's interests, but many lords were simply too negligent to notice usurpations until a generation or so had passed, by which time "immemorial custom" had usually sanctioned the usurpation and obtained the force of law. Although the extent to which lords lost or were forced to sell or rent their demesne to peasants has been overestimated, and considerable demesne farming persisted through use of salaried labor throughout the Middle Ages, the lords were in a period of economic crisis by the second half of the twelfth century.

Lords thus began to take an active interest in the economic expansion in the second half of the century, hoping to turn it to their advantage. Since they could always get revenues from newly cleared lands and many duties remained incumbent on the person of peasant dependents, they encouraged new settlers to come to their estates. They estab-

lished villages with "elementary bourgeois liberties" or gave such
charters to villages previously in existence. These places were still agrarian villages economically, and the liberties were given to the persons
living in the town and not to a separate town government, which was
rarely established by these charters. Lords obviously hoped that these
settlements would grow into genuine towns to rival the older centers and
attract capital to the lord's domain. Some, particularly those founded
before 1200, did become large, but most did not, for too many were
founded after the towns had absorbed a disproportionately large share
of the population. Temporal lords often made *pariage* (wager) contracts with ecclesiastical princes, with the one furnishing the land while
the other publicized the new foundation among daughter houses and
peasants on overpopulated estates. The central Middle Ages thus witnessed a redistribution of population and an increased degree of freedom among the peasants.

Some scholars have argued that the towns contributed to the growth
of peasant emancipation by reviving a money economy and giving
the peasants a market for their goods. This view is basically correct,
but must be nuanced. Village markets were thriving before towns developed—some villages indeed became towns—and the important fact
to remember is that the peasants received a much higher price for
grain in the towns than on the village markets. The higher prices
led to regional inflation, which in turn allowed the peasants to pay
their duties in cheap coin.

Social Consequences of Rural Economic Expansion

Such a fundamental economic change would obviously cause altera-
tions in the social structure. The peasants now had new opportunities
for advancement. Those who lived on the edge of forests and cleared
their lands might obtain freedom from servile duties, as lords com-
muted services for money. The various peasant classes had tended
to merge into serfdom in the period after Charlemagne, but freedom
and servility are always relative matters. Only a slave can be totally
at the mercy of a lord. The serf did labor services and paid rentals
in kind, but much of this was a result of the primitive state of the
economy. Why pay money when produce, which nearly every peasant had at his disposal, was what the lord really needed and wanted?
Much the same is true of labor services, which went out of existence

not only when lords began to need money—as commodities became needed for the noble life style which could not be produced locally— but when the supply of landless laborers was large enough to give lords some alternative to demesne labor services by tenants.

Certainly it seems evident that if the medieval peasant had a golden age, it was the first half of the twelfth century. Previously landless peasants might clear and hold land. Duties were lessening, and in most areas population pressure was still not sufficiently severe to bring dangerous pressure on the means of subsistence. Those who wanted to clear or expand lands already cultivated could do so, and generally at favorable conditions of tenure, for "elementary bourgeois liberties" normally gave freedom and specified fixed rental payments for the peasants. These charters usually also guaranteed the peasant's right to sell or otherwise alienate his tenement. Periods of prosperity tend to leave as many behind as they further, and peasants could create large holdings or even petty local lordships by purchasing lands from less fortunate or less intelligent neighbors.

But the classic picture of peasants gradually gaining freedom through purchase of charters of emancipation and performance of clearance work, in return for which they might be enfranchised, must be modified seriously. At the same time, servile status per se meant much less in the central Middle Ages than earlier and was no barrier to personal advancement. The case of England has been seen by some as an exception to continental developments, but recent studies suggest strong parallels between English and French peasant conditions. The Norman conquest has been credited with the revival of a moribund English economy, but this view is almost certainly erroneous. Anglo-Saxon town development was probably ahead of most regions of the continent. The conquest depressed the substantial English free peasantry into "villeinage," a term meaning either free or servile peasants in France but always designating a serf in England. The Domesday survey in 1086, however, which records tax payments and military service owed to the king, shows extremely high population density and numerous free peasants, particularly in eastern and southwestern England. There is evidence of new land clearance in the twelfth century, and some hint that this may have lightened peasant services. The English peasant was the equivalent of his continental counterpart by 1150 at the latest: servile in the sense of being justiciable in a lord's court rather than the king's, owing rental payments and labor to the lord, but also having some freedom of movement, a mark of free persons even when exercised by the unfree.

Thus there were means of advancement for peasants through normal economic means and usurpation. Even the village *maires* were sometimes serfs. We find also a peculiar class of "sergeants" who were usually free in England, but might be servile in France. Some were *maires*, others not, and some prospered more than others. As class distinctions became more finely enunciated in the thirteenth century, sergeants either sank into the upper reaches of the peasantry or became petty local squires.

The sergeants were the closest French equivalent to the German *ministeriales*, a class once thought much more unique to Germany than was actually the case. The *ministeriales* originated among the household serfs from whom lords recruited specialists who performed valuable services, such as messenger duties, carrying services with goods from one manor to another, and the like. Some early *ministeriales* even performed castle guard, for only in the twelfth century were prohibitions issued against unfree persons bearing arms. The German kings in particular used them for numerous important tasks, and the *ministeriales* had developed class consciousness by the early eleventh century. In parts of Germany they might change masters if their own lords did not grant them fiefs.

Since fiefs generally involved the ban power (power of command over persons), the *ministeriales* approached the nobility. Yet they remained servile in law until the thirteenth century. In effect they were a service nobility, just as the ancestors of the nobility of blood of the twelfth century had been in the Merovingian age. With the power of command and the profession of arms, the *ministeriales* held two prerogatives of the nobility, lacking only free status, which was not long in coming.

In addition to the royal *ministeriales*, who formed the core of the petty nobility of the late Middle Ages and created immense headaches for the towns and greater lords by brigandage, the great ecclesiastical foundations had *ministeriales*. Since most larger towns of Germany grew up on the land of a bishop or abbot, the landholding *ministeriales* of the town lord later made up a substantial part of the city patriciate. Although they began to identify with the townsmen as they had commercial contacts with them, the ministerial elements gave a landholding character to the urban patriciates of Germany quite similar to those of southern France and Italy and less like those of northern France and the Low Countries. Many prominent men of the German towns were still paying "quitrents of recognition," small payments to lords in acknowledgement of technically servile status, in the fourteenth and fifteenth centuries, although this had absolutely no practical effect on their business or freedom of movement.

The Reaction of the Thirteenth Century

The tendency of peasants to gain freedom was reversed in some areas as early as the last quarter of the twelfth century. The best land had been cleared, and as even marginal land was being used up, the clearance movements were less important as a means of gaining freedom. Villages might buy collective freedom, but the price was usually so high that the peasants subjected themselves to economic, as opposed to personal servitude. Lords also were paying more attention now to scientific estate management. The reintroduction of Roman legal studies contributed to a depressing of the peasantry. Peasants who did not have access to the courts of the state were considered servile, but this distinction had little practical effect in an age of minimal state power. Certain labor services or payments, particularly mortmain (payment of the best beast to the lord when a peasant died) and formariage (payment for the right to marry outside the manor), were considered prima facie tests of servile status unless the contrary could be proven. The concept was current until the very end of the Middle Ages that a person subject to a tax on his person, as opposed to a percentage tax on his property, was unfree, and many lords had the right to impose such taxes on their dependents. Once paid, it became a sign of servitude. Lords tried to impose head taxes not only because they were a sign of serfdom, but also because in an age of overpopulation the number of heads might be worth more than the value of the property in land rentals. Further fiscalization of lords' rights comes with the fixing of *banalités* in most parts of Europe in the twelfth century. In a sense this was a sign of technological advancement, for in the Carolingian period such primitive manufacturing was done in the peasant household. Now lords built mills for grinding grain, winepresses, breweries, and the like and forced the peasants to patronize them and pay high fees.

The development of tests of servile status was furthered as some persons were expressly termed "free," often leaving the rest unfree. This is particularly true in Germany, where peasants were being depressed into serfdom in the twelfth and thirteenth centuries largely on grounds of paying the head tax. The reaction was also severe in England, but while in France the peasants seem to have escaped the reimposition of serfdom to the extent that characterized England and Germany, some areas, particularly in the mountainous and infertile east and south, knew a resurgence of serfdom in the thirteenth century.

Part of the problem too was ambiguity in the charters. A person might gain "freedom" from certain obligations without gaining the juridical freedom which would have made him justiciable in a royal court. Particularly as local lords made their control over local government more firm in the thirteenth century, for what seem to have been essentially financial reasons, the dependent status of many peasants was confirmed. We must not overemphasize; the gains made during the eleventh and early twelfth centuries were not obliterated, but merely weakened. Many regions, such as Normandy, the Low Countries, and parts of England, still preserved a largely free peasantry. But the fact remains that there were always only two escape routes for peasants who could not make a living on the farm—the status of *ministerialis* and eventually the lesser nobility, and migration to the town—and by the mid-thirteenth century at the latest neither was open to servile persons.

The Fortunes of the Nobility

The social status and economic position of the European nobles were changed dramatically by the economic expansion. As their fixed rents became worth less and less, their expenses increased. Scutage was convenient, but it was not cheap. The nobles were becoming domesticated. They were no longer the primitives who lived from one campaigning season to the next on the proceeds of their estates, but rather were individuals who participated in government in some limited way and were interested in nonmilitary pursuits. Luxury commodities were now available from the East, and the expense of obtaining them and keeping up a high life style further drained noble pocketbooks.

The nobles tried various expedients, such as encouraging colonization of their vacant lands, which worked only temporarily and could not solve their long-range problems. In southern Europe, particularly in Italy, we find a movement away from the Roman ethos that trade was degrading for an aristocrat. Municipal patriciates were composed of men whose main wealth was in land, but who lived in the town and marketed the products of their rural estates there. This began to change only in the thirteenth century, as city magistracies were dominated more by men whose business was more purely mercantile or industrial, and even they invested in land as soon as they were able, thus obtaining social respectability by entering the frame of reference, if not the sociointellectual milieu, of the noble. Most nobles of northern Europe, however, remained outside the town, except in cases where the individual's land was enclosed by the expansion of a city. Save only the *ministeriales,* the nobles of most parts of the north remained a nonbourgeois class until the late thirteenth century. Even thereafter the nobles continued to regard their special social prerogatives, such as bloodletting, as sacrosanct. They engaged only occasionally in trade, living chiefly on investments in rural and urban land.

Perhaps in conscious reaction to their growing economic difficulties, however, the nobles began to close themselves off as a juridical class as early as the beginning of the twelfth century. The social evolution of the post-Carolingian nobility still awaits a definitive genealogical study, but it seems clear that the population increase which affected all classes left its mark on the nobility as well. Since noble standards of life were higher than those of other groups, we expect and generally find more sons surviving to divide a single patrimony than was the case with peasant households. The rather small Carolingian nobility had dominated "government" in the tenth century, but these houses developed younger branches, which were soon endowed with the power of command and with lands. Thus the territorial principalities were fragmenting in the late tenth and eleventh centuries, as younger sons founded governments based on the castellany and became minor local barons. Some took high-sounding titles; numerous counts and dukes appeared who had no connection with the great crown fiefs of France or the tribal duchies of Germany. This was merely a way of gaining social prestige and hoping to increase one's acceptability to those above in the social ranking. Some great principalities managed to overcome the disunity and others did not, but all developed a rather extensive nobility, taking in perhaps 5 percent of the population as opposed to 10 percent in the Merovingian period, when social advancement was more totally determined by brains and brawn, particularly the latter. Each of these noble houses, great and small, was very conscious of its essential characteristics: noble birth, preferably on both sides of the family, knighthood and the practice of arms, and the power of command over persons.

No one of these, save the all-essential birth, created a noble. The connection between knighthood and nobility is extremely complicated. The term *miles* (knight) originally had no connotation of nobility, but merely meant a soldier who fought on horseback, but it took on overtones of social prestige by the eleventh century. A knight was not necessarily a noble, but by the twelfth century all nobles were knights.

The thirteenth century brings a still more peculiar development. By this time knighthood involved expensive state burdens, particularly in England. Knights were in charge of local government, the county courts, parliamentary service somewhat later, and often the local militia. England did not have a nobility properly so-called, for position was not invariably hereditary, and while one son usually inherited his father's title, only the eldest son of a parent inherited his social rank. England's upper class was an aristocracy, not a nobility. The late twelfth century saw a very rapid rise and fall in knightly fortunes in England, and one suspects that were the continent better documented a similar story might be told there. The burdens of knighthood were so expensive that many persons whose birth qualified them for knighthood simply did not bother to take the final step of becoming knights and remained squires. We find "distraint of knighthood" in thirteenth century England to force all landholders of incomes above a certain amount to become knights. This was generally an excuse to fine such persons and allow them to avoid service, for knighthood by this time had lost its military importance and had become fiscal, as nobles and aristocrats no longer monopolized the profession of arms. On the continent, where a "poor noble" was virtually unheard of in the tenth century, many "proud but poor" families are found by the thirteenth, marrying their daughters to bourgeois and in some areas barely above the economic level of the peasants, having power of command only over their own households.

As a defensive reaction, then, the noble class—threatened by economic pressure, the growth of the princely state, and the loss of its raison d'être, the profession of arms—gradually closed its ranks. This happened earliest in northern Europe, for here it was very difficult for new men to enter the nobility after the early eleventh century. The nobility remained open somewhat longer in southern France and Germany, but by the early thirteenth century most regions of the continent had witnessed the union of the greater and lesser nobles into an all-encompassing juridical class, with fixed rules of descent, inheritance, and status. The two levels were in no sense social equals until much later, and a baron whose daughter married a squire sustained some loss of face. The lesser nobility more often was penetrated from below by the bourgeoisie.

But no closed juridical class can perpetuate itself. Part of the population is always infertile, and constant inbreeding exaggerates this. Many noble families were dying out, and the rank needed replenishment by the thirteenth century. Kings began to sell patents of nobility to those who had enough money to buy, particularly bourgeois. Since knighthood was the equivalent of nobility, most such persons simply bought knighthood, and both knighthood and nobility lost most of their earlier meaning.

The European nobility was thus in a peculiar situation at the end of the thirteenth century. The greatest nobles had not been affected appreciably. They still had a near monopoly on important governmental offices, and most of their lands were still intact. The middling and lesser nobles had often been forced to sell land to the great barons or even to the bourgeoisie. Thus they either sank economically into the peasantry or perhaps went to a town, where at least their social pretensions were respected. Local squires could consolidate their power and rule virtually independently, or might be forced to seek new fortune by entering the royal bureaucracy and building new estates through royal favor. The nobility was becoming at one and the same time impossibly narrow and impossibly broad.

The standard of life of the nobles was improving in this period, but it was still something less than elegant. Many lived simply in earthen blockhouses or towers from which they could dominate the surrounding area. These castles often maintained only one room heated in the winter, in which bodily functions were performed before the eyes of all. The wealthier nobles and kings had "motte and bailey" castles in this age, with a tower surrounded by an inner courtyard, then with exterior walls and a great moat or ditch to guard it from the outside. Floors were dirt, and the walls were so thick that while

Illustration 9. Castle of the counts of Flanders, Ghent

Illustration 10. Castle of Godfrey of Bouillon, at Bouillon

summer heat was kept out, life in the winter was scarcely tolerable. There was plenty of room in such castles for the chickens, cattle, and pigs to run about at will. Save for the defensive structures and living quarters, construction within these castles was of wood. Although by the late thirteenth century some princely castles were being built with a view toward comfortable living, this was exceptional, and most nobles lived close to nature. They did, of course, have advantages not generally available to the rest of the population, such as plenty of meat—for hunting was both a sport and a forage for food with the nobles—a good supply of other foods, and a generally better balanced diet than many. They had ample firewood and homes which, whatever their inelegance, would not burn easily or be blown away.

The Development of Town Life

Town life worthy of the name scarcely existed in Europe in 1000, but by the mid-thirteenth century many cities had grown to a larger size than they were to reach again before the eighteenth century. All towns developed in close connection with an agrarian hinterland, although the nature of the relationship varied tremendously.

Urban development was most precocious in Italy. While the Italian towns were not direct continuations of the Roman, the Roman urban tradition was strong and contributed to an early revival of town life, with economic institutions strikingly similar to the Roman, after the Lombard invasions. Venice was to know a particularly spectacular growth. Beginning as a fishing village on the lagoons off the northern Adriatic, Venice took advantage of its situation as the logical point of embarkation for goods coming to and from Constantinople. Although the Venetians did not actively further the calling of the first crusade, we have seen that their economic interests and resident colonies had preceded the crusaders and given them some economic footing. The Italians were largely responsible for the tremendous influx of oriental commodities into western Europe in the wake of the crusades.

On the western coast of Italy, Genoa and Pisa were becoming wealthy even by the tenth century through trade with southern Italy, the Mediterranean coast of France, and the Berber principalities of northern Africa. The rivalry of these two cities ended only when Genoa defeated Pisa in battle in 1284. After Pisa's harbor silted, the city was annexed to the state of Florence in 1404. Although both had economic interests in the crusader kingdoms, neither rivalled Venetian influence in the east.

The cities of the Italian interior developed more slowly until the twelfth century. Rome was a peculiar case, dominated by the popes and with little independent commercial life until the thirteenth century, when banking for the popes became a major occupation of Sienese and Lucchese and later Florentine business houses. Most towns of the interior, such as Florence and Milan, were centers of agrarian exchange and had a crude industry, and many townspeople had rural property whose products they used in urban industry. The industrial development later associated with the interior cities was absent in the beginning. Florence, the most heavily industrialized, was chiefly a refiner of raw cloth bought elsewhere, generally at the fairs of Champagne from the Flemings, until the late thirteenth century. The great political power of the twelfth century Italian towns, as shown by their successful wars with Frederick I, came less from their economic strength than from their powerful positions in uniting rural nobles and urban rich, groups which in the beginning were not strongly differentiated in Italy and always remained closer than in the north.

The cities of northern Europe had varied origins, but most of the larger of them began as preurban nuclei around fortifications or ecclesiastical foundations. The chief urban areas were the southeastern coast of England, although this region fell behind after the Norman conquest; Flanders, Brabant, and northernmost France; and the German Rhineland and the eastern Low Countries. The rest of France developed large cities more slowly. These towns were quite primitive into the twelfth century. Even those with some industry were dominated by their markets for grain and other raw materials, for their chief need was the safeguarding of their food supply. All, furthermore, provided a place where farmers might market their produce at higher prices than on most rural markets. Most, even the largest, had no more than a few thousand inhabitants by 1100, but such indirect evidence as the expansion of town walls (we have no decent population figures for the cities of southern Europe before the thirteenth century and for most of the north before the fourteenth) suggests that many tripled or quadrupled during the tremendous economic boom of the twelfth century. Migrating workers kept close contact with countryside relatives, who might follow them into the city after a time.

Practically all towns of northern Europe, large and small, were on the territory of a lord. We have noted the development of some by deliberate seigneurial foundation. By 1050, however, most of the preurban nuclei were chafing at the maintenance of aristocratic prerogatives, lordly rights, tolls, personal unfreedom, and other hindrances to their ability to make contracts or to move about as they pleased, for the townsman could not be governed in his business dealings by laws which fit the agricultural occupations of the surrounding countryside. Hence we find a series of revolts, the "communal movements" (a commune is a sworn association of whatever sort, but usually with a definite purpose in mind) of townsmen which resulted in freeing most large centers from all but a nominal princely overlordship by 1150. The earliest known revolt of a town against its lord occurred at Cambrai in 967. The first communal charter which has survived was given to Huy, a little town in eastern Belgium, after what seem to have been peaceful negotiations with the town lord, the bishop of Liège. The townsmen wanted recognition of their separate status, while the bishop needed their money. The cities of the Rhineland played off princes against one another during the investiture contest. Since most of their overlords were bishops, they tended to support the kings against the pope and were rewarded by charters of liberties, most of which were granted in the reign of Henry V (1106–25).

It is somewhat strange that after these promising beginnings the German kings became comparatively indifferent to town development, preferring to rely on their princes to govern Germany by delegation. This did not hinder German town development significantly, however, for some princes, notably Henry the Lion, founded numerous towns, particularly in Saxony and the German East, which became quite prosperous in the late Middle Ages. Lübeck, Brunswick, and the German cities of modern Poland are striking examples of this. Some planned foundations in the west developed into larger centers, but this was less usual than in the still undeveloped east, for the west was already becoming overurbanized and was glutted with towns by 1200 at the latest.

The Flemish cities knew a precocious development. Located in a prosperous agricultural and sheep-raising area, they developed textile industries at an early stage which quickly outstripped the native Flemish wool supply. Even by the twelfth century the Flemish industries were quite dependent upon importing English wool, for England had

only a small native weaving. We do not know when they first tried
to obtain self-government, but a disputed succession to the countship
of Flanders in 1127 gave them the opportunity to gain extensive
liberties as they bargained among the several contenders. Although
the count still had a formal overlordship, the cities were virtually independent, and their political power was to dominate Flanders by the
thirteenth century.

Urban Society

The society of the earliest preurban nuclei was extremely diverse.
Although artisans and farmers were part of these settlements, there
was more money in selling commodities than in making them, and
the merchants accordingly dominated most cities at an early date.
The merchants formed their own guilds, organizations with power
of self-regulation, at first for protection as they travelled about together, and later for absolute domination of some towns. Artisan organizations are recorded in some German and French cities in the
twelfth century, but they rarely got a share in political power, and
in many places the artisans were forbidden to organize. The Italian
and some English cities had a different system, with merchant wholesalers of goods and artisans who made those goods together in a single
guild; the combined upper crust of these organizations was thus the
equivalent of the merchant guilds of many northern towns.

Virtually all town governments were dominated by the wealthy,
and wealth was concentrated in a small number of families. The merchant patriciates of the northern towns sometimes adopted quite crass
methods of self-perpetuation; the rulers of Ghent were three rotating
bodies of thirteen magistrates which chose successors to vacant seats
from among ruling families. Somewhat later, Venice inscribed the
names of families with a hereditary right to sit on the town council
in a "Golden Book." Such regimes were not generally noted for their
stability, but the Venetian was exceptional. Most Italian towns had
a somewhat broader base of government than their northern counterparts, although it was still aristocratic. The nobles had preyed on commerce in the early days, and some towns had to conquer them and
force them to become citizens of the commune and spend part of
the year in the city. Many lesser nobles, indeed, saw the towns as
a new source of wealth and disposed of much of their rural property.

Urban and rural upper class are very close in Italy, although the predominantly landholding character of the ruling bodies of the interior cities was to lessen in the thirteenth century as men of more purely mercantile interest came to power. Even here, there are exceptions. The government of mercantile, powerful Genoa was dominated throughout the Middle Ages by rural nobles. Most Italian towns had independent governments under consuls, or officials of similar designation, by the late eleventh or early twelfth century, and some have argued that the regime of town councils of usually 10 to 30 persons which characterized the towns of northern Europe for the rest of the Middle Ages was consciously modeled on the Italian example. Certainly consular regimes were set up in towns of southern and central France, but they were under stricter seigneurial control than the communes of the north. The towns of imperial Italy also knew the *podestà,* an administrator originally appointed by the emperor and later a municipal official, chosen from another commune to administer a particular city equitably for a limited term, usually six months to a year.

The towns were able to sustain tremendous immigration in the twelfth century as markets continued to grow with population. Most cities produced only crude manufactured goods for the immediate environs, for textiles and mining were still the only industries with a large export market over long distances. But this market was becoming glutted by 1200, and there was less work for townsmen. Guilds, which originally had been open occupational groupings, began to close off. The guild regime had been designed to provide protection and charity for the members of the trade, for example by maintaining poor relief, orphanages, and the like, and later acting as a sort of labor union in relations with employers. Somewhat later, toward the end of the twelfth century, the guilds became quite concerned with preserving quality of production of their particular specialty, and this preoccupation was eventually to lead to monopoly and cartels, especially in the fourteenth century. Technology, however, was so simple that save in the case of the luxury textile trades, some construction work, and the guilds of sellers of spices and other precious commodities, the concern for quality was merely a pretext, for anyone of remotely decent capacity could make such implements as were known. Guilds began charging entry fees and developing elaborate rules regarding mastery (a master was an artisan who had produced his "masterpiece" under the supervision of another master, and hence was fully accredited), apprenticeship, and conditions of employment of "journeymen," laborers who were paid wages by the day (*journée*) but were not yet masters. Even before they came to political power, the artisan guilds had become quite exclusive.

Lords continued, furthermore, to found new towns, chiefly in an attempt to rival other nobles and drain riches away from them. Europe was drastically overurbanized by the late thirteenth century, and accordingly many peasants were gravitating toward the smaller markets rather than those of the overpopulated older towns. The large centers were becoming a drain on the economy which their own mercantile function, often geared chiefly to luxury commodities which could generate great wealth, did not justify.

Accordingly, there were ferocious social conflicts in some of the great towns in the thirteenth century, usually pitting either lower artisans and the unemployed against the masters, or all, including the masters, against the merchant patricians who employed them and gave them work. This resulted in many guild regimes coming to power in the northern European towns by the fourteenth century, but these governments, as we shall see, were often as oligarchical as their patrician predecessors, since each guild, in a situation reminiscent of Italy, now had its own rich and poor. The development took a slightly different form in Italy, where the noble element among the patricians, the "magnates," was generally expelled from the town by the "people," a term designating the greater guildsmen who disliked noble disorders in the streets and social pretensions. "Magnate" indeed takes on the context of "outlaw" in the Italian cities from the late thirteenth century, a person supposedly with power and economic interests outside the town who harassed merchants; many, indeed, were to be exiled as "magnates" who had no connection at all with the nobility. Rarely were these strictly struggles of rich against poor in either northern or southern Europe. The merchant rich used the mob force of the mass of poor and occasionally even unemployed (although the poor artisans were extremely jealous of the unemployed, whom they suspected with considerable justification of wanting to take away their work), but then ruled without them. A greater class consciousness began to develop on all levels of society as the guildsmen took seats in the magistracy, usually apportioned precisely among certain guilds which had political recognition, and concentrated on mak-

Illustration 11.   Guild houses along the Graslei, Ghent

ing themselves richer, for government and graft tended to be synonymous. The guild organization meant so little that wealthy patricians
of the earlier regime often enrolled in the guilds for purposes of gaining
political rights and the capacity to participate in government.

Industrial Organization and Technology

Most urban industry was very simple. Carpenters, bakers, masons,
and the like used tools which would be quite recognizable to their
counterparts today, save that only exceptionally was any energy employed in the Middle Ages in such operations other than human or
animal power. The large-scale industries, particularly textiles, had a

form of what would later be called a "putting-out" system. Great merchants bought raw materials at wholesale prices, whether through cornering local markets or through guild imports from overseas, then sent them to various artisans, each of whom performed one aspect of finishing. The textile industry gives an excellent example of the ridiculous degree of diversity of occupations within the same industry; medieval industry was notoriously inefficient, and the guild structure compounded the problem, although it is true that such a regime provided at least some work for many persons. The wool was first washed, with the good separated from the poor. Then it was beaten to separate strands which were too short and treated with butter to make a "wet" textile of high quality. The wool was then combed and carded, spun, and wound. It was then woven, but this in turn required the operations of several specialists. The wool might be dyed before or after weaving. The dye was a valuable commodity which often had to be imported from afar, although crops for industrial use, such as woad, were grown in scattered localities throughout Europe. In the last series of operations the cloth was stiffened by fulling, in which the textile was stamped in earth to make it smooth, washed, and debuttered, then sheared to remove knots and threads which were too short from the surface of the cloth. Finally the finished textile was stretched by pulleys on a frame to a size in accordance with local regulations and again sheared. Then it was offered for inspection at the cloth hall. The entire chain of operations required the services of over 20 specialists, most of them working in their own houses or apartments with very primitive equipment. They were paid after completing each piece of work, and as a result work was not constant and indeed tended to be seasonal with the wool supply. There was a considerable problem of part-time labor in the urban textile industries, causing many workers to cultivate gardens in the town or surrounding villages.

Such procedures are not conducive to great efficiency, and the wastefulness of the guilds, together with their concern with minute regulations, must be accounted among the most significant reasons for the decline of some large towns in the late Middle Ages. Industrial technology did, however, make some startling advances in the central Middle Ages, most of them connected with the harnessing of water power. The water mill with a vertical wheel was very common in the countryside, as we have seen, but industrial uses demanded the camshaft and cam wheel, both of which were known by the twelfth century. These locked the water wheel to buckets for drainage work,

Illustration 12.   Medieval industrial technology: a smithy

hammers for tanning and fulling, and somewhat later even created the hydraulic saw. The camshaft also allowed the disengagement of the wheel when no energy was needed. The fulling mill, replacing stamping with the feet by use of hammers, nearly created an industrial revolution in England. There, as indeed in many parts of the continent, the older town fulling guilds distrusted mechanization on grounds of supposed inferior quality of workmanship, and industry consequently was shifting from the towns of eastern England to the villages of the west even in the thirteenth century. A similar flight of industry from town to countryside occurred, although in lesser degree, on the northern continent in the fourteenth century.

Iron forges were operated simply by fires in the early Middle Ages, and only in the fourteenth century do we find bellows moved through attachment to a water mill. Coal was still rare, however, although it was used at Liège and Newcastle by the thirteenth century, and this limited the heat which could be generated for ironmaking.

The use of such inventions, however, remained exceptional, for most artisans disliked machinery which replaced men in the labor force. Although medieval industry was more inventive technologically than the Roman, it still was undergoing an intellectual hardening of the arteries as the thirteenth century and its population problem wore on.

The Mechanics of Exchange

The business of the merchant was not easy in medieval Europe. Trade routes were dangerous and often were little more than soggy footpaths through the forest. Traders tended to use the rivers in the central Middle Ages as before, although there was some improvement in overland travel as kingdoms and even town governments improved the roads. The only all-weather pass over the Alps was the Brenner, although the St. Gotthard was opened in 1237, and many Italian traders went along the Mediterranean coast to reach the north. From there, they took the Rhône or overland routes to the great fairs of Champagne, the major international trading depot. Only in the thirteenth century could the dangerous overland route be avoided, as the Italians began building larger ships, capable of carrying several hundred tons of merchandise, and the Hanse merchants of northern Germany developed the larger and more efficient "cog." The development of the rudder in the twelfth century and of the magnetic compass in the late thirteenth permitted more accurate navigation, but it was only in the 1290s that direct sea connections were established between Italy and the north over Gibraltar. The Italians had only borrowed the sail, a virtual necessity for decent navigation unless one had enormous gangs of oarsmen or motors unknown before the modern age, from the Byzantines in the twelfth century.

Merchants came together at the great fairs. There were regional fairs, such as the "five fairs" of Flanders, for distribution within smaller areas, and these occasionally handled some foreign trade. Merchant associations, such as the Hanse of London, which grouped Flemish merchants who traded in England, were also important for long-distance trade. But the most important depot was the series of six fairs in the Champagne, a flat area east of Paris of easy access to the Italians and Flemish, who were the richest merchants of Europe. The fairs began with that of Lagny-sur-Marne in January and ended with that of Troyes in October, with each fair lasting around six weeks. Merchants tended to make a circuit from one to the other. At the conclusion of the trading season, they returned home and spent the winter months collecting or manufacturing new items for sale. Trade was conducted personally for the most part, but some written instruments did develop, particularly for credit operations. "Fair letters" were promises made at one fair of payment at a subsequent fair. These payments were negotiable in a sense, for if one merchant owed a debt to another, he might assign obligations owed him by a third merchant to pay his own debts. They were used as payment for commodities, however, and we have little evidence of borrowing at the fairs through use of these instruments. The kings of France at first encouraged the merchants to come and enrich France with their money. They even allowed the merchants and bankers to charge interest despite ecclesiastical prohibitions and freed them from many tolls and from criminal prosecution. The rapid coinage devaluations of the French kings in the late thirteenth century contributed to the decline of the fairs, as did the attempts of Philip IV (1285–1314) to tax and expel foreign merchants in his effort to make France less dependent on foreign financiers. The development of direct sea links between Italy and Flanders was the coup de grace to the trade of the fairs of Champagne, which began to decline after about 1260, although they were still quite important in international banking and finance until around 1320.

Credit is absolutely essential to an expanding economy. Without it, no one could finance a large venture in hope of making even greater gain; entrepreneurs had to borrow or go into partnerships. The partnership was the preferred form, for the church forbade the loaning of money at interest on grounds of Biblical teachings. Jesus in particular had been talking of the exploitation of Palestinian peasants by urban loan sharks, and the church itself was thoroughly involved in banking and finance as well by the thirteenth century, but the prohibition was a severe hindrance to all moneylending whether the purposes were worthy or not. The theory that one should loan one's brother money out of love and expect no more than total repayment was nice, but it did not work in an age when one would repay one's brother in an inflated coin and when the risk that one's brother might lose all his money through sinking of the ship, ambushing of the caravan, or similar misfortune was quite high. As a result, "Cahorsins" from southern France and "Lombards" from the north Italian towns loaned money at interest; most remained Christians, although the Church regarded their activities as highly sinful. These persons often doubled as pawnbrokers, loaning on collateral. Their interest rates were from 20 percent to 40 percent, and even so the rate of failure of these persons, and in particular of those who loaned large sums, is astronomically high, so great were the dangers. Jews provided credit for townsman and prince alike, until they were expelled from most parts of western Europe in the late thirteenth and early fourteenth centuries. Kings declared periodic confiscations of Jewish property, but this merely meant that the Jews had to hand over large sums for "protection." The church tried to bring Jews who loaned at interest before Christian courts, and this was sometimes allowed by the civil authorities, but only exceptionally. Other informal sources of credit were developing. Moneychangers who took deposits

which they then repaid on demand, and which they might invest as
they saw fit in the interim (although many merely kept the money
in trust), are found in Genoa by the late twelfth century. The Knights
of the Temple of Jerusalem performed a similar function for crusaders
and pilgrims to the Holy Land; from the time of the crusades of
Louis IX to Africa in the mid-thirteenth century until Philip IV liqui-
dated the order in 1307, they were royal bankers, although basically
as storers of funds rather than as financiers.

The partnership in various forms was much favored by the Italians,
for it usually did not involve interest. The true partnership made each
partner liable for the debts of the others, and accordingly was somewhat clumsy. Merchants might make loans among themselves and
conceal the interest. By the twelfth century we find "companies," organizations with unlimited liability for all partners but tending to be
family operations. Although they soon began accepting capital from
outsiders, most remained small until the thirteenth century, when a
few of them became extremely prosperous. Such companies often extended credit, with interest open or concealed, and as such expanded
into banking. The artisan ideal of division of function was never taken
over by the businessmen, for the companies large and small invested
in various commodities and services and loaned money. The great
companies perfected the "sea loan," given for the duration of a voyage,
but to be repaid only if the voyage were completed successfully. This
was declared usurious by the pope in 1232, although it had been
approved at first, since there was risk involved and gain was not certain. The aspect of certainty was the primary point of contention,
and it led to the development of very sophisticated business techniques
in the late Middle Ages, as businessmen made money while saving
their souls. The sea loan actually was very similar to the legitimate
commenda, in which the party who carried out a voyage invested
a percentage of the cost, while a moneylender invested the rest but
stayed at home. Profits then were divided according to a prearranged
scheme which rewarded the one party for his labor.

Life in the Medieval Town

Historians know more of town life than of rural, largely through
accidents of document survival. The cities were obviously popular,
in view of the migration to them. One can only wonder at the caliber
of rural life which would have made the towns seem so attractive,

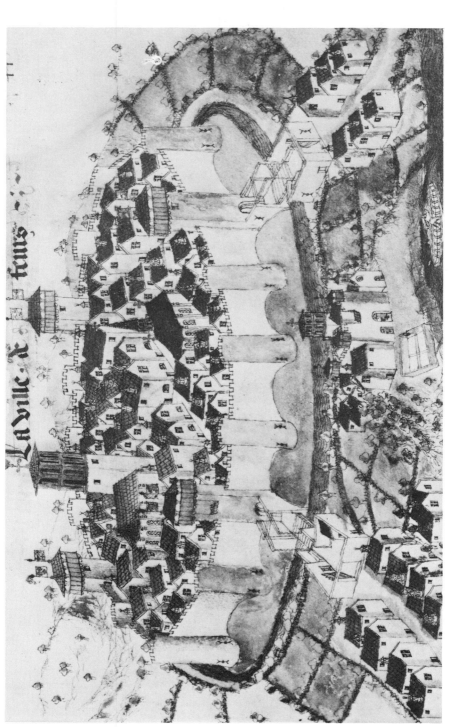

Illustration 13. The city of Feurs-sur-Loire

Illustration 14.   Medieval town scene

and indeed most cities preserved a very agrarian appearance. Many bourgeois had stables, some chickens and pigs, and gardens either inside or outside the walls. The livestock of the citizenry was a persistent problem for town magistrates, who issued repeated ordinances forbidding the inhabitants to let their horses and swine run loose in the public streets. The towns were overcrowded and filthy, with narrow, crooked streets. Most streets in the older nuclei towns were not laid out according to a definite plan. Houses were built in the merchant settlement, and paths which later became streets united them, although in the planned foundations a street plan in rectangles or squares usually was established before settlement. Urban land was quite expensive, and the richer townsmen owned most of it. Landholding in the town was often a legal characteristic separating the patricians from lesser mortals, and is similar to the landholding mystique which is so evident in the countryside, for the townsmen and nobles alike gained social respectability through landownership and collecting rents. Some

Illustration 15. The town hall of Damme (Flanders)

Italian rich owned entire quarters of cities. One could even argue that the patricians had a sort of power of command over persons, although it was informal and economic. Buildings usually contained several stories, each overhanging the other, so that slops and missiles thrown from above would land in the street. Glass was very unusual in houses before the fourteenth century; greased parchment or fabric was more ordinary. Furniture was rudimentary and totally functional. There were often large suburbs in which the workers (and the unemployed, if they were lucky) lived in rude huts. The city walls were several feet thick and had narrow gates which were drawn at night and in time of danger. The cities had curfews after dark, and anyone outside his house was presumed engaged in illicit activity. The towns were incredibly noisy, as bells tolled the beginning and end of each working day and usually at intervals between, and the dulcet voices of artisans, patricians, and fishwives filled the cosmos.

The nocturnal prohibitions extended to work as well as criminality, for the artisan was supposed to make his wares in the open, under the watchful eye of the prospective buyer. Artisans might work as many as 18 hours during a day in summer, although earlier darkness and lack of supplies which had to be imported cut this time substantially in winter. Since no work was done on holy days, and only half days were worked on many Saturdays and festival eves, the urban artisan in the Middle Ages had a normal work week of about four and one-half days, when he was working at all. There was a tremendous press on the streets, for the towns were overpopulated, and much ordinary activity which now can be done in or from the domicile required a personal trip to bank, shop, or market. The cities were invariably permeated with noxious odors. They had only the most elemental sanitation systems, usually amounting to the streams flowing through them, until a few towns began building drainage canals in the late Middle Ages and regulating the forms of waste which might be deposited in the streets. Unfortunately, town magistracies were extremely small, and the cities were very violent and dangerous, particularly as social conflicts became exacerbated from the late thirteenth century.

On the somewhat less mundane level, many larger towns and some smaller had magnificent cathedrals, which took centuries to build and which were a severe drain on the economy of the town, although the bulk of the cost was usually borne by the local bishopric, rather than the town government. Most cities had a town hall of which the burghers were extremely proud. These structures, with the walls, were a symbol of municipal independence. There were some princely castles, and by the thirteenth century some wealthy townsmen of the north were building houses in stone, but most private dwellings were wooden firetraps. The Italian patricians built in a brick tower style, creating strongholds from which they waged private wars with rival clans. The medieval town was the scene of much action of varying type, and as such attracted not only the shrewdest businessmen, but also the leading intellectuals of the age. But the natural habitat of medieval man, rural and urban, was in the midst of violence, stench, disease, and dishonesty.

10

MIND AND MATTER

THE EUROPEAN intellectual world was in ferment by 1050, the beginning of the age called the "Renaissance of the Twelfth Century" by many scholars. In terms of sheer originality of intellectual endeavor, this period was the most productive of the entire Middle Ages. It unquestionably surpasses the so-called Italian Renaissance of the fourteenth and fifteenth centuries, a time during which, despite remarkable advances in painting and sculpture, most intellectual activity was directed toward uncritical admiration and recitation of the works of Greek and Roman authors.

Several developments furthered the change in intellectual climate. First, the intellectual centers of the new age were the towns, rather than rural monasteries. Cathedral schools taught even the basic subjects to a much wider studentry than had the monastic schools of the early Middle Ages, whose curriculum rarely went beyond the rudiments of the divine services and bare literacy in Latin. As population expanded, productive limits grew so that a class of persons could be supported which did not grow its own food; the necessary economic base of an intellectual class was thus created. The social changes which we have noted in chapter 9 produced both population movement and change of class status. Men were able to wander about listening to lectures by the great masters of the age. Since the masters were usually itinerant and lectured for only part of the year, a large floating population of "wandering scholars" drawn primarily from the lesser nobility and the bourgeoisie, but also with a few peasants, was being created.

Furthermore, men now had a motive for becoming educated, for learning was a route to advancement in business and in the princely bureaucracies. All of society was becoming more literate, if not exactly more learned, and the vernacular (non-Latin) languages were written down to a much greater degree in the central Middle Ages than before.

Increased contact with the east and particularly the increased familiarity of northern Europeans with the legal and medical schools of Italy were important in producing this rebirth, but one must beware of attributing too much to these influences. The Crusades in particular were of only tangential significance. Most original Greek texts came to the west only in the early thirteenth century, after the fourth crusade, and the Byzantine east did little for the recovery of texts of Latin authors. Most Latin works not known in the twelfth century were only recovered during the manuscript-hunting craze of the Italian Renaissance. Greek philosophy and literature were known before the thirteenth century only through fragments of two of Plato's most mystical dialogues, the partial Latin translations of Aristotle by Boethius, and particularly the work of the Spanish Moslems, who had translated Greek works into Arabic, from which language the Christian west rendered them into Latin. The changes introduced by the double translation produced inaccuracies which contributed to the growth of intellectual forms of heresy (a very different phenomenon from the unlearned heresies which were the main concern of the church, as we shall see).

Literature in the Central Middle Ages

The twelfth and thirteenth centuries witness increasing secularization in forms of literature. As literacy became more widespread and tastes became more sophisticated, people were developing interest in good stories, poetry, and the like. The changes cannot be seen purely in the context of increased use of the vernacular tongues, for some vernacular literature survives from the early Middle Ages, particularly in Anglo-Saxon and Old High German. The Norse sagas were recited orally for centuries before finally being written down in the central Middle Ages. Vernacular literature certainly became more widespread after 1100 than before, but some of the most secular work of the twelfth century was written in Latin. The better distinction thus seems to be between the various audiences for whom the literature was written, and to a lesser extent between literary genres, rather than between Latin and the vernacular. In an age when formal education was increasing in quality and quantity, one would hardly expect Latin to fall out of use as a mode of literary expression. Only in the thirteenth and fourteenth centuries did Latin become confined largely to ecclesiastical treatises and works designed for an international audience, whether of scholars or diplomats.

Considerable literature was written for and even by the members of the aristocracy, both in prose and verse and almost entirely in the vernacular. One would naturally expect this, for the nobles had the money and life style which would cause them to patronize poets and singers around their courts, while the intellectual interests of most townsmen, however wealthy they might be, were still confined to the dirty story.

Patrons of the arts usually like literature which glorifies their past or present way of life. For the nobel this was the *chanson de geste*—song of the deed. These are national epic poems in a sense, with the action taking place at a particularly heroic moment in the past. Such are the *Cid* of Spain, dealing with the reconquest from the Moslems; the German *Nibelungenlied*, concerning the period of the great barbarian migrations; and the French *Song of Roland*. Despite the historical base, the stories are largely apocryphal except for the *Cid*. Although they were sung long before being written down, they are important historical sources only for the period during which they were finally put onto parchment. They have a common theme of the relation of a ruler to his knights, and a principal motif is the conflict of loyalties and the nature of fidelity to lord. The *Song of Roland,* for instance, while depicting the battle of Roncevalles, in which a rear guard of Charlemagne was ambushed while returning from Spain in 778, sees it through the eyes of the nobles of the late eleventh century, who were still very much warriors. Roland was bold and arrogant. There is little subtlety of motive in this epic, for all hinged on the fight. Roland fought to the death, too proud to save himself, not to mention his men, by sounding his horn to summon reinforcements from Charlemagne. The imagery is crude and bloody. There is scarcely a mention of a love interest, for the poem concentrates on bravery, loyalty, and Christian sentiments. *Roland* reflects nicely the concept of the knight serving Christ that was becoming current in the crusading period. The *Nibelungenlied,* on the other hand, written in Austria around 1200, a century and a half after the *Song of Roland,* shows much more subtlety in delineation of character and motive. It is much less bloody and is full of the ideas of courtly love and chivalry, emphasizing good manners and refinement to an extent that Roland and his brave followers would have found strange. These two *chansons* thus reflect changes in noble life and manners of the central Middle Ages.

The romance was also an important form of literature for the knightly classes. It was a sort of fictional epic, with an occasional moral message. The romances are the source of the courtly love tradition, governed by complex rules of the game. The most important were those of the "Arthurian cycle," dealing with the legends surrounding the king who supposedly defended Celtic Britain against the Germanic invaders, although many romances featured other heroes. Honor was the major motivating force in most romances, and slights to one's honor were questions of life and death. Courtesy, skill in the fine arts, the ability to speak well, and the like were important, as indeed was military prowess, although most romances did not emphasize this aspect. The romances stressed platonic love much more than carnal, and the ideal and unattainable lady was often a central figure. Many romances had great literary merit. Chrétien de Troyes, who wrote *Stories of the Grail* and several shorter romances in the twelfth century, particularly *Erec and Ywein,* was one of the finest of medieval poets. His slightly later German imitator, Wolfram von Eschenbach, produced the epic romance *Parzifal.* We must emphasize, however, that the romances portrayed an imaginary world. Many aristocrats who listened to them liked to think that they actually were such paragons. All evidence suggests, however, that while the nobles were becoming increasingly refined, they were a far cry from the knights in shining armor of the romances who besieged castles and slew dragons for the honor of the lady.

Lyric poetry, particularly that of the troubadours, was of great importance in the history of western literature. The earliest center was in southern France, and it was influenced by Arabic poetry from Spain as well as some secular Latin lyrics. Much of this was love poetry, but the troubadours and the trouvères, their somewhat later equivalents in northern France, also sang of war, youth, and the beauties of nature. The troubadours were not wandering minstrels, but were generally nobles themselves, although the best of them were *ministeriales* or other members of the lesser nobility. The earliest troubadour of whom anything is known was Duke William IX of Aquitaine, and such great princes as Richard I (1189–99) of England wrote poetry. Much of the troubadour poetry was composed at the court of Richard's mother, Eleanor of Aquitaine, granddaughter of William IX. At Eleanor's formal "Court of Love" in Poitou, her daughter by King Louis VII of France, Marie de France, composed *lais* of considerable power and beauty. The German *Minnesang* (love song) tradition developed somewhat later, in the very late twelfth and early thirteenth centuries, and as one might expect from the time lag, it was somewhat more sophisticated than the work of the troubadours. The *Minnesang* reached its culmination in the work of the *ministerialis* Walther von der Vogelweide (d. 1228).

The non-noble world was beginning to produce its own literature for the first time in forms which have survived. The medieval world was becoming more conscious of social class and standing than before. Various groups were forming into ranks or orders; the guild movement must be seen as part of this. The scholars who attended the cathedral and other schools were a peculiar group, and they formed their own order as well—the order of vagabonds. As they wandered between schools and lecturers, they sang their songs, but as clerics and educated men they sang them in Latin. The mythical character Golias was their hero. Several manuscripts of these songs have survived. The most famous of the "Goliardic poets" was the "Archpoet," who may have been Rainald of Dassel, chancellor of the emperor Frederick I. The students had very secular concerns, and the joys of tavern and bed were much more to their taste than the ephemeral delights of courtly love.

This literature, although written in Latin, was very secular in spirit. Many of these students were of lower and middle class backgrounds, and they were putting into more or less cultivated verse the very earthy thoughts and desires of the nonnoble classes. This is even more true of the so-called *fabliaux* (fables), written sometimes in prose and sometimes in verse. These were tales which circulated in town and countryside, almost certainly embellishments of actual events if our knowledge of manners and morals is any indication. Their favorite subject was sex, particularly the priest caught in carnal delights, for there was a strongly anticlerical element to much literature of the bourgeois and peasants, and the misfortunes of the elderly lecher whose bride sought youthful pleasures.

Schools and Universities

As intellectual life became centered in the towns, and particularly in their cathedral schools, changes were made in curriculum. The basic course of the "seven liberal arts" consisted of the *trivium* and the *quadrivium*. The *trivium* included the elementary subjects of grammar, rhetoric, and logic, dealing with correct exposition and construction of language and propositions, while the *quadrivium* took in the more specialized and advanced subjects of astronomy, arithmetic, music, and geometry, each of which dealt with quite a bit more than today—music, for instance, included part of what we call physics. Within the basic course of the *trivium,* schools had tended to emphasize correct declamation and learning by rote through grammar and rhetoric before the twelfth century, but emphasis now shifted to logic, and particularly dialectic, the branch of logic in which thesis and antithesis are used to create a new synthesis, which in turn is juxtaposed with another antithesis, and so on. Old attitudes were questioned and more play was given to human reason in this way, although in some schools, particularly at Chartres, studies of classical authors continued to dominate the newer disciplines and techniques. Probably no important thinker of the twelfth century was a religious skeptic; certainly Peter Abelard, who is sometimes considered an early type of the rationalist, was a devout Christian. They did, however, believe that man, through the use of his reason, could obtain a deeper meaning and a more profound understanding of revealed truths whose basic accuracy was never denied or even questioned.

Perhaps the most characteristic expression of the formal educational change of the central Middle Ages, and particularly of the shift toward dialectic, is the establishment of the universities. Specialized schools had existed in Italy from the early Middle Ages. Medical studies are attested at Salerno by the tenth century, and the law schools of Bologna by the eleventh. Medieval medicine was always quite elementary, but legal studies were much more advanced. Particularly after the recovery of the *corpus juris civilis* of Justinian, beginning with the Digest in 1076, the study of Roman law made tremendous advances.

The Latin *universitas* means a guild, and the earliest "universities" were guilds of masters (teachers who had become masters of the seven liberal arts) or students. Two features distinguish the university (taking the modern sense of the term) from other educational institutions, particularly municipal and cathedral schools: they granted to their licenciates a "right to teach anywhere," and only papal grant empowered them to do this; and they had at least one faculty dealing with subjects above the basic arts curriculum, such as canon law, civil law, medicine, or the "queen of the sciences," theology.

The university at Paris is often seen as the prototype of the northern European university, but this is not strictly correct. It is true that the German universities were founded on the model of Paris in the fourteenth century, but this was a conscious imitation, not an organic development. The university at Paris grew out of the several cathedral schools on the left bank of the Seine, particularly that of Notre Dame. The popularity of the lectures of Peter Abelard, and the resulting fame which dialectical studies had at Paris, contributed to its rise and had attracted several thousand students from all parts of Europe by the early thirteenth century. The English universities of Oxford and Cambridge, however, were not outgrowths of cathedral schools, for the closest episcopal city was some miles away in each case.

The masters of Paris had directed much of their early struggle against the pretensions of the chancellor of the cathedral school of Notre Dame, who was in the theological faculty and not a member of the masters' guild. The chancellor tried to undercut the masters' authority by granting licenses to persons not examined and approved by the masters and by charging fees for the license. His powers were purely formal by the mid-thirteenth century, however, for the masters received support from the pope.

Much of the early difficulty of the university of Paris was due to the similarity of the masters' guild to other guilds of artisans. The masters wanted absolute control over their affairs, and in so doing they controlled the university as a whole. The masters were those who had gone through the arts curriculum and were licensed. Many masters then returned home and found jobs as teachers, civil servants, and the like, but others went on into one of the "higher" faculties, of which theology was by far the most important at Paris. In this case they usually continued to teach arts for a few years to beginning students, who might incept at age 14. Thus they continued to regard themselves as members of the faculty of arts while they studied theology. The arts faculty consisted of four "nations," each with its own officials, but with little connection with modern ideas of nationality. The masters as a whole chose a rector of the arts faculty, and the rector even now is the head of many European universities. Governance of the university was in a general assembly, in which the nations in arts had one collective vote apiece, while each of the three higher faculties had one. Arts thus could dominate the entire structure.

The issue of guild control was involved also in the right of the masters to strike. In 1229 they left Paris, and during their absence the chancellor appointed several mendicants (on the mendicants, see below, p. 203) to chairs in the theological faculty. These men had not been examined by the Paris arts faculty, for the Dominican and Francisan orders maintained their own arts schools, and the arts faculty thus considered this a breach of guild control. The mendicants continued to hold the chairs, however, and a new strike in the 1250s brought matters to a climax. The pope eventually confirmed the masters' rights to examine such persons before they entered the theological faculty, but the mendicants were allowed to keep their positions.

The university of masters at Paris is often contrasted to the university of students at Bologna and other Italian centers, but the distinction is fictive. As we have seen, the Paris masters of arts were students in the higher faculties, men of about age 22–34. Bologna had no arts faculty until the fourteenth century, for the students there normally got their arts training from a municipal or cathedral school, both of which were much stronger in Italy than in northern Europe, or later from mendicant foundations. They were of the same age and educational level as the Paris masters. They had a degree of control over the faculty which is quite picturesque to the modern mind, dictating conditions and subjects of lecturing and even details of faculty personal conduct through control of the pursestrings. Professors were dependent upon student fees for their support until quite late in the thirteenth century at Bologna, and only in the fourteenth did the city establish enough salaried chairs to end student control. Indeed, the guild system at Bologna did not pit organizations of students against those of professors, but rather citizens of Bologna (professors) against outsiders (students).

Conditions in the universities were not very conducive to learning. Although stationers' shops were near the university halls, parchment was expensive. Masters often designated certain students to take notes on their lectures, and students might group together to buy books. It is true that comparatively few books were used, since the method of inquiry was commentary on the basic texts, whether the corpus of Justinian, the Bible, the *Decretum* of Gratian or the *Sentences* of Peter Lombard (twelfth century treatises on canon law and theology) or the various works of the church fathers. But the physical circumstances forced the student to spend a tremendous amount of time in learning what his modern counterpart would consider a very small body of knowledge. Periodic disputations were given on various points in the curriculum, amounting to exercises in logic combined with citation of memorized sections from the basic authorities to prove one's point. At the end of the arts course the student was examined by the faculty, gave a lecture of his own as a sort of masterpiece upon entering the guild, and joined the select company of the masters of arts.

This method of inquiry amounted to an oral "gloss." Basic texts, whether theological, legal, or philosophical, were considered authoritative, but variations could be made upon these sources to bring them into line with contemporary practice, updating them while still preserving their authority. Such changes were inserted in the margins or between the lines of manuscripts, and eventually some glosses were published as a necessary commentary on the basic text and became authoritative in their own right. Such were the various *Glossae Ordinariae* of canon and civil law. Much has been made of the influence of Roman law in the Middle Ages, largely through its revival in university studies. More properly stated, the influence was that of the glossators, who were adapting contemporary or such past experience as they knew—their only sources of cognition—to Roman legal maxims. Roman law has been used to justify everything from royal absolutism to parliamentary democracy, from freedom of all to slavery; the question was merely who was paying whom to dredge up citations which could be used for a given purpose.

The university structure had spread throughout France by the end of the thirteenth century, although Paris always remained the leading authority in arts and theology. The first university in the German Empire was founded at Prague in 1347, for the emperor, Charles IV, was king of Bohemia. The leading rival of his house, the Hapsburgs, founded the university of Vienna in 1365 to rival Prague. The foundation of these and several other German universities in the late fourteenth century reflects the growing nationalism of the late Middle Ages, for princes disliked sending their citizens into France for study that they should be getting at home. The international character and prestige of the universities was very much in decline.

The kings favored the universities and gave them numerous concessions, for they valued the presence of educated men in their bureaucracies. While the townsmen disliked students, there was little that they could do to replace student power on the local marketplace. The students, particularly in northern Europe, where most were clergy or at least in minor orders (through the grade of subdeacon), were outside the civil legal structure and could be tried only in their own or episcopal courts. Immunity from civil prosecution enabled the students of Oxford to put the town under a virtual reign of terror in the fourteenth century, and they were always sure of royal support.

The universities were important sources of social mobility. Sons of great nobles, who inherited riches and positions at court, rarely attended them, and indeed some felt pride in their ignorance. But a lesser noble whose fortune had been lost, a townsman, or a peasant who could get through the university course could make tremendous advances through a position, particularly in a royal bureaucracy or in one of the increasingly lucrative learned professions. In an age before printed books, the arts course was clumsy, as we have seen, and normally required 20 years of going to disputations and lectures. This meant that all but the wealthy students had to find patrons. Towns sometimes supported local scholars at Paris or Bologna, and these men entered city service when they returned. More often, a scholar would be appointed by the pope to a vacant church living, from which he would draw considerable revenues. All peasants had to pay tithes of produce to the local priest, who also controlled the landed endowment of his church, and while such measures were also incumbent on the other classes, they had more ready avenues of escape through concealment of income. The whole procedure was quite unfortunate in that many parishes never saw their priests and were given only illiterate vicars to read the divine services, while the nominal priest learned theology and rioting at Paris, but it was a sort of scholarship for poor students. Indigent scholars also were often taken in by "colleges," which originated as hostels. The earliest at Paris was founded by an anonymous Englishman in the 1180s, but the most famous was the

Sorbonne, founded by Robert de Sorbon in 1257. English colleges date from a somewhat later period. Since so many students lived and ate in the colleges, masters eventually began giving lectures there for convenience and economy, for the university had no fixed buildings and merely rented rooms as needed throughout the city. With this, the college as an educational institution was born. English universities today are a series of colleges with most functions duplicating, while the Sorbonne is the faculty of sciences and letters of the university of Paris.

Issues and Intellectuals

It would be mistaken to claim that "individualism" in the modern sense originated during the twelfth century, but this age does witness the emergence of towering personalities in the intellectual world for the first time since the Carolingian period. Such men as St. Anselm and Peter Abelard are interesting not only for what they said, but for what they were.

The new learning could be used both to buttress the old faith and to test it by trying to ascertain new truths within the overall structure of eternal truth that was assumed. The best example of the former trend is characteristically an early figure, St. Anselm of Bec (d. 1109), for most later logicians were more innovative. Anselm has been called the first creator of a theological "system" since St. Augustine. In *Cur Deus Homo? (Why Did God Become Man?)*, a study of the atonement through Jesus, he emphasized the human quality of Jesus as a means by which man could be saved from his sins. Only through union of man with God in Jesus can humanity achieve salvation.

Anselm is also important as the first man of the Middle Ages who thought it worthwhile to prove that God exists. In his most significant works, the *Proslogion* and the *Monologion,* he examined the nature of God and the role of human reason in finding eternal truth. In his "ontological" (drawn from an argument concerning the nature of being) proof, he argued that in denying the existence of God, the unbeliever admits that God or something like God exists. He defines God as that than which nothing greater can be conceived, for God exists outside the human understanding. The argument is weak, for it presupposes unchanging limits to human understanding and assumes that God is everything beyond, but his idea was influential. In a sense it is the intellectual antecedent of Descartes' "I think; therefore I am," considered by many to be a foundation of modern empirical philosophy. Anselm, however, always kept reason in a subordinate place. He said that "I believe in order to understand," making God, as fundamental principle of the universe, the presupposition of the use of reason, without which all mental activity is meaningless. Later logicians would reverse these priorities and understand in order to reinforce their beliefs.

Anselm, with most thinkers of his day, became involved in the debate over the nature of universals, and came down firmly on the side of the inherent reality of ideas, or general concepts. The Greek philosopher Plato, through his imitators the Neoplatonists, dominated the thought of the early Middle Ages, just as Aristotle was to dominate the period from the mid-thirteenth century. Plato conceived of reality as consisting of a hierarchy of general ideas or forms, highest of which was the idea of the good. Particular objects had no inherent reality; they were real only insofar as they partook of the general idea. For example, good men are not inherently real; they obtain reality only insofar as they reflect the ideal of goodness. The question was raised in the Middle Ages of whether these ideas had inherent reality, or whether they were an intellectual convenience by which man binds together objects with certain common characteristics. Aristotle adopted this position, which was a sort of moderate "realism," so called from belief in the reality of ideas. Nominalists (from the Latin *nomina*, names), of whom there were few in the twelfth century, argued that general concepts were mere names and hence lacked objective reality. This controversy had important implications for Christian thinkers. The realist subsumed the individual within an abstraction; for example, is the individual soul real or does it merely partake in a larger oversoul? If the latter, is it or can it be immortal? The nominalists tended to argue that reality came only through empirical perception, and thereby threatened the ideas so basic to medieval man of divine revelation and eternal ideas.

Peter Abelard (1079–1142)

Peter Abelard is perhaps the most fascinating and important intellectual personage of the twelfth century. He seems almost a prototype of the "new" type of man found in the twelfth century. As he stated, he "followed the peripatetics," a reference to those who followed Aristotle about and heard his teachings. He moved from school to school, and the popularity of his lectures drew so many students to Paris that he was in a certain sense the father of the development of the cathedral schools there into a university. Although he was born of a Breton knightly family, he became basically a townsman, spending the happiest years of his life in Paris.

Abelard described his fascinating and tragic career in an autobiography, *The History of My Calamities*. He arrived in the Paris region and successively antagonized several of the most learned men of the age by his great talent and his insufferable tendency to seek the limelight and embarrass them publicly in disputation. He was assaulted on several occasions by devotees of his rival intellectuals, but finally founded a school of his own. During his stay in Paris there occurred his famous love affair with Héloïse, the niece of a canon of the cathedral of Notre Dame. The church had finally prohibited marriage of the clergy in 1123, after frowning upon it for centuries. Abelard could still marry, for he was only in minor orders, but if he did it would mean giving up the normal professional career of the intellectual, culminating in a rich abbacy, a bishopric, or a place in a royal bureaucracy. He was willing to marry her anyway, but she objected to harming his career, and only after bearing him a son did she agree. As it turned out, Abelard had no choice, for the girl's uncle became upset and had him castrated by thugs, and canon law forbade the ordination of eunuchs. Abelard persuaded Heloise to enter a nunnery, and after a condemnation of his theology as heretical he became abbot of a monastery in the Breton backwoods. In his misery he wrote his autobiography. Eventually he was released from his abbacy, during which his very life was threatened by his monks, and returned to Paris. He was condemned for heresy in 1140 at the instigation of St. Bernard. Old and sick, he died at the abbey of Cluny in 1142, en route to Rome in search of vindication.

Abelard propounded a common-sense solution to the controversy over the reality of universals, although the issue continued to be debated. He argued that one should make a distinction between the meaning of a word, which was the true universal, and its sound. This was the premise of most later Christian philosophers, including Thomas Aquinas. Abelard was also important in the development of systematic theology. His *Sic et Non* (*Yes and No*) created a storm, for Abelard took points of canon law, the Bible, and the writings of the church fathers on particular questions and juxtaposed them. In contrast to others who used this method of inquiry later, however, he did not try to solve their contradictions, but left this to test the intellectual expertise of his readers. He was trying to stimulate inquiry by use of the dialectic, reason used rightly and for right ends. Abelard never doubted the truth of the various sources and considered the contradictions apparent rather than real. But such subtleties were not appreciated by the conservative theologians of the day, such as St. Bernard.

Abelard was not an "Aristotelian," for only a small part of Aristotle's writings had been recovered in the west during his lifetime. He would not have known what the term meant, but his work anticipated the later reception of Aristotle. Indeed, Abelard is more important for new attitudes and a spirit of intellectual inquiry than for what he actually did and said.

The Reception of Aristotle

The recovery of Aristotle's writings, first from the Arabic and later from the original Greek in the late twelfth and early thirteenth centuries, was a development of paramount importance. We must examine the nature of his work in order to understand why the church found some of his doctrines so obnoxious, even when they were placed in a Christian context. Aristotle urged the use of reason for the understanding of both the material and, insofar as he concerned himself with it at all, the immaterial world. Rationalism of this sort was not new to the Middle Ages even before Abelard, but Aristotle, who was basically a biologist rather than a metaphysician, had placed his emphasis on the world of matter. Still, the reservation of a sphere of activity for faith alone, leaving reason to handle the terrestrial world, could have been made, and eventually was made, with only slight modification of Aristotle's doctrines.

There were, however, ideas implicit in Aristotle's work and carried to their logical conclusion by his Moslem commentators which did contradict Christian teaching. In particular, the Spanish Moslem Averroës (1126–98) and his followers developed Aristotle's doctrine of the mortality of the soul, which they thought died with the individual human being as its essential form. They also emphasized the immortality of the world of matter, since the world was the manifestation of the deity who (or which) had created it and which Aristotle tended to view as an abstract prime mover rather than a personal God who intervened directly in the affairs of mankind. The activities of the "Latin Averroists" at the university of Paris in the early thirteenth century, culminating in Siger of Brabant (d. 1284), brought all Aristotelian philosophy into disrepute. Siger, who participated in disputations with St. Thomas Aquinas in the 1260s and 1270s, was more an Averroist than an Aristotelian in a sense in proclaiming that while the dictates of natural philosophy and reason are absolutely true for the world of matter, they may conflict with the eternal verities which alone are true for the world beyond. This doctrine of the "double truth" was totally unacceptable to the church, although William of Ockham, who obtained a significant following in the late Middle Ages, was to propound something rather close to it.

The use of Aristotle by significant orthodox Christian thinkers really began with Albert the Great (1193–1280), a Dominican of Cologne who wrote a vast amount on many subjects, including science and metaphysics. He was not totally Aristotelian, for he used elements of all sources to prove his essential points. He was less logical than his more famous pupil, Thomas Aquinas, but also broader in scope.

St. Thomas Aquinas

Born into an Italian noble family in 1225, Thomas of Aquino was to carry the *Summa,* the universal summary of knowledge on a given subject, and "scholastic" methodology, so called because it was used in the schools (*scholae*), to their highest form. Thomas' method was a refinement of the technique used by earlier scholastics. He cited propositions, various authorities which might seem to contradict them, then contrary arguments supporting the side which he himself held, then finally express refutations of the points raised against the original propositions. He has been seen as the quintessential medieval philosopher, and certainly his career as a Dominican friar and as teacher in the theological faculty at Paris placed him in the forefront of the intellectual activity of his age.

Thomas' works, particularly the *Summa Theologica* and the *Summa contra Gentiles,* set forth what he considered an exposition of Christian philosophy as seen through Aristotelian categories, buttressed by writings of the church fathers, the Bible, and canon law. Aquinas viewed the use of reason as innate to man and a natural product of his activity. Indeed, if man does not use his reason he fails to realize his divine potentiality. The personal God implanted free will in man, and man can choose whether to exercise this will in accordance with the will of God. The use of right reason, also implanted by God in each man, is determined by the will of man. Hence both reason and faith have their spheres. Aquinas basically accepted Aristotle's doctrines for the world of matter, and his work hence loses a certain originality and spontaneity when we realize that often he is merely writing an elaborate justification of the works of "the philosopher." But he had to modify Aristotle in a direction toward Augustinianism, or even Platonism, in his ideas concerning God and eternal truth.

Aquinas' basic problem in his application of Aristotle to Christianity was to delimit the respective spheres of faith and reason. He saw the world as a reflection of its creator, but not as part of a process over which the will of God had no control. Reason can lead us to an understanding of the world of matter, and as such to a limited extent of the divine purpose. Sense experience thus was primary for Aquinas' epistemology. Man knows what he sees and feels. Yet Aquinas also admitted the inherent reality of ideas and of such general concepts as the soul. Man could attain only a partial truth through his unaided reason, but he needed faith and grace for an understanding of divine law and eternal truth. God had posited a fourfold category of law: eternal law, which is the mind and will of God; divine law, which is the eternal law as revealed in the scriptures and in the works of divinely inspired men; natural law, a behavioral norm in accordance with divine law but which applies to all peoples, both Christian and not; and human law, the activity of the state or legislator. Human law must be in accordance with divine and natural law to be true law, but Aquinas provided no other remedy than tyrannicide (and that under the most extraordinary of circumstances—and the treatise in which he suggested even this may be the work of someone else) for a ruler who acts unjustly. Divine law can be attained only through faith, while the eternal law cannot be known in this world. While reason can prove the existence of eternal law, it cannot grasp its essence. Natural and human law are derived by man through his reason, aided by faith in the scriptures and other divinely inspired writings.

In a larger sense, Aquinas is speaking here not only of law, but of the respective spheres of faith and reason in all human endeavor.

Aquinas' "Christian Aristotelianism" encountered strong opposition even before he died in 1274. The reaction of the church against the use of Aristotle perhaps culminated in the condemnation of propositions of the Latin Averroists and Siger of Brabant, and several doctrines of Aquinas, in a famous proceeding by the bishop of Paris in 1277. Thomas was regarded as authoritative only in the sixteenth century, although he was canonized in 1323. Much of the reaction against him amounted to Franciscan antipathy toward a Dominician, for it is noteworthy that virtually all his major critics were Franciscans. Perhaps the most characteristic is St. Bonaventure (1221–74), minister general of the Franciscan order, whose work was in the Augustinian tradition. While Bonaventure did not deprecate the use of reason per

Illustration 16.
A Romanesque exterior: the west choir of Worms cathedral

Illustration 17. English Romanesque: Durham cathedral

Illustration 18.
A Romanesque interior:
the church of Ste.
Madeleine at Vézélay

Illustration 19. A Gothic façade: Exeter cathedral

Illustration 20.
A Gothic interior:
Cologne cathedral

Illustration 21.
Exterior buttressing:
Winchester cathedral

Illustration 23.
Gothic art:
the last judgment,
from the west façade
of Bourges cathedral

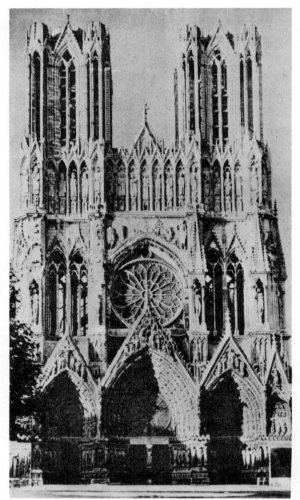

Illustration 22.
Reims cathedral

Illustration 24.
Gargoyle, from cathedral
of Notre-Dame, Paris

se, he disliked the tendency which he attributed to the Aristotelians to overemphasize the role of reason in man's total being and correspondingly to underestimate the sphere of faith and emotion. Somewhat surprisingly to the modern eye, the Aristotelians also had difficulties with some scientists, who criticized them for overconcentration on the mundane. The Oxford Franciscan Robert Grosseteste (c. 1168–1253) was an admirer of Aristotle and even translated Aristotle's *Ethics* from Greek into Latin, but the fundamental emphasis of his work was Neoplatonic. He was interested in the "light metaphysic," in which light is viewed not only from the partly symbolic standpoint of divine illumination, but also from the scientist's view, and Grosseteste performed valuable scientific experiments with optics. His pupil Roger Bacon (d. 1294) has achieved even greater fame through supposed magic and a totally fictive invention of gunpowder. Bacon was a man of considerable talent, but he fell into trouble with the church, and his reputation as a magician comes largely from totally far-fetched speculations in astrology and alchemy.

Gothic Architecture

The development of Gothic art and architecture is a reflection of the preoccupation of the men of the central Middle Ages with light and with straight lines reaching toward heaven. Romanesque, the style usually associated with the early Middle Ages and the basic form of most Italian church architecture, was normally in the basilica form. The walls were heavy and thick, with few windows. Rounded arches placed the entire weight of the nave ceiling on the walls, with little opportunity for side aisles, windows, or height. Gothic did not grow out of Romanesque, although many churches, such as that of Worms, show features of both styles. The earliest building in the Gothic style was the abbey church of St. Denis, constructed in the twelfth century under the direction of Suger, councillor of Louis VI and VII of France. Gothic was characterized by the pointed arch, which allowed higher structures to be built. The weight of the nave ceiling now rested on interior pillars which created a side aisle, rather than on the walls. From these pillars, ribbed vaults intersected across the ceiling, dispersing the weight of the structure more evenly. The walls themselves were quite thin and intersected to provide windows, which were filled with a gorgeous stained glass, the technique of which has unfortunately been lost. The exterior walls were often supported in addition by "flying buttresses," structures attached to pillars totally outside the church and then to the exterior wall.

The building of cathedrals was a point of civic pride for many communities. Some apparently bankrupted themselves by the constant expenditure on these churches, whose construction might take centuries. Towns vied with each other in height of construction, but also in the art work which decorated the façades with scenes from the Bible and Christian tradition. Some churches overstrained their structures and collapsed, such as that of Beauvais. Gothic style was to become increasingly ornate, decorated, and flamboyant in the fourteenth and fifteenth centuries, with the original straight, angled structures embellished with fluting and fussiness. The Gothic cathedral of the thirteenth century, however, is a magnificent monument to the structural and geometrical knowledge of medieval man and to his capacity to enslave himself to an ideal. Stone might have to be brought hundreds of miles by oxcart, and the cities maintained regular crews of architects and masons who spent entire lifetimes working on these churches. When one remembers the technology of the day, the achievement of the "cathedral builders" becomes even more impressive.

11

RELIGIOSITY AND THE
CHURCH IN THE CENTRAL
MIDDLE AGES

INTELLECTUAL LIFE and religion were obviously very closely connected in the Middle Ages. The church was part of the intellectual "renaissance." As the popes emerged victorious from the investiture contest, they needed to define orthodoxy. It has often been noted that while the great popes of the eleventh century were monks, their successors in the twelfth and thirteenth centuries were canon lawyers, anxious to fix norms of belief for all Christians. A certain loss of spontaneity was the inevitable result, although much of the most fruitful intellectual endeavor of the central Middle Ages resulted from the continuing attempt of the church to define proper doctrine.

First and foremost, this period witnessed a great revival of the study of theology and canon law. Peter Lombard, an Italian pupil of Peter Abelard who became bishop of Paris in the mid-twelfth century, wrote the *Four Books of Sentences,* containing opinions from authoritative sources on various questions. His very name symbolizes the international character of the universities and is a good example of how occupation, origin, or personal characteristic might become a patronymic in the twelfth and thirteenth centuries. His method, however, reconciled divergences of opinion when he found them; he learned from his master's calamities.

Canon law consists of church statutes, papal pronouncements, legal procedure, and in general all questions of church practice and morality. It is more specific than theology and is concerned much more with this world than with the next. Collections of canon law certainly existed before the twelfth century. As early as the mid-ninth century an anonymous compiler produced the "False Decretals," in which authentic papal decretals (statements on church law which became authoritative) were mixed with spurious. Around 1100 Ivo of Chartres produced the best of the earliest collections of canon law, the *Pannormia*. A new era began, however, when around 1140 the Italian monk Gratian produced his *Concordance of Discordant Canons,* known as the *Decretum*. It is a code of laws and an exposition of their principles, arranged analytically according to categories of questions, quoting the necessary canons. This was the first work of the great *corpus juris canonici*, body of the canon law. Other official collections of subsequent canons were made in 1234, 1248, and 1317—so rapidly were the popes being drawn into legal business—with the result that the church had amassed an enormous body of law to define norms of behavior and belief by the late Middle Ages.

The Investiture Contest, however, was the last time that any movement of religious emotion or enthusiasm ever received the support of the medieval papacy in more than a formal sense. Emotion and religiosity were dangerous, for they might lead the unwary into heresy. The church structure was becoming increasingly rigid. From the time of Gregory VII and particularly Urban II, papal courts had taken most of the pope's energies, and the problem had become acute by the time of Alexander III (1159–81), who combined this with a quarrel with the emperor Frederick I that seemed unnecessary to many and helped give the impression of an essentially political papacy. Satires on papal greed appeared in the twelfth century, such as the *Gospel According to the Mark Silver*. The church was coming into disrepute and was losing the allegiance of many.

Much of this was for purely practical reasons. An informed body of persons is less likely than the uneducated to accept any body of dogma uncritically, and educational levels were rising. This is not to imply that anybody's religion was becoming very sophisticated by modern standards. All, orthodox and heterodox alike, believed in demons and spirits. Miracle tales are only slightly less abundant in twelfth and thirteenth century writing than in that of the early Middle Ages. Many carried charms of various sorts to ward off evil spirits.

The worship of relics is part of the same religious primitivism. The Maypole dance is merely one instance of fertility celebrations at the rite of spring derived from ancient pagan cult life. The most worldly of businessmen sought to buy salvation by ferocious acts of penitence in their last hours. The practicalities of medieval religion were sorcery and demonology, with the mass merely considered another piece of magic to ward off the ever-present spirits of evil and doom.

Nonetheless, education brought grievances against the formal church hierarchy, although not against the old and established religion. Most moral theology was based in greater or lesser degree on St. Augustine and the other church fathers. Augustine, as indeed Jesus, had written and lived in a time when there were few towns, and when businessman and profiteer tended to be synonymous terms. Hence the church became very concerned with formulating abstract "just prices" for articles, without consideration given to risk, supply, and demand. It forbade outright the loaning of money at interest. Thus many merchants who desired to live Christian lives found themselves alienated from the church, although not excluded—for they still could buy penance—as a result of the increasing rigidity of usage and dogma.

As the church lost its earlier monopoly on literacy, laymen, particularly merchants, had to read and write. With this, they became sufficiently educated to know a smattering of scripture. Such men were not trained theologians, but they knew enough of the Bible to see the enormous contrast between the life of Jesus of Nazareth and the lives and sometimes ideals of the great church princes and the often corrupt local clergy. Hence we find a resurgence of anticlericalism on all levels of society, but particularly among the merchants. The church's reply was some of the most ferocious social criticism which the Middle Ages was to know, in railing especially at the ungodliness of peasants who, to keep from starving, denied the church a tithe of their produce. The feeling grew that since the church seemed unworthy, good men, whether clergy or not, might take over the functions of the church and achieve their own and others' salvation with or without recourse to the sacraments of the church. An important feature of the religious milieu of the twelfth and thirteenth centuries is the ethical emphasis of the heretical movements as opposed to the legal emphasis of the church.

Finally, we have noted that the central Middle Ages witnessed increased social mobility and more rapid communications. Men were wandering about, preaching, teaching, and learning. Ideas spread more rapidly than before and found a much wider and readier reception. We begin to find mass movements of religious hysteria or enthusiasm at the time of the first crusade, and this tendency continued for the rest of the Middle Ages. Entire regions became subject to waves of emotionalism as they fell under the sway of a popular preacher. Much of the difficulty of the church in the central Middle Ages can be explained as its reaction to heresy and deviation from established norms of belief.

The Monastic Movements

There were two sides to the ecclesiastical changes of the central Middle Ages. There was a very orthodox reaction to some of the excesses of the intellectuals, but this reaction took the form of a mysticism which in its turn fostered some of the outlooks, if not the doctrines, that the heretics were to embrace. Much of the new enthusiasm came from a revived monasticism. The monastery of Cluny had established an order on a Benedictine model, but with the abbot of Cluny having almost total control over the various daughter houses. But the Cluniacs became conservative, particularly as wealthy patrons tried to buy salvation by endowing the monastery with rich properties. In addition, since they did not entirely sympathize with the tendencies of the reform papacy of the eleventh century, they seemed somewhat behind the times, although the order prospered and remained morally pure.

Even as early as the late tenth century the life of the hermit became very popular in Italy. St. Romuald (d. 1027), after starting life as a Cluniac monk, wandered and preached. He had wide influence, although he founded no order, and some of his disciples rose to high places. The monastic life was always more popular than the eremitical, and there was a tendency that we have seen to apply monastic rules as standards to lay endeavor. The popes were particularly insistent against simony and in favor of clerical celibacy, as we have seen. Ever concerned with definition, they wanted every religious group to have a rule according to which its members would live. By the end of the twelfth century, this was to involve the popes in troubles with laymen who wanted to lead lives of piety but in their own way. For the moment, the popes concentrated on turning communities of canons

Illustration 25.   St. Bavon's abbey, Ghent

(the clergy attached to cathedral staffs) into canons regular, canons with a rule. Hence many cathedral staffs assumed the rule erroneously ascribed to St. Augustine as their standard from the late eleventh century.

Monastic life continued to be popular with secular patrons. Although the amount of land granted to churches and abbeys dropped off in the central Middle Ages from its earlier levels, this is not to say that the grants stopped, and it may simply reflect the fact that the available land was being used up and could no longer be donated without great loss. Increased emphasis on the family tie in the central Middle Ages also made all persons more reluctant, and at times legally unable, to disinherit their children without the latter's consent. But communities which started in stark poverty, always considered a mark of particular holiness as an imitation of the life of Christ and his disciples, were soon given heavy endowments, became rich, lost their initial enthusiasm, and began to lose out to new monastic groups of greater ascetic fervor. The whole matter was cyclical throughout the Middle Ages.

A classic case is the early history of the Cistercian order, the most famous of the new orders produced by the monastic revival of the central Middle Ages. It was founded around 1075 in Burgundy, center of many spiritual movements, by a Benedictine named Robert. His abbey at Molesme was revered as a holy place and became wealthy.

Dissatisfied, the abbot and a few monks went to Cîteaux, not far away. When the monks of Molesme claimed that their abbot had left without permission, he had to return, for the secular patrons were getting restless in fear that the monastic prayers for which they had paid so dearly would lose their celestial efficacy. But the new community, from which the order was to derive its name, struggled along, and its fortunes were transformed in 1112 by the entry of Bernard, a young Burgundian nobleman, who was to be the virtual spiritual dictator of western Europe during the 1130s and 1140s. Bernard spent three years at Cîteaux, then established the third daughter house of the Cistercian order, Clairvaux, of which he became abbot. The Cistercian order spread throughout Europe through his personal influence.

Earlier monastic movements, including the Cluniac foundations, had no institutional basis from which to control daughter houses. Much depended on the character of individual monks and particularly abbots. Each house of the Cistercian order, however, was subject to an annual visitation by the abbot of Cîteaux, and Cîteaux itself was to be visited yearly by the abbots of the four eldest foundations. The visitors had power to remedy any abuses. There was also a chapter general of all abbots of the order at Cîteaux to decide policy.

Other orders were founded as well. The Cistercians encouraged preaching and conversion, a return to old mores and enthusiasm. Missionaries were encouraged. Partly under Cistercian influence, the order of Premonstratensian canons was founded in the early twelfth century by St. Norbert of Xanten. The Premonstratensians intended to lead lives of poverty and wander about converting, but the authorities disliked this as unfair competition for local priests and bishops—a complaint which would be made later of the mendicants and some of the great heretical movements. Although the Premonstratensians eventually lost their enthusiasm, they performed valuable works of conversion among the Slavic populations.

The church encouraged chivalry, the fighting for Christian ideals, and as a result the orders of "crusading knights" developed in the kingdom of Jerusalem in the early twelfth century. They were dedicated to the defense of the Latin kingdom and the protection of pilgrims and crusaders. The Knights of the Hospital of Jerusalem continued a precarious existence and controlled some lands in the east even after the crusader state fell. They assisted later crusaders against the Turks. The Knights of the Temple of Jerusalem, called the Templars, soon became bankers as they safeguarded the possessions of the pious in the Holy Land. They became bankers of the kings of France, and their chief historical importance was in finance, not in holiness. The order was dissolved in 1307 by King Philip IV of France, on the ostensible grounds of moral turpitude of the Templars, actually because he wanted to possess the Templar treasures. He was disappointed, for Templar financial organization was simple, and the order had been little more than a storehouse of funds, without substantial investments.

A third crusading order, the "Teutonic Knights," had a spectacular career which illustrates nicely the result of mixing religion and politics. As it became obvious in the thirteenth century that the Kingdom of Jerusalem could not survive, the Teutonic Knights, entirely of German extraction, moved into eastern Europe. With the cooperation of the Poles, they began fighting the Prussians and spreading Christianity along the shores of the Baltic. They governed the lands which they conquered, and they were rulers of Prussia by the late thirteenth century. They encouraged colonists from Germany to settle. The Teutonic knights were not easy taskmasters, and there were periodic revolts which resulted in the extermination of most of the native Prussian population and its replacement with Germans. Towns grew up and joined the Hanse (on the Hanse, see below, p. 234), but generally remained independent of the Teutonic Knights. In the thirteenth and fourteenth centuries the order expanded into Estonia, Latvia, Lithuania, and finally Poland. A check was finally administered to the Teutonic Knights by the dynastic union of Lithuania and Poland in 1385, and German expansion eastward was ended in 1410 when the Poles and Lithuanians defeated the order severely. Further struggles in the fifteenth century reduced the power of the order still further, but the work of the Teutonic Knights had made the population of the Baltic regions of eastern Europe largely German, which it remained. Finally, in 1525, the Grand Master of the Teutonic Knights became a Lutheran and made East Prussia a secular duchy hereditary in his family, the Hohenzollern.

St. Bernard

Perhaps the ideal representative of the monastic or spiritual side of the "twelfth-century Renaissance" is St. Bernard of Clairvaux, a religious mystic who was completely out of tune with the rationalistic movements of his day. His rivals, such as Abelard, won admiration for their intellectual powers, but most persons were not intellectuals. They were hypnotized by the personal force of the tall, thin, red-haired Bernard, whose fiery oratory won numerous converts to the monastic life.

Bernard repeatedly proclaimed his desire to be left alone to a peaceful life as a monk, but this was impossible for a man with his temperament. He was extremely combative and could not understand that there might be legitimate disagreement with his views. Appeals came to him as judge from everywhere in Christendom; he was virtually a substitute pope. Although he recognized the supremacy of the papal office, his hectorings extended to bishops and popes alike, especially when one of his pupils became pope as Eugene III in 1145. Once he had convinced himself that a cause was right, he left no stone unturned to see that justice as he saw it was done, and his polemics reveal a most unattractive man. When there was a divided election to the papacy in 1130, Bernard became convinced of the justice of the cause of Innocent II, elected by a minority faction of cardinals who held a rump session of the college before the scheduled meeting, against Anacletus II, personally a much more worthy character who was elected later on the same day by a majority of the cardinals. Bernard persuaded the kings of Europe to support Innocent, and the German emperor intervened with armed force. Innocent is now recognized as the legitimate pope. The disastrous second crusade also owed much to Bernard, who saw the holy sepulchre in danger and by his skillful oratory persuaded kings and princes to go to the Holy Land.

Bernard would not have considered himself anti-intellectual, but he often thought that the use of reason per se hindered the mystical ministrations of faith. He emphasized the humanity of Jesus, following in Anselm's footsteps, and was an important force in the growing veneration of Mary as a divine figure in her own right. This movement taken several degrees further would become heretical in the late twelfth century as men emphasized Christ as an ethical being in contrast to the less than ethical church establishment. Bernard emphasized the inner life; but the inner life which is not properly guided by the wisdom of the church can lead to heresy.

Bernard's most famous battle was against Abelard. Much of this was personal antagonism between two supreme egotists. Bernard's egotism, however, was couched in his humility, of which he was inordinately proud, while he felt that Abelard was concerned only with his own fame and the glorification of reason. They quarreled at several points, and in 1140 Bernard procured Abelard's condemnation as a heretic over a question involving free will and grace, after Abelard had stated that intention was more important in a person's conduct and moral responsibility than the outward act. Bernard deliberately garbled Abelard's words, and finally stated his real intention as the downfall of a man who placed reason above the mysteries of faith. This also was untrue; Abelard was simply more interested in propositions which were capable of rational demonstration than in those which were not.

The Growth of Heresy

Hence it is not totally inaccurate to say that some of the great heresies were merely extensions of an intellectual attitude fostered by persons high in the church, until those high persons realized the direction toward which their ideas might lead. Some of the earliest heresies were the work of men with diseased minds, generally in urban environments with few priests, places whose inhabitants had little contact with the church hierarchy and disliked what they did see of it. These movements were sporadic, but they accompanied outbursts of mass religious hysteria, such as a pogrom of the Rhineland Jews in the early stages of the second crusade.

Perhaps the most famous, if not the most important, of the heretics of the central Middle Ages were the Cathari ("pure"), or Albigensians, a name derived from their major center, the town of Albi in the county of Toulouse in southern France. They propounded a dualist heresy apparently derived from eastern influences. All creation was divided into realms of light and darkness, each ruled by its own god. Life on earth was a struggle between the two gods, but the world of matter itself was evil or dark. The Cathari saw salvation in the total purification of the body from matter; hence they abstained from sexual intercourse and all its food products, although they could eat plants and fish. The world would end eventually in a battle between the two gods. The Cathari had two grades of devotion: the perfect, who lived completely according to their vigorous scheme, and the ordinary "believers," who merely served the perfect. Change from believer to perfect might come on the deathbed, while the rest of one's life could be spent as one wished. This doctrine in turn provoked some moral looseness which brought the Cathari into disrepute.

The Cathari included much if not most of the population of southern France at the turn of the thirteenth century, with many princes and clergymen as well as ordinary laymen. Accordingly, the popes moved circumspectly. Finally, the murder of the papal legate at the court of Count Raymond of Toulouse in 1208 caused Pope Innocent III (1198–1216), perhaps the greatest of medieval political popes, to call a crusade. Philip II of France refused to take part, but the landless barons of northern France responded quickly. As they moved from one success to another, however, the king decided to prevent them from reaping the rewards, and accordingly gave direction of the crusade to his son, the future Louis VIII. Matters seemed ended by 1229, but the count of Toulouse apostasized again and there were renewed crusades. Albigensian resistance was finally broken in 1244, and the daughter and sole heiress of the count of Toulouse was married to the younger brother of Louis IX of France. They were childless, and when the brother, Alphonse of Poitiers, died in 1270, much of southern France escheated to the French crown.

Innocent also used the occasion of the Albigensian trouble to establish the Inquisition. Before this time, control of heresy had been in the hands of local ecclesiastical authorities, who were to find heretics and destroy them lest they contaminate others. But heresy was such a problem by the late twelfth century that most bishops were unable to cope with it. There is evidence too that many were indifferent to the heretics as long as they were discreet and caused no trouble. Using the murder of 1208 as a pretext, however, Innocent III established courts throughout Europe directly under the pope for apprehending and trying heretics.

The Inquisition has been much overplayed as a force in medieval life. It is quite true that torture was used and that one was presumed guilty; indeed, the way to escape the stake was by recanting errors, whether one had held them or not. But torture was used in most secular courts as well, and only occasionally did the Inquisition really get out of hand. Conrad of Marburg carried out a vicious pogrom as papal inquisitor of Germany in the early 1230s until he himself was murdered, after which the furor died down. Robert le Bougre, whose surname suggests that he may have been a former heretic or perhaps Beghard, was quite active at the same time in northern France. The Inquisition in Italy received the full support of the emperor Frederick II and prospered. After imperial power declined, papal authority and local city administrations kept it in force, although comparatively few persons were burned. It simply petered out in the north. After a brief flareup in France in the early fourteenth century over a supposed threat from the Beguines and the "Spiritual Franciscans," the Inquisition became a royal court. There were periodic outbreaks of inquisitorial activity in time of crisis, but there was never a coherent program which was well administered. While innocent persons certainly were massacred, the very fact that heresy continued to spread is evidence that the Inquisition was ineffective.

The Doctrine of Apostolic Poverty

It is very difficult to draw a fine line between heterodoxy and orthodoxy by the early thirteenth century. Indeed, a much more powerful force than the Inquisition in reestablishing a sort of calm was the growth of the mendicant orders, which had much in common with some of the most despised heretical groups, particularly the Waldensians.

Peter Waldo had many similarities to St. Francis of Assisi. He was a wealthy merchant of Lyon, in southern France, who began to have qualms of conscience about his riches, while Christ, his disciples, and many persons of Waldo's own time lived lives of stark poverty. Accordingly, he and a group of twelve disciples renounced the world in 1173 and began to preach the gospel. Peter Waldo did not know Latin, but he had the Gospels translated into Provençal, the language of southern France, and the diffusion of the scriptures added weight to his arguments. The idea of "apostolic poverty" espoused by the Waldensians is particularly important, for they preached that one must live this way in Christian charity in order to gain God's approval.

Only in the Waldensian insistence that absolute poverty was the only avenue to salvation was this doctrine extraordinary. The fundamental problem with the Waldensians was their lay status. As laymen, they had to obtain the permission of the local ecclesiastical authorities before they could preach, and this permission was frequently denied. They felt a divine calling to preach, however, and continued to follow the dictates of their consciences and to fall afoul of the church. Furthermore, while the Waldensians were well versed in the scriptures, they did not know theology and canon law. Accordingly, many of them quite innocently began to preach heretical doctrines which seemed justified by the Bible, but which the church had anathematized. When they refused to cooperate with the pope, they were condemned in 1179. Their preaching became increasingly heretical after this. They taught that laymen might administer the sacraments, denying implicitly that the power of the keys resided in the episcopal hierarchy, and argued that the church in its corrupted state had no efficacy in the next world. Although the Waldensians were persecuted by the Inquisition, colonies of them continued to exist throughout the Middle Ages and indeed in the modern period, and their preachers troubled local authorities.

The Mendicants

Francis of Assisi differed from the Waldensians in being less anticlerical and more willing to accept papal direction. St. Francis' movement seized Europe a generation after the Waldensians, and by this time the papacy was less struck by the novelty of the same ideas.

Francis was born Pietro Bernardone around 1180 at Assisi, in northern Italy. His father was a prosperous merchant who dealt with French traders, and the young boy affected French manners to the point of being dubbed "Francesco" ("Frenchy"); from his popularity the name went into all languages of Europe. He told later of his dissolute youth, but this may simply have been an ordinary young manhood, for Francis always had a morbid fascination with his own "unworthiness." He seems gradually to have become convinced that his way of life was sinful, although he formally renounced the world around 1207 by giving up his possessions publicly and leaving his father's house, evidently after hearing a sermon preached by a Waldensian.

The sincerity of Francis' conversion and of his desire to lead a simple life of poverty, preaching, and conversion is beyond question. Italy was overly urbanized, with a wealthy church. The clergy took in a higher percentage of the population than today, but the tremendous demographic expansion of the twelfth century had left the church totally unable to meet the spiritual needs of the townsmen. Even in the countryside the church was topheavy and rich, without enough parish priests.

Francis' movement began as a simple preaching group in the vicinity of Assisi. For reasons which are uncertain, he drew up a rule and asked papal approval of it in 1211. This rule has nothing to do with the formal rule of 1223 for the Franciscan order; it is simply several Bible verses, the "sell all that thou hast and give to the poor" passages from Matthew and Luke. Innocent III did not approve this rule per se, but he did give indirect approval by allowing Francis and his followers to lead lives of absolute conformity to the Gospel. Innocent did, however, require the Franciscans to choose a superior through whom they might deal with the ecclesiastical authorities. They chose Francis, were tonsured, and became priests.

Francis' order filled a genuine spiritual need. The man himself was the object of personality identification for the poor and oppressed multitudes. He became a legend in his own lifetime for his simple, childlike faith and his empathy for nature and all humankind. By concentrating their work chiefly in the always volatile towns, the Franciscans helped to defuse the issue of heresy, particularly in northern Europe. The order was so large by 1220 that Francis himself was no longer able to control it. The Franciscan rule of 1223, borrowed to some extent from the Dominican organization, provided a graded hierarchy of provinces under papal control. The minister general was elected by a chapter general which met every three years. In close similarity to the Cathari and the Dominicans, there were three grades of Franciscans: the friars (from *fratres,* brothers, as Francis thought of himself and his followers), a second order for women, and the tertiaries, who pursued lives in the world but were closely affiliated with the Franciscans.

With growth came prosperity and expansion of design. The later development of the order has little to do with the founder's career. Francis died in 1226, revered but without influence. Numerous persons were attracted to the Franciscan order who did not share Francis' affinity for the meanest and dirtiest wretches of the world. Francis furthermore had an unfortunate talent for picking associates who worked against his ultimate aims. This is particularly evident in his choice of his twelve disciples, several of whom were totally unworthy and schemed behind Francis' back for control of the order, and in his dealings with Cardinal Ugolino, who became pope as Gregory IX (1227–41). Ugolino genuinely admired Francis and thought that the poor man's movement could do great service to the church, but

Francis the man was utterly beyond his comprehension. He tried to introduce Francis to the "right people," persuade him to give up his preaching, for Francis always had in mind a lay fraternity of the poor and simple, and gain his consent to the foundation of an order. To his credit, Francis always resisted to the best of his ability, but he considered Ugolino his friend to the end. After Francis' death, Ugolino as pope set aside his will and declared heretical the teaching that Christ and his disciples had led lives of absolute poverty.

The Franciscans soon became intellectual leaders, despite Francis' distaste for secular learning, and several chairs in theology in the universities were reserved for them. According to papal decree of 1230, the friars might hold property through intermediaries. Shortly after the founder's death, the order split into two branches: the Conventuals, who preferred to follow the rule of 1223 and subsequent broadenings, and the Spiritual Franciscans, who wished to keep strict adherence to the ideals of apostolic poverty. Although the Conventuals have received a bad press from historians, it is hard to fault them too severely for desiring to modernize Francis, for his ideal in its purest form was totally impractical for the world in which he lived and in which he conceived his mission to be. It was entirely possible for perfectly sincere men to be attracted to Francis' saintly personality and his ideal of church reform without carrying them to his extremes. The Conventuals, however, tried to make life impossible for the Spirituals and branded them as heretics.

The Dominican order was as important in the Middle Ages as the Franciscan, although the personality of St. Dominic comes through the sources much less clearly than that of Francis. Dominic was a Spaniard who spent some years working against the Albigensian heretics. He became convinced that the only way to combat heresy effectively was for orthodox missionaries to match the heretics in purity of life and knowledge of creed. Hence he established an order which adopted the rule of the Augustinian canons in 1215, changing this in 1220 to a new rule very similar to that of the Franciscans of 1223. The Dominicans were much more willing than the Franciscans to follow papal direction, and the popes tended to favor them for that reason, but the Dominicans never got the popular allegiance which the Franciscans received, and the two orders thus tended to be opposite edges of the same sword. The Franciscan movement was not directed against heresy per se, but fought it in fact, since many who might earlier have been led astray now found a place of their own within the church. The Dominicans were more completely orthodox as scholars and teachers. They became very important as inquisitors, giving rise to a popular derivation of their name as "hounds of God" (*domini canes*). Their emphasis on the necessity of learning led them to found schools. They, with many Franciscans, were very important in the universities in the late Middle Ages.

The Circle Is Completed

The Spiritual-Conventual division of the Franciscans was to produce much personal acrimony and unholy bickering, together with extremely interesting ideas. Authority in the order alternated between the factions until there seemed to be a definite reaction in favor of the Spirituals in 1248 with the election as minister general of John of Parma, an Italian who taught theology at the university of Paris— so involved in the world of intellect were even the Spirituals. But John was forced out in 1257 over an incident involving one of the most interesting phenomena of the intellectual history of medieval Europe, which one historian has called "the pursuit of the millennium."

Ideas of the millennium, the eventual end of the world, were quite common throughout the Middle Ages, but in the late twelfth century the Italian monk Joachim of Flora put some new twists on them. Joachim considered himself less a prophet than an explicator of what the scriptures really meant. Taking the mystic numbers 7 and 3 as his base, he devised a scheme of 42 months containing 1260 days of the history of mankind. The history of the world was divided into three ages, corresponding to the Father, Son, and Holy Spirit. Each age had 42 generations, 21 of beginning and 21 of fulfillment. According to his time reckoning, the reign of the son was to last until 1260. He was predicting not the end of the world, but the beginning of the age of the Holy Spirit. The adherents of Joachim among the Franciscans, almost entirely of the Spiritual branch, took this to mean that they would be the agents of the Holy Ghost in the new age, when human wickedness would end. But a storm arose in 1254 with the publication of the *Book of the Everlasting Gospel* by an intimate of John of Parma. This work, consisting of works of Joachim of Flora

Illustration 26.   A flagellant procession

with explanatory glosses, had an antisacramental and antipapal tone. Among other things, it predicted that a simoniac would obtain the papacy in 1260. The Spirituals were compromised, and John of Parma had to give way as minister general to St. Bonaventure. The Spiritual Franciscans also began prophesying in their own right, foretelling the failure of the crusade of St. Louis of France. This sort of thing endeared them to no one. They maintained a separate existence despite some persecution, and the Italian Spirituals were organized into a separate arm, the *Fraticelli* (Little Brothers) in the early fourteenth century. A papal commission investigated the Spirituals in 1311 and pronounced them orthodox, but they were persecuted again under Pope John XXII (1316–34).

Joachitism seems also to have been connected in some way with what to modern minds is one of the most singular forms of medieval piety: the outbreak of self-flagellation. This had been known for centuries and was used as a form of penance in monasteries, apparently in the hope that men would escape some punishment in the hereafter by flogging themselves on earth. But in 1260, the very year which Joachim had predicted would begin a new age, organized flagellant processions appeared in some Italian cities. They were usually led by priests, but occasionally by prominent men of the town. Although rich and poor participated, the poor tended to dominate the proces-

sions. It is true that matters other than Joachitism led to psychological
disorder about this time: there had been a famine in 1258 and a
plague in 1259, and in 1260 the illegitimate son of the emperor Frederick II, Manfred, seemed about the recapture his father's empire.
Still, the sources indicate that the number mysticism surrounding 1260
had wide popular adherence. When 1260 passed and the world continued as before, the Italian flagellant movement subsided, although
it was to reappear during the disasters of the fourteenth century. In
southern Germany and the Rhineland, however, Italians organized
flagellant processions of the urban masses in 1261–62, but they were
soon suppressed on suspicion of heresy, only to reappear in time of
crisis.

As the real world closed in on the Franciscans, and as Spiritual
and Conventual alike seemed to become concerned chiefly with vying
with each other and with the Dominicans, the real meaning of Francis'
rule came to be exemplified better in the lives of two groups that
had no connection with the Franciscans: the Béguines and Beghards.
The Béguines were laywomen, generally in or near cities of northern
Europe, who wanted to lead lives of quiet piety and charity. There
were some common houses, but they might live in their own homes
as well. Most were orthodox, although an occasional heretical Béguine
tended to give the entire movement a bad name. Most large cities
of northern Germany and the Low Countries had Béguine convents
and even entire Béguine parishes by the late thirteenth century.

The Béguinages were originally havens set up by rich women for
poor relief, and for widows and unmarried girls who wanted to lead
lives of quiet meditation. Sometimes they took up weaving as an occupation to prevent idleness, but this occasionally brought them into
conflict with the local textile guilds. The ideal was compromised here
eventually, as with the Franciscans, for the pope used the discovery of
some heretical Béguines in the early fourteenth century to force them
to assume a rule and go under the protection of the Dominicans or
Franciscans. The tendency toward heresy was more pronounced
among the Beghards, who were very roughly a sort of male equivalent
of the Béguines, but with much more revolutionary ideas and often
with connections with the "Free Spirit" heretics, antinomian and anticlerical, who were common in the Rhineland during the fourteenth
century.

Heresy, in short, was endemic in a religious society which was becoming more learned and in which physical mobility was increasing. Much of the difficulty, one suspects, was simply the papal ability now to find out about aberrant beliefs when they occurred. The popes, to their eternal discredit, were much more concerned with persons who wished to live pious lives without papal interference than with cleaning up corruption within their church or even preserving the good moral name of the papacy itself. The conflict of ideal and reality, with the pope usually on the side of reality, would come close to destroying the church in the fourteenth century.

Part III

EUROPE IN CRISIS: THE LATE MIDDLE AGES

12

ECONOMIC DEPRESSION AND SOCIAL CRISIS

Europe entered a period of social and economic crisis in the late thirteenth century from which it did not recover until modern times. The crisis was reflected in political and institutional change, as we shall see. An earlier generation of historians placed primary responsibility for the disaster on the "Black Death" of 1348–50, and there can be no doubt that this plague prolonged and intensified the difficulty. But the basic nature of the crisis was of long standing, with roots in the economy of the thirteenth century or perhaps even the late twelfth. Population began to decline as early as 1250 in some regions, and the "prosperity" which an earlier generation saw in the thirteenth century economy contained seeds of disaster.

Part of the change can be explained by the role of the towns. Europe was overurbanized in the thirteenth century. Migration from the countryside had swelled urban populations to such an extent that most large centers had substantial proletariats. Lords continued to found new towns in the late thirteenth century, particularly in Germany, but none of these settlements became large in the Middle Ages, for most surplus farm labor migrated to previously established centers which had a reputation for high prices and a good labor market. This condition became stifling in the late thirteenth century, for such a primitive economy as that of the Middle Ages could only support a limited number of persons not engaged directly in production. Many cities could not even support the persons already within their walls by 1250, for the population of Europe as a whole was becoming poorer and markets for town manufactured goods were diminishing. The urban economy was to be hit less severely than the rural by the catastrophe of the fourteenth century, for as decline of population released pressure on the means of subsistence, a higher standard of living resulted for the survivors, and markets for luxury items made in the towns again increased relatively. But the towns, specializing in luxury wares, were losing their original function as centers of agricultural exchange to local village markets in the late thirteenth century. Many goods which could have been exported over a large area remained in essentially local commerce as the towns failed to fulfill their primary function of transfer and consignment. The towns acted chiefly as consumers of rural produce, and indeed many farmers seem to have starved themselves for the sake of getting high prices from the town grain monopolies. Only with the fourteenth century, however, do we find large scale interregional export of food and the beginning of a tendency for some areas to specialize in large-scale farming while others were industrial. After originally serving as a powerful force for the amelioration of rural conditions, drawing surplus population away from the countryside and furthering an exchange economy, the towns had thus begun to stifle the countryside and had become a drain upon it.

As the towns lost markets but became overpopulated in relation to the economy as a whole, the bourgeois of northern Europe, although not the south, began to lose interest in new markets, which seemed impossible to obtain, and concentrated their attention on preserving markets which they already had. In particular, this took the form of restrictive guild regulation. Most towns of northern Europe were ruled by a large guild containing both wholesalers and retailers in the thirteenth century. Other forms included large guilds which began as artisan unions but developed wealthy upper strata which were merchant oligarchies in effect, as in the towns of Italy and some of England. But artisan organizations, often repressed by the merchants in the thirteenth century, came to power increasingly in the cities during the fourteenth century. The guilds had begun as charitable organizations which later developed the character of occupational groupings. To say the least, they did not promote industrial efficiency, for guilds demanded separate functions and separate workers for numerous jobs which could be performed by one person. The great export guilds, such as those of the textile industries, usually dominated the magistracies of the larger towns, but they always had to share power with smaller guilds, particularly victuallers and makers of small items for local consumption, for the towns were still occupied in large part with feeding their own citizens and providing manufactured goods to nearby farmers. The visions of these "small guildsmen" were even narrower than those of the export workers, and the guilds which monopolized the city's food supply had a very important role in all town policy, particularly after the plagues. The guilds were generally at one another's throats, and even those within the same overall field did not realize the benefits of unity, preferring instead to fight pitched battles on the local marketplaces. Although guild regulations usually insured that goods of proper quality were made, so that the guilds would not get a bad name and their market suffer, this increasingly became a pretext for town action against others who might compete for a shrinking market. This is particularly true of town attempts to stifle rural industries in the late thirteenth century and for the rest of the Middle Ages, when some urban as well as rural entrepreneurs began using rural labor because it was cheaper—for the farmers it was a second source of income—and making dents in town markets, less over long distance than in the immediate economic hinterland. Especially after the Black Death, guilds limited membership, as population imbalance became worse and the artisans were competing for an ever shrinking market. This did not mean that only sons of masters could work, but rather that only they could control work, renting stalls, providing raw materials, and the like to persons who actually did the labor. A ceiling thus was placed over the heads of most immigrants to the towns. They were journeymen, day laborers, but not masters, a term which takes on an increasingly petty bourgeois aristocratic cast in the fourteenth century. The statutorily hereditary character of the guilds was much mitigated in practice, since no group could maintain itself as a closed caste, but mobility was hindered.

The Agricultural Depression

The fundamental aspects of the economic crisis, however, must be sought in the rural sector. Here the basic problem was a technological gap resulting in a press on natural resources. Although the increased use of iron implements had been an important element in the economic growth of the central Middle Ages, recent studies have shown that the great expansion of medieval mining only came in the second half of the thirteenth century. Before this time, many and perhaps most peasants and townsmen used tools made entirely of wood or stone. In view of this extremely primitive technology, most of Europe had reached its productive limits by 1275, and some regions even earlier. We have noted the press of population on the land. All available area was under cultivation, and much marginal land had been put under the plow during the great expansion of the twelfth and early thirteenth centuries. Such lands could not be maintained continuously, and they fell out of use. The three-field system was no unmixed blessing. Since manure was the only fertilizer known until some chemicals were used in the fourteenth century, nutrients were taken out of the soil and not returned. A serious problem of soil exhaustion loomed, and all evidence suggests that seed yields on grain, always low, declined during the thirteenth century. But population continued to grow, and a Malthusian crisis seemed imminent. In some areas, particularly Italy, where reasonably reliable population figures have survived from the thirteenth century, the land was drastically overpopulated even in terms of what these areas can support in the twentieth century. Even in tiny peasant households with small tenements, salaried laborers were often used in the thirteenth century to cultivate the land and particularly to fulfill labor obligations to the lord. This indicates extreme overpopulation and much part-time labor. Some of the lag was taken up by importing food from regions which still grew abundant grain, such as eastern Germany and Picardy-Artois, which fed much of northern Europe in the late Middle Ages, and Africa and southern Italy, which fed the overpopulated cities of Tuscany and Lombardy. But inevitably under such circumstances, people began starving and population declined. Population declined more rapidly, however, than was necessary to equalize the food-population ratio. Hence within a few years there were too few people to cultivate the land then under the plow. Some marginal land thus would be withdrawn from cultivation, but to such an extent that a new hunger problem was created and a vicious circle continued. There is evidence that this was happening in some areas as early as the turn of the fourteenth century.

This problem probably would have worked itself out within a generation or so had it not been complicated by natural disasters. Famines had not been unknown in the comparatively prosperous central Middle Ages, but most were regional and could be relieved by some minimal export of grain from areas which were not affected. Many more famines undoubtedly occurred than we know of from surviving evidence. Farming is a very risky business even in the twentieth century. Farmers now have safeguards which were unknown in the Middle Ages, but tremendous suffering still can be caused by bad harvests and diseased crops or animals. Even in comparatively prosperous times during the Middle Ages such disasters meant much starvation.

But Europe seems to have undergone a fundamental change of climate in the second half of the thirteenth century, accentuating in the early fourteenth, involving longer winters and cooler, wetter summers. Europe still is in this climatic phase, but the condition can be combatted now. Beginning in 1310, however, Europe had a series of bad harvests. In 1315 there was an almost total crop failure in northern Europe as torrential rains fell throughout the summer. Food had to be imported from southern Europe, but it was not enough to prevent mass starvation. The disaster lasted three years, moving across Europe from west to east, and was followed by a plague. Sporadic bad harvests continued, and another monstrous famine occurred in 1340, this time affecting all of Europe. By this time the population was significantly lower than in 1250 or even 1300.

The population of Europe was undernourished in the best of times. We have seen earlier that the diet of most was grain, chiefly wheat and rye. The carbohydrates were supplemented with some poultry and eggs, but there was little milk, since it soured so rapidly and little was known of refrigeration. The upper classes had meat from their hunts, but the farmers who had animals for slaughter usually sold them on the town market, where they would bring high prices. Indeed, the need for animals to sell and to pull plows was so severe that providing grazing space for animals put further pressure on the arable. Despite the habit of slaughtering animals in the winter that were not needed for breeding purposes, the animal population of Europe limited the food resources of humans. This was only relieved after the Black Death, when so many tenements fell vacant that the land could be used only by grazing animals, and this development in turn improved the diet of most Europeans. Similarly, large amounts of bean crops were grown from the mid-fourteenth century, but this seems to have been less the result of increased knowledge of balanced diet than a reaction to falling grain prices and the need to produce commodities which brought a better price than wheat or rye. Europe thus backed into better nourishment in the last century of the Middle Ages, but

this effect was absolutely minimal in the period before the Black
Death. A chronically malnourished population is extremely subject
to disease. Plagues tended to follow famines.

Political conditions also contributed to economic disorder. Europe
underwent a series of wars in the late Middle Ages which totally
devastated the French countryside. Although there were sporadic
truces, they were probably more disastrous for the economy than the
periods of fighting, for most soldiers were hired mercenaries by the
mid-fourteenth century and had nothing to do but pillage when their
commanders turned them loose. Inflation of the coinage is also of
great significance. Europe had been on a monometallic silver standard
from the Carolingian age, but the silver coins had been much debased
by the twelfth century. Byzantine and Arab gold coins were used for
large international transactions. New silver coins were issued in the
early thirteenth century by the Venetians and Florentines, and finally
by Louis IX of France in 1266. The improvement in coins made
merchandising much safer, for businessmen could carry much less bulk
in coin, or even negotiable instruments, with them as they traveled.
Gold coins also were minted in the thirteenth century, beginning with
the *augustalis* of the emperor Frederick II in 1231 and followed by
the Florentine gold florin and the Genoese *januino* in 1252. Louis
IX issued a gold coin soon after, but the overminting of gold led
to inflation as production declined in the late thirteenth century. This
was made worse by deliberate debasement, particularly from the
1290s. Prince debased the coinage to pay their obligations in cheaper
money, particularly in wartime, but even under normal circumstances
to avoid consulting assemblies for taxes. They could also take a profit
on seigniorage, the bullion remaining in the treasury after a coin had
been reminted with the same face value but a cheaper precious metal
content. Prices tended to follow the debasements, but there was an
interim period during which many were caught selling their goods
for coin whose value diminished rapidly within a time space of only a
month or so. Inflation became extremely severe as the fourteenth century wore on.

The Black Death

The great plague thus was not the sudden bolt out of the blue
that some have seen, but its effects were disastrous on a population

Illustration 27. Burial of victims of the Black Death at Tournai

weakened by famine and chronic malnutrition. Several types of disease were rampant, but the most important were bubonic plague, carried by fleas feeding on rats, in which the symptoms are high fever and pustules on armpits or groin, and pneumonic plague, attacking the lungs and hence the much more contagious and invariably fatal of the two. Coming to Italy on ships from the east in August 1348, the plague spread until 1350 in northern Europe, when it began to die down. Had the series of economic disasters closed with the plague of 1348–50, Europe might have recovered fairly easily. The pressure on the means of subsistence had been removed with one blow, for this plague alone killed between one fourth and one third of the total population of Europe. Statistical evidence has proven the obvious fact that the age groups most severely struck by the disease were the weakest, young children and the aged. The least affected group was the young adult and middle aged, those of child-producing age. Hence the population lag could have been overcome within a relatively short period, and birth rates did rise somewhat immediately after the plague as parents tried to replace lost children. But Europe did not recover for some time, due largely to three factors: psychology in its manifold aspects, migration patterns, and above all the recurrence of the plague. There was another in 1357–58, and the disease returned in 1360–61, 1368–69, and 1374. Thereafter the cycle slowed, and the next major plague occurred in 1400. Italy was visited in 1424, but the disease did not spread to northern Europe. A general plague and famine next occurred in 1438–39. Thus as population was replaced in the second half of the fourteenth century, it was carried off in the next plague before it could reproduce itself in turn. Long-range recovery was thus impossible until the last years of the century. The population of Europe may have been reduced by as much as 50 percent by the series of disasters.

Such a demographic catastrophe would obviously have a tremendous effect on economy and society, although consequences varied from region to region. In a sense it merely hastened trends already present in the declining economy of 1250–1340. Disease invariably spreads more rapidly in areas of high population density than in more open regions, and the towns accordingly had a much higher percentage of loss than the countryside, but they more than made this up by migration. The relative overpopulation of town vis à vis countryside became worse after the plagues. The result was that when the next plague struck, the artificially high town populations caused a correspondingly high loss of persons, a tendency which would have been less pronounced if population had been less mobile and had remained on the farm.

Why did farmers migrate to the towns? The first and most obvious answer is psychological. Understanding little of contagion and the nature of disease, medieval man longed to be with his fellows when the day of judgment arrived. Many entire peasant villages were wiped out by the plagues, and the occasional survivor might feel that he had nowhere else to go. But there are also economic explanations. Town guilds were powerful and wages were generally quite high, a formidable attraction. Unfortunately, the guilds tried to keep out newcomers. Many who went to the towns could not find work, and costs of living in the towns were as relatively high as wages.

The basic problem, however, was a "crisis of overproduction." As entire families and entire villages were destroyed, immense territories fell out of cultivation. It is true that this allowed some consolidation of holdings, and peasants who survived the plagues would be less likely than their ancestors to have a tiny plot too small to support their families. But there was a limit to what one person or family could till. Furthermore, as families holding land at hereditary quitrent died out without heirs, lords could renegotiate and lease for a term of years,

raising the rent each time the lease came due; there is evidence, indeed, that they did this by the late thirteenth century, as death rates
started to rise. But with an immediate lack of persons to cultivate
the fields which were available, hunger loomed for a year or two in
the wake of each plague. Peasants hoarded their produce, preferring
to eat it themselves rather than sell it to townsmen. But then land
was put back into cultivation, and it was a normal psychological reaction to overproduce for the next rainy day. Lords were having most
of their demesnes cultivated by salaried agricultural laborers, persons
holding no tenancies, rather than by forced labor services of their
tenant farmers by this time. Many tried to reimpose services on their
tenants as conditions of tenure to get land back into cultivation. This
did not work in the long run, for the forced labor system was inefficient. Lords paid fantastically high wages to the landless laborers,
however, and in reaction "statutes of laborers" throughout Europe
tried to fix wages at preplague levels. Although some attempt was
made to enforce these laws, it was impossible. The landless laborer's
position improved immeasureably throughout Europe in the period
after the plagues; indeed, wages of skilled and unskilled laborers
tended to equalize in both town and countryside, as masters sought
bodies to work and produce, while in the thirteenth century there
was a much clearer differentiation between the two groups.

Ill understanding economic forces, lord and peasant alike were too
concerned with production for the next plague. The resulting surplus
drove grain prices down. Agricultural areas near large cities were producing chiefly for a town market by this time. The towns hoarded
grain between plagues, usually buying it at low cost during periods
of overproduction and feeding the multitudes during scarcity. But the
decline in grain prices meant that the small, independent farmer could
not sell at a profit even when he consolidated holdings after a plague.
Lords were hurt less badly, since they had more cash reserves than
the peasants and could sustain losses easier, but there was a definite
tendency in the wake of the plagues for the lords to alienate their
demesnes still further, as they were caught between falling grain prices
and the rising costs of labor.

Unable to sell his grain, the farmer might turn to other forms of
agriculture, as we have seen, or leave the land to avoid the "price
shear." Large scale farming became quite common, particularly in
eastern Germany, where the lords were able to reimpose servile duties

on their tenants and farm systematically on a large scale for export, underselling their smaller competitors in the west.

In short, all social classes were in crisis during this period. As migrants for whom there was no work streamed into the towns, the situation with the proletariat was made worse. Tastes were generally becoming higher after the plagues. Conspicuous consumption by townsmen and by the princes and nobles, who were increasingly living in the cities, was merely the outward sign of a deeper psychological and social malaise. Differentiations of wealth were increasing in the towns and probably in the countryside, as rich became richer and poor stayed that way, and the desire to live before the plague carries you off produced a new market for town luxury goods. Similarly, the middling range of peasants, those with land but modest means, were being forced off the land, while wealthier farmers consolidated and expanded into other forms of agricultural activity. Some of the middle group made ends meet by going into weaving or some other form of artisan work. Indeed, the extent of rural artisan production was always significant, although hard to measure since most of it never reached market. Manorial customs of the early Middle Ages often ordered weaving and spinning for the lord. Although it was not ordinarily done for the lord by the fourteenth century, peasants still made most of the coarse cloth which they themselves wore for field work. Furniture and most farm implements were primitive and might be made on the spot, and baking, building, and brewing were as rural as urban. Conflict of interest came only when towns claimed the right to the exclusive manufacture of some commodities, which the countryside then refused to buy. Most rural areas near large towns succumbed to the political power of the urban militias in the late fourteenth century, if not earlier, as princely power declined and could not protect them.

There was crisis also among the nobles. We have noted that many were simply unable to maintain their earlier degree of real economic prosperity, especially in a sumptuary age of rising standards for all, to such an extent that some laws were issued forbidding low-born persons to dress or act "as ladies or gentlemen." The great nobles tended increasingly to become courtiers around the princes of the rising nation states and to appropriate much of the state revenue for themselves; a classic case of this is the dukes of Burgundy, brothers and uncles of French kings in the late fourteenth and early fifteenth centuries, who were able to create a state in the Low Countries and eastern France which threatened the mother country. The lesser nobles sank to a level approaching the peasantry. Noble and clerical monopolies of important places in government were being lost. Most royal office-holders in Languedoc were bourgeois by the late thirteenth century, although the nobles continued to hold the high positions, but the townsmen were increasingly becoming a nobility of service which would be very important in the modern period.

The problem of the nobles was complicated by social attitudes. We have seen that the nobles' attempt to close their ranks to new-comers was a biologically losing battle. Standards of noble status became quite fluid in the fourteenth and fifteenth centuries. Princes granted "patents of nobility" from the late thirteenth century as a means of getting money and rewarding their faithful followers, but only the bourgeois could afford such luxuries. Criteria were becoming increasingly economic and amounted to whether one was recognized as noble by others considered noble. Knighthood equalled nobility in many regions, and knighthood was very easy to obtain by purchase. The entire aspect of knighthood was made a farce by innovations in military technology. Gunpowder and cannon were used in Europe by the 1320s, and would eventually make obsolete most castles and any fighting with bow and arrow. Admittedly, the new weapons at first were more dangerous to those firing them than to the intended victims, but even infantrymen with the longbow were winning battles for the English over the French mounted knights, who had less mobility and accuracy of aim. Modern students often associate heavy plate armor with medieval knighthood. It was used by some, although it was so heavy that the knight could scarcely move himself, and if he fell the weight of his armor would kill him. More often this armor was used for show, in a period when knighthood had become a social distinction rather than a military function. The feudal host was called for the last time in England in 1385 for a ceremonial occasion. Nonetheless, it is striking that other groups wanted to imitate the noble and join his class. Society continued to have a noble standard of values even as the nobility itself was weakening.

The extent of apparent noble impoverishment, however, can be deceptive. Faced increasingly with the political rivalry of other groups, particularly the bourgeoise, who had more economic power in terms of what the prince needed than they, many nobles became town dwellers in the late Middle Ages even in northern Europe. The institutional structure of most fourteenth century monarchies was considerably stronger than the monarchs themselves, and the nobles often managed to make themselves local squires or representatives of the royal bureaucracy, particularly in England but also in France. In the wake of the disintegration of public order in the late Middle Ages, such men often made their way by oppressing peasants and preying upon commerce, particularly in Germany but also in the west. Among the nobles as among the townsmen, there was consolidation of wealth into fewer hands in the late Middle Ages. An aristocracy of about 250 persons, many of them related by marriage, held some 20 percent of the land in England in the fifteenth century.

Social Revolts

It is not surprising that revolts of the "oppressed" occurred frequently in such an age. Urban revolts were endemic, with the "in" guilds battling the "outs" in the great industrial centers. Rarely was a municipal magistracy able to maintain itself without hiatus institutionally or in terms of social composition throughout the late Middle Ages. In Flanders the weavers and fullers, largest guilds of the textile industry, fought each other with overtones of a national struggle against the kings of France and the counts of Flanders, while the balance of power was held by smaller guilds which prospered in local commerce. The so-called "democratic" revolt of Jacques van Artevelde at Ghent (1338–45) at the outbreak of the Hundred Years War (on this conflict, see below, p. 254) represented no more than a realization that the Flemish textile industry was dependent upon raw wool imported from England and that the supply could be guaranteed only by an Anglo-Flemish alliance against France, while the count of Flanders wanted to remain loyal to his liege lord, Philip VI of France. Artevelde established neither a democratic regime in Ghent nor a popular government in Flanders, where loyalty to the count was still strong. His power rested chiefly upon the suppression of countryside by town, and he was eventually assassinated by personal enemies. The Flemish cities were racked with other internal struggles during this period. The fullers were dependent for wages upon magistracies dominated by weavers, and tended to rely on the count, whose return from exile they supported in 1349. The 1350s witnessed domination of the great city governments by fullers, who were a minority group within the textile industry, until ferocious struggles at the end of the decade returned the weavers to power. There is evidence of collusion between the Flemish insurgents and the Paris rebels led by Etienne Marcel in 1358, although the Parisians lost control after Marcel was assassinated in that year. The revolt of the "Maillotins" (hammers) in the French towns in 1382–83 was directed at the regents of the young king Charles VI (1380–1422), who had in effect reimposed, in the form of a head tax, the hearth tax abolished by King Charles V (1364–80) on his deathbed. During the same period the great Flemish cities again revolted against their count, in a war lasting six years and totally devastating Flanders. The uprising at Rome under Cola di Rienzo (1348–55) amounted to a sort of fanciful desire to bring the popes back to Rome from France (on the "Babylonian Captivity" of the papacy, see below, p. 261) and to reinstate the institutions of the Roman republic. It ended in excesses and the murder of Cola di Rienzo. In heavily industrial Florence, the "Ciompi," the mass of artisans who were in no guild, allied with the less prosperous guildsmen in 1378 and forced their way into a participatory role in government, although the upper classes continued to dominate. But since even the poor workingmen had an interest against the unemployed, they allied with the aristocrats to drive the Ciompi out in 1382. Social and political conflicts were less severe in the German cities, although they did occur.

Of the numerous peasant uprisings, three in particular have caught historians' imaginations: the revolt of maritime Flanders between 1323 and 1328, the "Jacquerie" of France in 1358, and the revolt of the English peasants in 1381. The revolts show several common characteristics. The peasants in revolt were usually comparatively prosperous and independent, although this is less true of the Jacquerie than the others. The Flemish peasants were prosperous, but resented being forced to pay ransom for the great nobles who were captured during wars with France ending in 1305. The peasants, in addition to having little use for the nobles, had to pay a disproportionate share, for the great towns rigged the assessment. The famine of 1315–17 had struck the coastal regions of Flanders severely, and a break in the dikes in 1321 had caused suffering. But these grievances were comparatively minor, and the revolt itself began as a purely political quarrel of the city of Bruges against the count of Flanders, who had tried to limit the monopolies of Bruges at Sluis, its port on the coast. A series of minor peasant outbreaks near Bruges followed, but this was soon settled. Revolt then broke out again in the winter of 1324 and spread to much of western Flanders. Bruges assumed control of the revolt with purely political intent, for there was no social quarrel involved. In the last stages of the revolt, after 1326, the disturbance took on the connotation of a revolt against the entire social order, with millennarian overtones. As far as is known, no previous peasant uprising had taken such a deliberate and conscious radical turn. The success of the peasants in sustaining a revolt for five years, after which they were routed by the king of France and the count of Flanders, was due in large measure to support from the large city, a characteristic of other successful peasant revolts of the fourteenth century.

In terms of overall effect, the French Jacquerie (from Jacques, or James, the nickname of the "typical" French farmer) of 1358 was less serious than the Flemish revolt, but it is more just to term it a social conflict. Royal government practically collapsed after the English defeated the French knights at Poitiers in 1356, and the ravages of the "free companies" hit the peasants severely, as we have seen. As in Flanders, a ransom payment was involved, for King John II of France (1350–64) was captured and held captive by the English. Paris had revolted under Etienne Marcel, one of the richest men of the town, in a situation similar to that of Artevelde. The peasants were in close contact with Marcel's regime, and the association discredited Marcel in the rest of France and led to his murder. The revolt extended through most parishes of north central France, accompanied by outrages and massacres. It is hard to say whether there was central direction or merely isolated outbreaks of the oppressed, but the revolt was quickly crushed.

In contrast to the Jacquerie, the English peasants' revolt of 1381 had both much more organization and a more highly developed and articulated social motivation. The English peasants were only beginning to come out from under statutory serfdom in the fourteenth century, somewhat later than many of their continental counterparts, but servile ties seem to have had less practical effect in England than elsewhere. The statute of laborers after the plague was a sore point, as was mismanagement of the war, made worse when King Edward III (1327–77) was succeeded by his ten year old grandson, Richard

II (1377–99), who was controlled by unpopular uncles. Violent anti-clericalism also played its role. The luxurious lives of the great clergy were noted; papal exactions had hit the lower clergy, who preached to the multitudes and inflamed them. The doctrines of John Wycliffe obtained great currency, and indeed became a sort of ideology of the peasants. Wycliffe and his followers, the "Lollards" (mumblers—the term is also used for continental heretics with no known connection with the English), preached that all could hear and interpret scripture, for all men were equal. The peasants carried this further, saying that it was time to chase out rich prelates, bad lords, bad judges, and crooked lawyers, and return to a state of primitive equality.

But the outburst in 1381 was caused primarily by tax questions. Parliament had authorized a poll or head tax on all adults over age 14 in 1377. The rate was 4 d., just over a day's wages for ordinary farm labor, and although there was some grumbling, it was not serious. This tax was a departure from the older practice in being based on heads, rather than on property. The head tax was a basically servile exaction, although it had been losing this stigma in the fourteenth century. Another tax was ordered in 1379, this time on a graduated basis, but in 1380 the rate was tripled and the tax less fairly administered. There was large-scale evasion, and in early 1381 commissions were set up to make inquiry. Rumor spread that a new tax was to be levied without parliamentary consent, and revolt broke out in May. It was most serious in Kent and Essex (southern and southeastern England), which were among the most prosperous parts of the country. Characteristically, the townsmen led the revolt in Kent, the prosperous peasants in Essex.

England was undergoing a severe agrarian crisis, as was all of Europe, and it is hard to say whether the poll tax was simply a pretext. At any event, the peasants, led by Wat Tyler (who from his name may have been a tiler or a tailor, but there is no evidence that he was a farmer) and the vagrant priest John Ball, took London, assassinated the archbishop of Canterbury and other dignitaries, and held the city in terror for two days. They were dispersed only after Tyler was killed and the youthful Richard II had claimed to side with the peasants and promised redress of their grievances. This was a pretext, for as soon as order was restored Richard revoked the charters of emancipation granted to the rebels. The practical effect of the revolt is hard to pinpoint. There was a proscription, but the enfranchisement of the peasants was not significantly delayed, although, as we have seen, the fact of freedom might mean little beyond added dignity.

Aspects of Recovery

The countryside began to pull out of the plague depression toward 1400, although definitive betterment only became totally apparent toward 1475. The change took the form of a rapprochement, both economic and to a certain extent social and juridical, between town and countryside within the framework of the national state. Italy was perhaps the region most severely hit by plagues and famines, but it was also the first to exhibit significant signs of recovery.

Some land which had gone back to forest was again cleared in the late fourteenth century, in some cases to such an extent that over-production became a threat and prices were driven down. Most of the labor was provided by unskilled, salaried workers rather than by persons clearing on the edge of their own tenements as in the twelfth century. Much capital for these enterprises was provided by townsmen, who had become substantial rural landlords in northern Europe during the fourteenth century as they had always been in the south. Part of their motive was social, for possession of land with the power of command over persons was one way to move into the nobility, but it also had its economic side, although it was of less advantage for the townsmen than for the economy as a whole. Land was a safe investment, without some of the risks of commerce; just as an earlier generation had invested its commercial profits chiefly in urban land, so now the bourgeoisie invested in farmland. Land prices stayed high in the fourteenth century, so that only bourgeois landholders had enough capital to expand their holdings substantially. Returns were not great, for rentals tended to be low until the fifteenth century, as lords offered favorable rentals as inducements to keep tenants on the land.

The economic imbalance of town and countryside was accentuated in the fifteenth century. Regions produced even more than before for the market of a particular overpopulated town, where prices were much higher than in the villages. Specialization of types of crop became the rule. For the first time in the fourteenth and fifteenth century, numerous animals were raised not only for meat, but also for dairy products and leather, as diet became diversified and tastes more elevated. Vineyards also were expanded, often financed by bourgeois capital.

The leading "industry" in many pre-industrial societies is textiles, for everyone needs something to cover the body. Before the fourteenth century only the Flemish and Italians had produced enough fine woolen cloth to have much effect on international markets. But now sheep raising and weaving were diversified. Regional sheep-rearing associations were formed which would simply move from one grazing area to another. Spain knew a revolution of this type around 1300, when sheep were imported from Africa and bred with those of Castile to produce the merino, which still produces one of the finest wools in the world. Regional associations of sheepowners were united in Castile by this time into an organization later called the Mesta. The government gave privileges to the Mesta in return for financial rights, and the flocks of the Mesta made a yearly grazing rotation throughout Castile and later Spain. There were violent conflicts with the peasants, whose fields were being ruined. The export of wool gave a tremendous short-term advantage to the Castilian economy, but the Mesta so ruined the arable land—sheep pull up grass by the roots, creating problems of erosion and soil exhaustion—that the agrarian economy of Spain was irreparably damaged.

Increased grazing of sheep also had profound effects on the English economy. There had always been substantial grazing, particularly in the north and west, and the wool was exported chiefly to Flanders. With the decline in arable under cultivation, lords turned increasingly to livestock farming and indeed began to enclose common fields for pasture, creating further tensions with the peasants. In the middle and late fourteenth century, the English kings encouraged the use of native wool in textile manufacturing for export, even to the point of putting a high export duty on wool to hinder its being shipped outside the country. They also gave a monopoly on wool export to the "Merchants of the Staple," who raised prices still further in their sales not only to the Flemish, but also increasingly to Dutch textile exporters. The new industry had produced a major shift in the English agrarian economy by the early fifteenth century: while the eastern counties and "Midlands," home of the "classic" manor, had earlier been the most prosperous parts of England, they now declined in favor of the south and west, near the great weaving centers.

The Italian textile cities had engaged chiefly in refining coarse cloth imported from Flanders in the late thirteenth century, but they soon began to develop their own industries. They surpassed the Flemish industry in luxury textiles in the late Middle Ages. Indeed, the Flemish cities found their markets increasingly in Germany and the east, for the newer cities of Brabant, and even some smaller towns of Flanders which were barely more than agrarian villages, took a larger share of the Mediterranean market than did Ghent, Bruges, and Ypres. Ghent and Bruges maintained their prosperity despite the textile decline: Bruges through its commercial monopolies, and Ghent because it controlled the shipment of grain from Picardy-Artois into Flanders along the Lys and Scheldt rivers. Here as elsewhere, particularly Italy and Holland, a natural economic superiority often did not suffice the great cities, and they had to preserve their domination over the hinterland through sheer physical force.

Trade and Commerce

Several commercial regions were developing in Europe during the late Middle Ages. The economy of southern Germany was becoming prosperous, particularly through the banking and mining activities of Nuremberg and especially Augsburg. Territorial fragmentation was so severe in Germany that it was hard for the German towns to reach more than a local market, for tolls were exacted all along the route. Urban defense leagues and town political power alleviated the problem to a degree, however, and the expansion of the iron and silver mines of southern and central Germany and under German direction in the Slavic southeast gave commodities much in demand to German commerce. The south German cities had easy access to the Brenner Pass across the Alps, and from there to Venice and the world market.

The Italian cities were the commercial leaders of the world. The Venetians had expanded their interests in the east, even controlling Cyprus after the crusader kingdoms had fallen. They concentrated especially on importing precious spices and minerals needed in the west. The Venetian monopoly of commerce with Byzantium was an important source of the city's prosperity until Constantinople finally fell to the Turks in 1453, but this did not significantly diminish Venetian activity, for the Italians had foreseen the fall and had diversified their activities along the great trade routes of Asia Minor and Syria. The Genoese had been the rivals of the Venetians for the riches of the eastern Mediterranean, and although they lost first place to the Venetians in the late thirteenth century, they were still quite powerful. In particular, their territories in Asia Minor were the only known sources of alum, a mordant used in dyes, until it was discovered in Italy in the 1470s.

Most Italian trade with southern Germany developed in the fifteenth century. In the thirteenth and fourteenth, the Italians were active at the fairs of Champagne and later at Bruges, the port of Flanders. The 1290s indeed witnessed what one scholar has called a "commercial revolution." The fairs of Champagne were declining, partly because Philip IV of France overtaxed the merchants and partly because better trade routes were developing. Furthermore, commercial techniques were becoming sufficiently advanced that businessmen were able to stay at home and conduct operations through employees or partners in other cities.

The Italians pioneered the partnership, as we have seen, and the great companies thus formed loaned money. Private individuals also made fortunes by loaning money to princes and managing their finances, in operations usually lacking the connection with merchandising that characterizes the great companies. Such persons made their loans in return for security on royal fiscal incidents and rights, such as the revenues of certain ports or markets. They controlled royal mints and collected tolls. Nonetheless, it is somewhat difficult to understand why they did it. Edward III of England simply defaulted on his loans to the Bardi and Peruzzi firms of Florence in the 1340s. This caused their fall, since they operated on a very small cash reserve. A king could, however, withdraw the invaluable trading concessions of the Italians, who in effect were monopolizing merchandising and the carrying trade as well as finance in many parts of northern Europe in the fourteenth century. He thus had all the advantages, and if "national interest" prevented him from paying his debts, there was little recourse for his creditors. The Italian habit of loaning money to impecunious princes continued and figured largely in the decline of the famous Medici bank in the late fifteenth century.

The extension of credit for commercial transactions, however, usually involved interest, which was forbidden under most circumstances by the church. There were various devices for concealing the rate. One might engage in a contract which specified only a "certain sum" to be repaid. Even more important was the development of the bill of exchange from the late thirteenth century. It was similar to the "fair letter" which had evolved at the fairs of Champagne, but it did not involve purchase or exchange of goods. Bills of exchange were important both as a means of concealing interest on loans and of speculating on the monetary exchange rates.

Playing games with the exchange rates would have been virtually impossible before the late thirteenth century. Coinage was not stable, and there were many different currencies before kings and great princes were more or less able to get a monopoly on minting in northern Europe in the late Middle Ages, with the Italian cities doing the same in the south. As debasement by princes accentuated the natural inflation, prices tended to follow, but at an uncertain rate. In addition, there was tremendous variation in the exchange rates allowed by local moneychangers, who were not basically international operators. The element of uncertainty prevented accusation of usury by the church, for one might lose and be paid in cheap coin if the rate dropped too far.

Accordingly, one drew a bill which specified repayment at a given time and place, usually several weeks or months hence, in a different coin. The bill would then have to be redrafted to get the money back into the currency of the purchaser. Eventually the bills could be endorsed and transferred. The result was a tremendous increase in the amount of loaning and fiduciary money in the fourteenth century, a fact which tended to inflate the currency still further.

The use of bills of exchange as credit instruments presupposed contacts in a foreign port who could honor the bill. The Italians maintained resident colonies, often under their own law, in the important ports of the world. They also had "correspondents," businessmen of the locality in which repayment was to be made, who could handle commercial contacts for them, including bills of exchange. Correspondents were also common in the northern towns, where a German merchant and a Fleming might handle business on each other's behalf in their respective cities, but the businessmen of northern Europe did not adopt the more sophisticated techniques of the Italians until the modern period. Except in the case of some south German houses, their "companies" were even more strictly family operations than the Italian. Indeed, the ties of the extended family were becoming stronger throughout Europe in the wake of the uncertainties of plague and war, and this undoubtedly had its economic effect. Northern business-

Map 6. Medieval Italy, with Major Cities

men were strikingly unimaginative. A merchant of Ghent who had
dealings in Bruges had to send a messenger or go there himself. The
closest thing to speculation on the exchange rate that they developed
amounted to speculation on the death rate. A man in need of money
would sell for a lump sum an annuity or "rent," a smaller amount
to be paid each year until he died. If he lived long enough to pay
more than the original lump sum, he lost the wager, while the purchaser of the annuity lost if the seller died a year later. Annuities
could also be sold on a hereditary basis, binding the descendants.
Towns also sold annuities for the lifetime of the purchaser as a funding
of debt, in a sort of primitive bond issue, but such devices are quite
crude. The Italians totally dominated the money market and international exchange in the late Middle Ages.

The economy of northern Europe was in the process of reorientation
in the late Middle Ages. New economic regions were becoming important, such as Scandinavia and Portugal, and Brabant and later Holland were assuming the importance which Flanders had held earlier.
The export trade of most of northern Europe was handled by the
Hanse, the league of north German towns. The number of towns
fluctuated, but was about eighty at its height. We first find evidence
of the Hanse in the twelfth century under the leadership of Cologne,
but the league was led by Lübeck as it became extremely powerful
in the thirteenth and fourteenth centuries. Strictly speaking, the league
only existed as a body from the mid-fourteenth century, with "diets"
or unions of representatives of the various towns and statutes regulating affairs of common concern. The Hanse had resident offices in
England, Norway, Russia, and above all at Bruges, the "marketplace
of the medieval world," exporting timber, furs, grain, and other raw
materials from the comparatively undeveloped east and importing
manufactured goods. The political power of the Hanse was tremendous. After a quarrel in the 1350s with the Flemings over commercial
privileges, the Germans blockaded Flanders. So dependent was the
county on the German trade that there was severe hunger, and the
Flemings had to meet most of the German demands. The Germans
were rivals of the Danish king for the commerce of the northern is-
lands, and defeated him in open war between 1367 and 1370. From
these giddy heights their power declined somewhat in the fifteenth
century as they faced increasing competition for their near monopoly
of seaborne commerce. The English and Dutch both took to the sea

in greater numbers and were able to limit the prerogatives of the Hanse towns in the carrying trade.

The city of Bruges, in western Flanders, was the commercial meeting place of north and south. Flemish foreign trade at this time was almost entirely in German and Italian hands, while the Flemings concentrated on industry, particularly cloth. The great patricians of Bruges, however, did make fortunes through monopolies on commodities coming through their port for reconsignment to the interior of northwestern Europe. Bruges had resident offices of the Hansards and the great Italian banking houses, in addition to the smaller offices of the local moneychangers. Since the Italians in particular concentrated in Bruges, others, especially the English, who wanted more distant markets for their own products tended to come there. The English established their staple on wool in Bruges for a time, but it was moved to Antwerp and then Calais in the 1350s. Bruges was the only place in northern Europe where one could take advantage of the commercial techniques developed by the Italians, for the "wandering merchant" still characterized much of the northern urban economy. The economy of Bruges was to stagnate in the late fifteenth and early sixteenth centuries, but the city knew its golden period in the late Middle Ages as the center of riches, princes, and patrons of the arts.

Governments and the Economy

Princes began consciously to develop economic policy in the late Middle Ages. The fundamental aim of each was to make his land as economically self-sufficient as possible. This meant promoting the basic industries within the country, importing as little as possible. Every possible means was adopted to keep gold and silver within the land, and some princes even forbade their export. These prohibitions severely damaged foreign trade, particularly in the fifteenth century. Such considerations explain the change in the textile policy of the English kings. Although England had a sizeable textile industry even in the thirteenth century, it was primarily for domestic use, for the English exported much of their best raw wool. As we have seen, the rulers actively promoted textile exports from the fourteenth century.

The chief target of prohibitions of gold and silver export was the papacy, as papal fiscal exactions increased and were resented. Such embargoes could be powerful political weapons, as in the quarrel be-

tween Philip IV of France and Pope Boniface VIII at the end of
the thirteenth century. But the fundamental economic policy of most
princes and even town governments was woefully shortsighted,
amounting to borrowing on the short term and chronic indebtedness.
Direct taxes were tried occasionally, and we shall consider them in
the next chapter. Most princes lacked resources adequate even to enforce the financial means theoretically at their disposal. Protectionism
to the point of xenophobia, heavy borrowing, ruinous inflation, and
loss of public confidence in government, or perhaps better stated the
development of a general public interest in government during a
period when it merited no confidence, are the marks of public fiscal
policy in the late Middle Ages. The wonder is not that commercial
decline followed agrarian decline, but rather that despite these dis-
advantages and attitudes, and despite the unfortunate economic policies of most princely governments, the economy of the towns probably
suffered less than that of the countryside.

13

GOVERNMENT AND POLITICS

Henry VI, emperor of Germany and northern Italy and lord of Sicily and southern Italy through his wife, left an infant son when he died in 1197. A minority regime for such a vast empire was unthinkable, and rival factions in Germany accordingly supported the claims of Philip of Swabia, brother of Henry VI, and Otto of Brunswick, son of Henry the Lion. The young Frederick II became a ward of Pope Innocent III. Innocent wanted to end the Hohenstaufen threat of encirclement of the papacy and accordingly tried to play the rival German factions against each other. He developed the singular doctrine that the spiritual function of the pope permitted him to choose between rival candidates for the imperial throne on grounds of "suitability" for the dignity. After delaying long enough to make certain that the situation in Germany would be impossible for whomever he chose, he finally opted for Otto. A civil war broke out, and Philip of Swabia was assassinated in 1208 when he was on the verge of victory. Otto then was recognized as king throughout Germany, but he soon showed himself a much less docile tool of the pope than before. Innocent then had to turn to Frederick II, who assumed his throne in 1212. Otto was eventually defeated in a coalition with his English relatives against Philip II of France at Bouvines in 1214. Frederick promised never to unite Germany and Italy, and although he never gave up his claims to Germany, it worked according to papal desire in practice. Frederick was totally a product of Italy and the Italian way of life and despised Germany. His Constitutions of Melfi gave to the king and his administration absolute power in Italy at the expense of the nobles. The Golden Bull of Eger in 1213, however, legitimized all usurpations of power in Germany since 1197. In 1220 he guaranteed the privileges of the German ecclesiastical princes, and in the Statute in Favor of the Princes (1231) he gave to the German lay princes the exercise of regalian rights and guaranteed them freedom from imperial interference. The princes built up coalitions with and against one another and founded little states which they were no more able to keep united than the emperor had been in his vast territory. Frederick II even renounced the attempt of his son, the putative emperor Henry VII, to ally with the towns against the princes and attempt to keep Germany within the sphere of imperial power. The extreme territorial fragmentation of Germany thus dates from the period of Frederick II, who was quite willing to leave the German princes alone if they would not trouble him in his Italian designs.

For in fact Frederick's preoccupation with Italy, even abandoning Germany, presented a greater threat to the popes than an emperor who had to spend much of his time in the faraway north. He fought the popes constantly, and an unbiased view must concede that the holy fathers pursued him with a most unchristian ferocity, further damaging their own moral standing in Europe. Frederick became involved in a war with the Lombard towns and their papal ally, as his grandfather had done, and the results were the same, although at first it seemed that he might succeed.

Frederick II was more important as a personality than as a ruler. He was a scientist of sorts, a dabbler in alchemy and astrology, and legends surrounded him during his lifetime. He prepared a book on falconry which contained intelligent zoological information on birds. His court was a center of medical studies, and he founded a university at Naples which he hoped would rival Bologna in importance. But he left only a weak and short-lived heir in Conrad IV (1250–54). The real heir of Frederick's realm was his bastard son, Manfred, who had married into the royal house of Aragon, the rich Spanish coastal kingdom. Manfred was reconquering his father's realm in Italy when he was killed in battle in 1266. Conradin, teen-aged son of Conrad IV, was defeated and executed when he made a similar effort in 1268. The popes had summoned Charles of Anjou, younger brother of King Louis IX of France, to help them against the last Hohenstaufen. He did so and carved out his own realm. The pope had found an overly powerful protector, and at Charles' death in 1285 the popes were looking elsewhere for relief. Sicily had revolted against Charles in 1282, and the Aragonese monarchy had taken up Manfred's claims. Naples and the southern part of the Hohenstaufen kingdom became a separate principality under a branch of the royal house of Aragon in the early fourteenth century. The rest of Italy was left to the power of the great cities, for the popes left Italy in the early fourteenth century and would return only after an absence of 75 years.

Late medieval Germany knew few successful institutional developments. After an interregnum of 19 years, the German barons chose Rudolf of Hapsburg, duke of Swabia, as emperor in 1273. Rudolf's center of power was in Switzerland and southern Germany, although he managed to expand his household possessions into Austria. But imperial elections usually alternated between baronial houses in succeeding years, so that no one could form a lasting dynasty. Continuous Hapsburg power only comes in the late fifteenth century. Imperial authority was at a minimum under such circumstances. The imperial domain was tiny, and the Hapsburgs and Luxembourgs, their chief rivals, viewed the designation chiefly as a means of increasing family properties. The Luxembourgs, originally from the Low Country principality of that name, married into the royal house of Bohemia and became kings. They, more than the Hapsburgs, dominated the imperial throne in the fourteenth century, but they used it merely to gain a free hand in Bohemia. The emperor Charles IV issued the "Golden Bull" in 1356, giving to the princes in law the free rein which they already held in fact. Imperial elections were regularized with an electoral college of seven lay and ecclesiastical princes, and the elections thereafter became occasions of colossal bribery. The sphere of action of the Luxembourgs was enlarged when Sigismund, younger brother of Charles IV's son Wenceslaus, who succeeded his father in 1378, became king of Hungary. This in turn led to a resurgence of Hapsburg power, as the princes feared the Luxembourgs. At the end of the fifteenth century a major concern of thinkers in Germany, which then was beginning to experience the nationalist feelings which had seized England and France a century and a half earlier, was *Reichsreform,* particularly reform of the imperial office by giving it some power while keeping the local autonomy of the princes and by creating a meaningful imperial judiciary.

On the practical level, German political life disintegrated rapidly in the late Middle Ages. Towns formed regional defense leagues against robber barons, the poor knights who were trying to maintain a noble facade but only by turning to brigandage. This threat, together with the presence of numerous tolls, both at town gates and those which lords threw up every few miles, seriously damaged German commercial development in the late Middle Ages. The Hanse towns and the Teutonic knights were able to keep better order in northern Germany, but the Westphalian nobility did its share of damage.

Representative institutions of a sort developed in the German states, but this growth remained sterile. Organization of the provincial diets was by social class, generally with knights, clergy, and later bourgeois or some similar arrangement. Their degree of power varied with the principality, but generally they were scarcely more than a thorn in the side of the local princes and had little independent authority until the late fifteenth century. The princes had to consult them to get extraordinary aids, but since many German barons were little more than rich landlords who could suppress and extort from an increasingly servile peasantry in the late Middle Ages, such occasions rarely arose.

The City-States and Local Administration

We have noted the increasing imbalance in population and wealth between town and countryside in the late Middle Ages. This imbalance was reflected in a growing political power of towns over their immediate agrarian hinterlands, particularly as guild regimes came to power in the cities. Part of the ability of the towns to create city-states came from superior physical force. Towns maintained militias, while most rural communities had a small guard at best, and the townsmen could run roughshod over the prerogatives of the rural communities as soon as they realized the very real advantages of doing so. No medieval city-state developed in a region in which the nobility was strong enough to resist town pretensions, but some territorial princes, who were less able to control local affairs than were their own aristocrats, had to tolerate considerable town power within their borders.

The city-state appeared earliest in Italy, where many of the great men of the towns were originally rural landholders. Town expansion into the countryside was done chiefly for self-defense in the beginning, for the towns were at the mercy of any stronger force that could raid merchant convoys or cut off supplies of food or water. Accordingly, most towns throughout Europe maintained jurisdiction over a certain territory outside the walls. The famine and plague period of the fourteenth century made it even more imperative for towns to secure their food supplies, and they thus forced peasants who might be inclined to hoard to bring their grain to the town market. The large towns of Italy had forced the nobles of the countryside to recognize at least a nominal town suzerainty at a comparatively early date, and this development in effect made the cities into territorial lords.

Hence most large Italian towns were administering the surrounding *contado* (countryside) along with the city itself by the thirteenth century. Town exploited countryside in some cases, such as Florence, forcing the rural areas to produce raw materials for the city but preventing rural communities from developing industry of their own. Tax rates in such centers were much lower for citizens of the town than for *contado* households, and as a result some persons from the countryside took out bourgeois status in the city while maintaining their residences outside. Other cities, notably Siena, imposed only a very benevolent rule on the surrounding countryside.

The Italian city-states soon found imitators. The great Flemish towns, some German cities, and somewhat later the Dutch began to suppress rural industry and make trouble for local princes. The northern towns usually did not go to the extent of the Italian in making the surrounding rural areas administratively part of a general town seigneurie. They generally tried to hinder the industrial and commercial development of the rural regions, enforced their own privileges outside the town, and occasionally taxed or imposed forced loans, but this was much less systematic than in Italy. In addition, as government became increasingly complex and expensive in the late Middle Ages, the towns, the major sources of money, got a substantial voice in the assemblies which princes were calling to approve measures of governance and vote supply. The towns and the economic regions which they dominated were very powerful, even when they were not totally free of external control.

Most town governments in the late Middle Ages were more efficient than those of agrarian villages and all but the best administered territorial principalities, but they were nonetheless woefully inadequate. Even after the guilds obtained nominal control, the rich cliques dominated. Composition of most magistracies revolved, but the electoral process was so tightly controlled that a few dozen families dominated

in most cities. The cities were able to operate with miniscule bureaucracies. Ghent had a total administrative personnel of less than 100,
including 26 chief magistrates, guild officials paid by the town, and
messengers, but rarely as many as 40 gendarmes. Order was thus at
a minimum. Furthermore, municipal governments were notoriously
corrupt. Most city finance in northern Europe was based on indirect
taxes on consumption: the tax on a particular commodity, such as
grain or beer, would be leased to a prominent townsman, who paid
a lump sum to the city and in return collected the tax on behalf
of the town. Even the town prisons were sometimes leased. Such an
arrangement gave wide berth to illegality, and many magistrates in
addition simply lined their own pockets with public funds. Matters
were less bad in Italy, where most communities used some form of
the direct tax on movable property as well as land assessments and
some tax farming. Most large towns throughout Europe incurred
heavy debts in the late Middle Ages and had to borrow. Some, such
as Florence, had begun systematic funding of the municipal debt at
a fixed rate of interest before the end of the Middle Ages, and investment in the city became a profitable source of income, particularly
for rich townsmen.

   Although the governance of most cities was oligarchical, there was
a considerable turnover of governing personnel. Immediate reelection
to the same magistracy was usually forbidden. In an attempt to rotate
power as much as possible among the members of the possessory
classes, the composition of city governments might change as frequently as every other month. Although some cities developed an executive in the form of a burgomaster or mayor in the late Middle
Ages, many, particularly in Italy, were plagued by a large number
of revolving councils, none of which gave firm direction of policy.
This inevitably meant that such towns had to give special powers
to one man in time of crisis, usually the head of a powerful local
faction or a military captain called from outside to defend the town.
Most Italian towns had fallen under the rule of a despot by the end
of the Middle Ages, and some indeed never knew a more democratic
form of government than this at any time in the medieval period.
Although the towns of Flanders continued to have some pretensions
of independence, they fell increasingly under the control of the counts
of Flanders, who became dukes of Burgundy in 1384. Many towns
of Germany and the eastern Netherlands, however, were able to use

the power vacuum created by the absence of strong princely authorities to continue to rule city-states of a sort throughout the Middle Ages.

Royal Government in England and France

Governmental and constitutional development in France and England in the late Middle Ages is perhaps more significant to the modern mind than the German experience, for much of it was preserved into the modern period. Representative institutions began to develop, and in contrast to Germany and Italy, we find the beginnings of national monarchies. Particularly in England, but to a lesser degree in France, it is no longer anachronistic to speak of government, administration, and even bureaucracy and judiciary in the modern sense by the mid-thirteenth century.

The organization of the bureaucracy continued along the lines we have described. Household departments proliferated and went out of court. The most fruitful English development in this direction had occurred by 1200, and much baronial effort in the late Middle Ages was directed toward obtaining control of the chamber and the king's remaining household, the last outposts of royal autocracy. The developments which England experienced in the twelfth century are found in France in the thirteenth. It is often said that while Philip II created the French monarchy, Louis IX (1226–70) sanctified it. Certainly royal prestige rose to a new level during his period. It was a comparatively peaceful reign, since England was ruled by the incompetent Henry III (1216–72), who was prevented by domestic problems from mounting a successful French venture. Quibbles over the English possessions on the continent dragged on until 1259, when Louis IX arranged a supposedly definitive settlement: Henry III would continue to hold Aquitaine, the last major Angevin outpost in France, but in fief of the French crown. Some historians have portrayed this as a master stroke of diplomacy, for Louis' successors were able to use the feudal tie as an excuse for sending officers into Aquitaine and antagonizing England, with the result that a new war for control of Aquitaine broke out in 1294. This explanation ignores the fact that England had always held its continental territories in fief of France, and Louis' action merely amounted to repeal of the confiscation decree of 1204–5 for Aquitaine, although not for the rest of the Angevin continental territories. Louis' moral authority was so great that he mediated between Henry III and his barons in 1264, naturally choosing the side of the king on grounds that he was divinely ordained.

Extremely pious and ascetic, Louis IX was a popular and saintly figure who was canonized shortly after his death. He was a minor when his father died, and he in effect allowed his mother to determine policy until she died in 1252, as she had done during his minority. He dreamed of recapturing the Holy Land from the Moslems. Ransomed in 1254 following his capture on crusade, he withdrew increasingly from public business, which was handled by his more down to earth wife, Margaret of Provence, his children, and his bureaucrats. Louis finally fulfilled his dearest wish, dying on crusade in Tunisia in 1270. He was fortunate in having no serious threats to his position at home or abroad by worthy opponents and in having capable people around him.

Louis' reign saw some fruitful developments. He or his regents increased royal control over the church and continued to tax the clergy. Inquisitors were sent from the royal court to check on the conduct of the royal bailiffs and seneschals, but this was only a stopgap and changed little. We have noted his reforms of the French coinage. Royal administration became more sophisticated during his reign and was extended into the newly annexed provinces. The "chamber of accounts" began its gradual separation from the royal court which would culminate in 1320. The *parlement* of Paris was specializing as the judicial session of the royal court. It was to become the supreme court of the royal domain, just as provincial *parlements* were of their areas, but it was accepting appeals from seigneurial courts by the mid-thirteenth century. The *parlement* and chamber of accounts took the form which would characterize them for the rest of the Middle Ages, however, during the reign of Philip IV (1285–1314), not that of Louis IX.

The Growth of Representative Institutions

Representative institutions were developing throughout Europe in the late Middle Ages, in territories large and small. We have noted the essential feudal background, particularly the idea of a contract which cannot be broken by one party and the concept of consent to extraordinary demands. Much too is owed to the revival of the idea of the state as something distinct from the person of the monarch.

This development is due largely to the revival of Roman law and its distinction between the sovereign and all others, although the public legal tradition of the Anglo-Saxons had much to do with it in England. Both in England and on the continent it was due in part also to the rise of nonfeudal groups, particularly the bourgeois, who in contrast to the earlier nonfeudal class, the peasants, had some political rights and a degree of self-government. The bourgeois also had money, which was easier to tax than land. The kings, particularly in France, burdened the towns with heavy taxation about which the cities could do little in the thirteenth century, since the bourgeois needed the comparative peace which the kings could provide. The situation was not helped by the nobles, who always tried to shift taxation to other groups. But particularly in England the cooperation of the townsmen in the collection of a tax was essential, for once a levy was ordered, the magistrates of towns which "had the farm" (the right to collect all duties owed to the king, as the sheriff did in the county) were to assess and collect it.

Representative institutions first became important in the Spanish kingdom of Aragon in the late twelfth century, when groups of nobles, clergy, and townsmen met to treat with the king. Similar assemblies, the *Cortes,* were meeting in the other Spanish realms by the thirteenth century. The king had the right to call them when he pleased, and many rulers actually favored the growth of these assemblies because they could use the bourgeois to limit the nobles, but they gradually lost power in the late Middle Ages through overdependence upon the king, the general decline in public order, which gave power to the nobles, and their own structural weaknesses, which were much the same as the French.

The early Spanish assemblies display an essential aspect of representative development which came both to England and France: the idea of proctorial representation, according to which one person may speak for another, negotiate on his behalf, and bind him to a settlement. Without this, only those who personally consented to measures would be bound to them, a very unwieldy system. Without proctorial representation, the English parliament would have remained the king's great council.

The kings of the early and central Middle Ages were expected to live on the revenues of the extensive royal domain, together with such regalian rights as tolls and market duties and the feudal aids and incidents, without making tax demands upon their subjects. This was an obvious impossibility by the late twelfth century in England, for the king had a large army of bureaucrats and justices even by then and needed money to support them. Real revenues from royal as from noble estates were declining in an inflationary period, and the king had to alienate much of the domain. The constant warfare of the period of Henry II was a drain on the treasury, as was the crusade planned by Henry and executed by Richard I. The defense of Aquitaine was very expensive.

There was a tremendous expansion of all royal bureaucracies throughout Europe in the thirteenth century. Writing was much more common in the administration by this time than before. The feudal structure of royal government became a façade for the professional civil servants, most of them from the lesser nobility and bourgeoisie, who performed the day to day functions of the increasingly specialized bureaucracies. Monarchs were in the social milieu of the great nobles who occupied most great offices but had little practical effect on administration. Kings were often unable to control their own lesser officials in the late Middle Ages, a fact which may help to explain the breakdown of royal authority.

While government was certainly becoming more complex, it still seems very rudimentary to us. The *parlement* of Paris had 20 councillors in 1314, but by 1343 the number had grown to 62, each with his own clerks. The French royal chancery could prepare about 35,000 documents annually in the 1330s, but this was an average of only about 140 per working day, or a rather easy task even for 20 clerks. Royal messengers in England, used in the absence of any sort of rapid communication, grew from one in the early twelfth century to 18 in 1236, 37 in 1264, and 60 by the mid-fourteenth century. Even cities which were well administered in terms of the day might do better than this. Twenty-one persons did messenger service for Ghent, a city of 60,000, in 1358, although these men had other duties as well. Accordingly, it is not surprising that general tax levies in the thirteenth century, an age of comparative peace, were unusual. There were only fourteen in England, although clerical tithes were assessed more frequently by the kings.

The king's need of a larger tax base thus was most apparent during wartime. John of England (1199–1216), faced with dissatisfaction at home and a running war in France, tried various expedients, such as repeated scutages and enormous aids. Adding to his troubles was a quarrel with Pope Innocent III over the archbishopric of Canterbury, the chief ecclesiastical seat of England. The cathedral chapter had nominated a candidate unacceptable to John; the king then proposed another candidate and the chapter ratified this choice. In Rome, however, Innocent III appointed yet a third man, Stephen Langton, an English theologian of some renown who had been trained at Paris and was an advocate of extreme papal power. According to old English custom, John was entirely within his rights in refusing to accept Langton, but it meant excommunication and interdict. This did not have immediate effects; parish priests were totally out of touch with the situation and probably scarcely knew what an interdict was, and they continued to hold mass. But it did have some consequences after a time, and a baronial coalition, tacitly encouraged by the pope, began to make trouble over the issues of the archbishopric and extraordinary taxation, for the barons were the parties most subject to John's attempt to raise money by feudal aids and incidents, rather than general taxation. John then capitulated and agreed to hold England in fief of the pope. This angered the barons, who fell away from the pope's side but continued to oppose the king.

The result was that *Magna Carta* (the Great Charter) was forced upon John in 1215 by the baronial coalition. It had little immediate effect. Innocent III promptly excommunicated the barons for revolt against their legitimate sovereign who happened to be the pope's ally at the time. John withdrew to the royalist strongholds of northern England and was beginning military action against the barons when he died in 1216, leaving a nine-year-old son.

Magna Carta was a document pregnant with future principles, but it had reactionary concepts for its day. It gave graphic expression to the idea that prior consent must be obtained before extraordinary levies are collected and limited the king's rights of wardship and marriage of heiresses, both notoriously abused under John. The king's just relief was set down for various categories of holdings, and scutages could only be levied by baronial consent. Judgment by peers—not jury trial, for the concept was totally different—was guaranteed for all free persons, a decided minority of the total population of England. The king's prerogatives against baronial courts were circumscribed. Whenever an extraordinary aid was needed, the king was to summon through the sheriffs two knights from every shire and two burgesses from every borough (this did not mean every town, for "borough" was an official designation applied only to certain places). Individual summonses were to be sent from the royal chancery to the great tenants in chief. A board of barons was set up to force the king to honor these provisions. *Magna Carta,* in short, was a document drawn up by the barons for their own benefit, against the centralizing pretensions of the monarchy.

The young Henry III had all his father's weaknesses and none of his talents as an administrator. He was a better man, but a worse king. Increasing dissatisfaction was fed by the knowledge that the opposition was weak. The barons came increasingly to feel that government was their business if the king were incompetent or ruled unjustly. Henry III developed an unfortunate predilection for foreign favorites who were disliked in England. He spent enormous sums trying to get his son Edmund crowned king of Sicily by the pope after 1254, and his brother, Richard of Cornwall, emperor after Frederick II died. Finally, the Provisions of Oxford (1258) stated that a "parliament" was to meet thrice annually and would include not only the king's advisors, but also a body of 12 men selected by the barons. A permanent council of 15 was set up to advise the king on matters of state. Shortly thereafter, when the king refused to abide by the provisions, there occurred the famous rebellion of Simon de Montfort, a French baron who had settled in England. Montfort briefly overturned the government in 1264, but the crown prince, the future Edward I (1272–1307), defeated the rebels in 1265. Edward was in fact the ruler during the rest of his father's reign.

Many of the trends leading toward representative institutions crystallized in the period of Edward I. *Magna Carta* did not create parliament, but it did create a machinery for advising the king through the barons. Edward I was a legal reformer, and he extended the bureaucracy into new areas as limitations on private jurisdiction continued. The royal government interfered increasingly in cases involving land transfer. Government was made more efficient, and surveys of obligations to the royal government were undertaken. In addition, however, the 1290s inaugurated a new period of wars with France, and the king needed more money than before.

It was common for kings to call assemblies to parley by the time of Edward I. The word "parliament" is derived from parley, but it meant different things at different times. The earliest assemblies called "parliaments" were assemblies which were called simply to petition the king and his council on some question. The petitioners then went home and left king and council to take action. Some of the early assemblies were quite comprehensive. In 1254 the king summoned the knights of the shires to meet with the prelates and barons. In a famous parliament called by Montfort in 1265, the burgesses were to meet with these groups. But before and after these assemblies, meetings were called of only burgesses, only barons, only knights, or any combination. These men presented their petitions and left. Some early parliaments were called for voting taxes, others not. Taxation was often arranged by individual towns or groups in negotiations with the king, and these dealings might not be called parliaments. But eventually the convenience of one assembly to handle petitions and grant money at the same time became apparent. The transition to this as the normal form of parliament, of great lords in an upper house and petitioners in a lower, comes in the early years of the fourteenth century. After the famous "Model Parliament" of 1295, which was a model for very little since it included the clergy, the prelates dropped out of the parliaments and voted revenues for the king in meetings called "convocation."

The procedure and composition of parliament were refined during the fourteenth century, and particularly during the reign of the weak and unpopular Edward II (1307–27). Parliament was a regular assembly by this time, although only the king could call it. Edward promised in his coronation charter to govern according to the laws made by the "community of the realm," not by the king himself. The knights of the shire and the burgesses met together regularly from this period in a House of Commons, while the great barons constituted the House of Lords. This derives in part from law, in part from the English social structure. The great barons, who were members of the king's great council, were to receive individual summonses to the assemblies, according to *Magna Carta*, while the others were to be summoned by the sheriffs to represent their groups. Means of choice varied from appointment by the sheriff or the local county court to something approaching election. In part also it was the result of the growing narrowness of the king's council, which now handled very specialized and often secret matters of state and did not include the entire body of the great barons, for the baronage in the "great council" of the twelfth century was now at best an informal body beside the "small council" of the king's advisors. The barons felt that they should be consulted. The bourgeois and the knights had a community of interest, but the knights felt little community with the barons in the loose English aristocracy. While in France such persons were considered part of the noble "estate" (social class), whatever the economic reality may have been, such was not true in England.

Several great constitutional advances were made in the time of Edward III (1327–77). In the early years of the Hundred Years War, the Commons obtained a general recognition of the principle of redress of grievance before they voted tax revenues. This had little practical effect, for they would find after they left the assembly that the king would do whatever he wished with their money. Practical implementation came later. They obtained their own speaker and freedom of debate during the final years of Edward III or the early period of Richard II. Parliament by this time was a genuine legislative assembly, and its petitions were actually drafts of statutes to be placed before the king and his council. It also was a political device, as ambitious men played off parliamentary factions against each other. The great barons, who were often lords of the knights, controlled membership in the commons to a considerable degree. The development of armed retainers by private lords in the late Middle Ages added nothing to an orderly legislative process. Parliament was in the vanguard of the fight against the king by the late fourteenth century, but the goals of the battle were ill defined save personal dislike of the king and his advisors. Richard II reacted in kind by attempting totally to downgrade the pretensions of Parliament in 1397. He executed some of its leaders, but Richard himself was deposed and executed in 1399 when Parliament began a century of turmoil by installing the house of Lancaster on the throne.

Parliament thus began as a device of convenience for the king. He could hear his subjects' desires, make judgments, and obtain money. Originally the representatives could only assent to the king's request, thereby binding their constituencies. They had no right to refuse the king in the beginning, but this had changed by the fourteenth century. Parliament was the voice of the free population to the king. It had extensive claims in the Middle Ages and was putting some of them into effect by the fourteenth century. But the convenience of having a single assembly to take care of the troublesome business was possible only in a small area—only small principalities on the continent, such as Flanders, developed workable representative institutions in the Middle Ages—with a strong king, a population accustomed to extensive participation in local government, hundred courts, and sessions of the "justices of the peace," local lords who had replaced the sheriffs as chief figures of local government by the late Middle Ages. The very strength of the English monarchy had created the organ which was to limit royal absolutism in the modern period.

Representative Institutions in France

France knew substantial variations on the English situation. The kings held a much larger territory, but it was poorly administered and as such required less revenue. The kings became tremendously wealthy by the annexations of the land of barons who remained loyal to the English after the split of 1205. Accordingly, the French kings were able to "live off their own," with such added expedients as taxing the towns, until the last half of the thirteenth century, and their fiscal troubles only reached crisis proportions in the reign of Philip IV (1285–1314), called "the Fair." Philip pursued a vigorously expansionist foreign policy, particularly against his two great crown vassals, the king of England in Aquitaine and the count of Flanders. He also tried to expand in the east, and may have hoped eventually to extend the borders of France to the Rhine. Philip also was centralizing the royal administration, trying to extend it into the provinces and break down regional particularism. All this required much money.

As in England, the French *parlement* was originally merely the king's council sitting in a judicial capacity, hearing petitions and advising the king on how to rule. But while in England the court heard petitions both by private individuals and by groups on matters concerning national policy, coming soon to specialize in the latter while leaving private petitions to the common law courts, the *parlement* of Paris remained in effect the supreme court of the royal domain, not acting on matters of public concern. It heard almost exclusively civil and criminal pleas.

The kings did experiment with national representative assemblies in the late thirteenth and early fourteenth centuries. They had summoned regional meetings in the various provinces of the realm during the thirteenth century, but this was cumbersome. They met with one or more "estates" or social classes. We have noted that all free men had the obligation to defend their homeland by serving in the so-called "general levy." Philip IV, desperately needing money, tried to tax each person rather than summoning him to the army. Accordingly, an "Estates General" met in 1302 after the Flemish townsmen defeated the French at Courtrai, both to vote taxes and to act as a public relations soundboard for the king in his quarrel with the pope (see next chapter). But although estates continued to meet periodically for the next few decades in Paris, the kings basically gave up the idea of national assemblies after the first half of the fourteenth century.

There are several reasons for this failure. France was very large, and it was hard to assemble a national meeting. Communications were poor, and regional peculiarities were felt very strongly. Furthermore, decisions of the national assemblies were mere recommendations, for only the regional assemblies had proctorial power to bind a constituency. Perhaps most significantly, the French assemblies met in three estates, the clergy, nobles, and bourgeoisie (the peasants were unrepresented in law, as in England they were in fact). The kings of France could negotiate separately with the estates and play them off against each other. Since each estate in an assembly had one collective vote, the great nobles dominated the lesser to a much greater degree than the English barons ever dominated the knights of the shire. The nobles also were able to push most taxation onto the shoulders of the bourgeois, who had no political allies and were easy sheep for fleecing, to such an extent that in the modern period the French nobles claimed total immunity from taxation. The English barons realized that by paying taxes they could control the monarchy's pursestrings. The French nobles contented themselves with an attempt to gain personal control of offices—the English, of course, did this also—but they never institutionalized a means of keeping control of the king.

Accordingly, the kings dealt with regional assemblies in the early fourteenth century. A general tax on hearths was levied in 1328 on the king's authority alone. A crisis was finally reached in 1356, when King John II and many nobles were captured by the English and held for ransom. Two general estates were called, one at Paris for northern France and one at Toulouse for the south. But these groups could not bind a constituency. The estates of Paris had control of the crown prince, the future Charles V (1364–80), until he fled the city. In 1357 they forced him to accept the "Great Ordinance," which provided for regular meetings of the estates, which were to choose the members of the royal council. The estates gave themselves control of the royal government by a standing committee when they were not meeting, including control over taxation and foreign policy. They also established a machinery for collecting taxes, and imposed several levies to pay the king's ransom: a hearth tax, some tolls on commerce, and the salt tax or *gabelle*. But the estates were compromised fatally by being associated with the revolt of Etienne Marcel and the Jacquerie (see above, p. 226). Prince Charles was again in control by 1360, and the estates, simply to avoid the necessity of coming to Paris and Toulouse, gave him control of the new levies and the machinery for collecting them. Local assemblies continued to meet, but the kings were able to divide and conquer. By now the kings were fully aware of the dangers of national assemblies to rulers, and accordingly worked against them. They got out of the habit of consulting anyone about taxes by the second half of the fifteenth century, and France entered the modern period with only a tenuous limitation on the absolute power of the king. The basic sources of the royal revenue were those granted in 1360–1, save that the hearth tax was abolished by the king in 1380 and replaced by the *taille,* which in northern France was a tax on the head of the hearth, in the south a land tax.

Lunacy, Chivalry, and Public Policy in the Fourteenth and Fifteenth Centuries

. The question of English Aquitaine (or Gascony, the region around Bordeaux, the name usually applied to the entire English possession in southern France in the late Middle Ages) was the ultimate cause of renewed war between England and France. Hostilities in the 1290s were brief, and the French thereafter were more concerned with the Flemings, who had aided the English but had been abandoned by them, than with Gascony. Some years of internal turmoil followed in both countries. The weak Edward II was deposed and murdered after a troubled reign in 1327 by a baronial coalition in favor of his son, Edward III, who only began to rule on his own in 1330. Philip IV was succeeded in turn by his three sons and the infant son of one of them, but the direct Capetian line died out in 1328. The barons chose a

grandson of King Philip III (1270–85) as Philip VI (1328–50), first
of the Valois dynasty, which would last into the late sixteenth century.
In so doing, they overlooked possible claims of Edward III of England
to the throne through his mother, a daughter of Philip the Fair, on
grounds that the so-called "Salic law" prevented royal succession
through females. No one took Edward's claim seriously at first, but
in 1337 Edward suddenly declared himself king of France—his successors were to do this until the nineteenth century—and prepared to
invade France in alliance with France's continental enemies.

The war, called the Hundred Years War because it lasted 116 years
until the final peace treaty in 1453, was not fought continuously.
Neither nation was financially, militarily, or emotionally prepared for
it. The English won a naval battle in 1340 at Sluis, off the Flemish
coast, and during that year the Flemish troops, financed by the
English, conducted operations around Tournai, on the northern border
of France. But truces were made thereafter and hostilities were only
resumed in 1345. In 1346 the English armies administered a crushing
defeat on a much larger French force at Crécy. This battle was of
great significance in the history of military tactics, for the English
infantrymen, using the longbow, decimated the mounted Frenchmen.

The English, however, lacked the capacity for a sustained occupation of large parts of France in default of substantial French help,
which was not forthcoming at this stage. Their armies on the continent
were rarely of more than 5000 men. The fighting continued desul-
torily, punctuated by armistices. Another battle was fought at Poitiers
in 1356 with the same result, for the French had not learned the
lesson of Crécy. This battle precipitated the constitutional crisis which
we have noted above. Both nations, exhausted by the fighting, agreed
to another truce in 1360: the French recognized the English claim
to Gascony and gave up Calais and Ponthieu, while the ransom of
King John II was fixed. It is perhaps worth noting, as a sidelight
on the singular chivalric mentality of this age, that the estates of
France made a down payment on the king's ransom and obtained
his release. Once he was back in France, however, they refused to
pay more. John had given his word as a chivalrous knight that his
subjects would bleed themselves white to redeem his sacred person,
and when they ungratefully refused, he voluntarily returned to captivity, dying in England in 1364. Posterity has known him as John the
Good.

Friction between England and France continued. The French could not allow the continued English presence in France, while the English king was more determined than ever to rule on both sides of the channel, although the popularity of the war with his subjects waned as soon as they realized that it would be expensive. King Charles V (1364–80) of France and his marshal, Bertrand du Guesclin, spent the truce period revamping their military structure and made some progress against the "free companies" which had been ravaging the countryside. When hostilities broke out again in 1369, the French were able to make a much better show of it. They were not able to drive the English out of Gascony, but they did force them to ask for an armistice. Yearly truces were made throughout the 1370s.

The late 1370s and 1380s brought peculiar situations. The war dragged on and was complicated from 1378 by the papal schism (see next chapter), for England and France supported opposing popes. Both countries were ruled by boy kings dominated by their uncles, and in the case of England, later by Parliament. Richard II (1377–99) was a peculiar figure, of unstable psychological makeup. He evidently desired peace with France and an end to the schism in one package, but his domestic troubles kept him from attaining it. A war party among the nobles, led by his uncle, John of Gaunt, hoped for a renewal of hostilities, but preferably only after detaching France's Spanish allies. John had a claim to the throne of Castile through his wife, but his campaigns in Spain in the 1380s proved fruitless.

Charles VI (1380–1422) of France went insane in 1388. Although he regained his sanity periodically, his lucid periods became ever shorter, and he was rarely in charge of the government. Power was divided between the king's uncle, the duke of Burgundy, and his younger brother, the duke of Orléans, with Burgundy generally favoring an anti-English policy and Orléans peace with an end to the schism. Burgundy tended to rule during the king's insanity; his interest in an expansionist foreign policy had been compounded in 1384 when he became count of Flanders through his wife. Soon thereafter he gained other territories and married his children advantageously to various princes in the Low Countries and western Germany. Orléans was more docile and managed the king more effectively, but he was assassinated by the Burgundian party in 1407. Civil war then broke out in France between Burgundy and Orléans.

The situation in England had changed totally with the deposition of Richard II and the accession of Henry IV (1399–1413), first of the Lancastrian dynasty and a man who owed his crown to Parliament. Henry IV had little opportunity for foreign adventure, but his son, Henry V (1413–22) was a moralistic prig who was convinced that he was divinely called to be the king of France. He renewed the war immediately and invaded a divided France. The English defeated French forces at Agincourt in 1415 and moved toward Paris, which had only recently succumbed to a reign of terror by the Burgundian party. On the verge of success, the English were helped immensely by the assassination of John "the Fearless," duke of Burgundy, by partisans of the Orléans faction in 1419. The Burgundians thereupon allied openly with the English, and with this help a peace was arranged in 1420. Henry V was to become king of France when Charles VI died, and would marry Charles' daughter. Northern France was immediately placed under English viceroys. Henry V died prematurely, however, a few months before Charles VI, and his son, Henry VI (1422–61) succeeded to both crowns as an infant. Henry VI was a well-meaning innocent who eventually went insane. Most of France still recognized the claims of Charles VII (1422–61), son of Charles VI. In the late 1420s the "maid of Orléans," Joan of Arc, came forth, claiming that she had seen visions and would crown Charles VII in Reims, site of ancient coronations and symbol of legitimacy. Under her leadership the French administered several defeats to the English, and Charles was crowned. She was captured in a skirmish in 1431 and was burned as a witch by the English, with Burgundian connivance. But the unnatural Anglo-Burgundian alliance was ended in 1435, leaving the English dangerously overextended, trying to govern a country several times the size of their own and with a hostile population. The English gradually lost ground even in southern France, which they had held so long. A peace was made in 1453 which left only the city of Calais to the English as a continental outpost.

The entire struggle had been totally unrealistic from the English point of view. The kings were burdening the population with ferocious taxes while losing much of their own authority to Parliament. While royal forces fought in France, England at home was torn by civil strife between the competing houses of Lancaster and York. The Yorkists placed Edward IV (1461–83) on the throne after deposing

Henry VI. This was the heyday of the indentured retainers, and the armies of each side ground the country into chaos. A definitive end of the struggle only came when Henry VII (1485–1509), the first of the Tudor dynasty, ascended the throne.

France was governed weakly by Charles VII, but against the background of emancipation from England it was not generally noticed. There were still serious problems with the nobles which were ended only under Louis XI (1461–83), the "spider king." Louis' particular enemy was the duke of Burgundy, whose lands by now almost formed a compact belt of territory north and east of the kingdom of France. The last of the independent Burgundian dukes, Charles the Rash (1461–77) was a good fighter, but he was no match for the cunning of Louis XI. He also had the bad taste to try to turn Burgundy into a kingdom, and this attempt to usurp the power of the king of France cost him much support within his homeland. He was killed in battle in 1477 and his empire fell apart. His daughter Mary later married the emperor Maximilian, and the Hapsburg family was to carry the claims of Burgundy into the religious wars of the sixteenth century.

The Iberian Peninsula

Save for the final conquest of Granada in 1492, the Iberian peninsula had been recovered by the Christians by the mid-thirteenth century. The leading kingdoms were Castile, the largest in size and the interior area, which had led the fight against the Moslems, and Aragon, smaller and richer, a coastal kingdom which included Barcelona, one of the richest cities of the western world. The late Middle Ages was a period of succession struggle in both, particularly in Castile, involving royal relatives in France and England. Portugal also made progress in the fourteenth century and became a kingdom. Castile and Aragon were to know a dynastic union under Ferdinand of Aragon and Isabella of Castile in the late fifteenth century, but a united monarchy of Spain would only be created by their Hapsburg descendants in the sixteenth century.

The political troubles throughout Europe in the late Middle Ages show graphically that even with the improved communications and more sophisticated governmental structures, it was very difficult to administer large territories from a central location. Princes had over-inflated egos and unrealistic ambitions as always, and their lack of realism was combined with just enough power to enable them to enforce their desires upon their subjects without in any way being able to carry off their foreign pretensions. The kings of the late Middle Ages were certainly less able men than some of their forebears, but in fairness to them it must be admitted that they faced enormous problems, many of them involved with the economic crisis. In fairness to them also, however, we must acknowledge that many of their difficulties were of their own making.

14

THE CHURCH AND
INTELLECTUAL LIFE

THE THIRTEENTH century was a turning point in the history of the medieval papacy. The popes' hands had been soiled by engaging in dirty politics against temporal powers in Italy for centuries, but matters now became even worse. Innocent III played secular governments off against each other and changed sides with alarming rapidity, but his successors descended to new lows in their battles with the emperors. As we have seen, Gregory IX was not above negotiating with the Moslems to foil the crusade of Frederick II. The popes openly allied with the emperor's rebellious subjects, and Innocent IV (1243–54) even called a crusade against a Christian prince. The popes managed to extirpate the Hohenstaufen and dismember their kingdom, but as we have seen, they soon had difficulties with new protectors.

Most popes of the late thirteenth century were weak but dogmatic men. Several were French during the Angevin domination of Italy. The tendency was for a worldly, political pope to alienate so many by his actions that he would be followed by a sincere, spiritual weakfish. When Pope Nicholas IV died in 1292, there was a lengthy interregnum, followed by the choice of Peter de Morrone as Celestine V in 1294. The new pope was a Spanish hermit, a simple man who was totally out of place in the world of high politics which the papal curia had become. He abdicated under severe pressure after five months. He was kept a virtual prisoner in the Vatican until he died in 1296, and rumors circulated that he was poisoned by his successor, Boniface VIII (1294–1303). Certainly the fact that the pope abdicated was something new, and cast automatic doubts upon the legitimacy of his successor.

Boniface was in his eighties when he became pope. He was not a conciliating figure. A member of the Gaetani family of Rome, archrivals of the Colonna who were to bring about his downfall, the new pope used his high position to further the interests of his family. His primary concern seemed financial rather than spiritual. He began the "jubilees" in 1300, promising plenary remission of sins for all who came to Rome at this time. Jubilees became very frequent, and plenary remission of sins for a single meritorious act, first used by Urban II for those who died on crusade, was abused from this time to take in the most elementary of good deeds, particularly those involving financial gain for the church. The popes were simply using up their moral capital.

Boniface VIII compounded this, however, by antagonizing the great secular powers of Europe. Edward I of England and Philip IV of France were preparing for war with each other, and each needed money. They tried a variety of expedients, including percentage taxes on clerical wealth. Kings for years had collected such revenues from the clergy after the churchmen themselves had voted the grant, but Boniface in 1297 held that papal consent for such taxation was necessary. Philip IV replied by placing an embargo on the supply of precious metals from France, thus denying substantial revenues to the papacy, and Boniface had to withdraw his objection.

A new quarrel developed in 1300. Although canon law held that only the pope could try a bishop, Philip IV, evidently trying to be provocative, placed the bishop of Pamiers on trial for the very secular crime of treason. The bishop was obviously guilty, but that was not the issue. The pope replied in a bull which referred to the king in patronizing terms, but royal agents then circulated a forged version of this document in which the pope seemed to claim that the king was subject to him in temporal as well as spiritual affairs. The French clergy, thus caught between religion and patriotism, supported the king on grounds that Boniface had exceeded his authority. They continued to vote subsidies for the English and Flemish wars. Boniface then issued the bull *Unam Sanctam*, in which he claimed that the temporal power was to be subject to the spiritual and that all human creatures desiring salvation had to acknowledge the supremacy of the pope.

In 1303 Guillaume de Nogaret, Philip's chief minister, attacked the pope before an assembly of French bishops, then went to Italy and made a bond with the pope's Colonna enemies. They surprised the pope at his summer residence at Anagni, abused him physically, and apparently tried to remove him to France. They were thrown out of Anagni by an enraged mob before they could do so, but the pope died soon after.

A tremendous propaganda literature surrounded the quarrel of Philip IV and Boniface VIII, amounting to a culmination of arguments used since the period of the Investiture Contest. Papal theorists, such as Giles of Rome, argued that the pope's power was derived directly from God and was passed on to secular princes only through him. The pope by this time was extending to other rulers the claims previously reserved for the emperors, for now his major threats came from the west. But secular thinkers, such as John of Paris and Pierre Dubois, argued that the state could be justified for its own sake, since God had made man a political and social animal and had anointed rulers directly. The state was no longer battling church claims to supremacy on the church's own terms.

Boniface's successor lived only a few months and was succeeded in turn by the Archbishop of Bordeaux, who seemed a compromise since Bordeaux was in English territory. He took the name Clement V and slowly made his way toward Italy, but he never got there. There were various problems in France which forced his attention. The French king threatened him throughout his journey by such amiable behavior as surprising the pope's retinue in Poitiers with armed royal guards. Clement was a man easily cowed physically, and he never forgot Boniface's fate. At the king's urging, he opened proceedings on the question of whether Boniface had been a heretic and whether his accession to the papacy had been legitimate. He also held hearings on the orthodoxy of the Templars (on this incident, see above, p. 164), but in both cases he procrastinated and never reached a verdict.

The Avignon Papacy

The church was entering a period of distress sometimes known as the "Babylonian Captivity," since the pope was not in the city of which he was bishop. The papacy was formally situated in Avignon, where the popes built a great fortress to keep out the hostile population, from the time of John XXII (1316–34). Avignon was owned by the papacy and was not French royal territory at this time, but to the world it seemed that the papacy had been captured by the French kings and was their tool. The behavior of the popes did nothing to dispel this. Clement V had created 24 new cardinals, of whom 23 were French and several were his relatives. This placed the Italian element in a minority, in an age when the cardinals were developing independent prerogatives and viewed themselves as the pope's great council, church princes with a right to advise and consent and a right to a very luxurious style of life. During the absence of the popes, the papal states in Italy got out of control, and only a series of military campaigns under papal sponsorship in the 1350s and 1360s brought them back to the point where the pope might safely return to Italy.

The popes were also devising new means of raising money, particularly under John XXII. Clement V invented annates, a tax of the first year's income from any see to which the pope made "provision," or appointment. This was extended under his successors, and in view of high death rates and the wealth of the church, annates became an important source of papal revenue. The choice of a bishop was theoretically made by "election" by the clergy and "people" of the diocese in the early Middle Ages, while the pope could only appoint to sees whose occupants had died at Rome. This was extended first to those whose bishops had died within a day's journey of Rome, then into categories of bishoprics, until by the mid-fourteenth century the popes could appoint many if not most bishops of western Europe. In addition to the obvious financial benefits to the papacy, for entry fees and annates were high, this meant that foreigners were occupying many important positions in churches whose national orientation was becoming extremely pronounced in the late Middle Ages, to the point that the German, French, and English churches were under an only nominal overlordship of the pope by the end of the fifteenth century; indeed, treaties of state specified royal rights and those of the local clergy in church appointments.

Particularly with John XXII, there were problems with the use to which the popes were putting their vast riches. John got into an unseemingly quarrel with the German emperor, Louis of Bavaria, for reasons which are still obscure and may have involved little more than a conflict of personalities. The disputed election which gave rise to it—John had backed the other candidate—was soon resolved in

Germany, but John opposed Louis to the bitter end and particularly opposed his expedition to Italy for the imperial crown in 1328. Louis' court became a refuge for various excommunicates, particularly intellectuals and Spiritual Franciscans who were dissatisfied with the pope, among others Marsiglio of Padua and William of Ockham. John XXII was a man of unimpeachable moral character and a good administrator, but the aspect of a very efficient fiscal organization, about one third of whose budget was spent on warfare against other Christians in Germany and Italy, was unfortunate. Indeed, movements of spiritual reform, although usually not positively heretical, concentrated on private devotions and were largely outside the church structure by this time. There was no St. Francis to save the church of the fourteenth and fifteenth centuries from itself.

Pope John was succeeded by the saintly Benedict XII (1334–42)—a man so saintly that he fell afoul of his cardinals, who considered him hard-hearted because he tried to end the practice of plurality of benefice holding and restrict the political ambitions of the church. In deliberate reaction against him, the cardinals chose as his successor the utterly dissolute Clement VI (1342–52), nephew of Clement V. Clement's successors were not strong figures, but at least they were moral men. Military prospects improved in Italy, and Urban V (1362–70) tried to return to Rome, but got only into northern Italy. His successor, Gregory XI (1370–78), nephew of Clement VI but a man of very different character, did get to Rome, but died there unexpectedly in 1378.

The cardinals were in a dilemma. Most were French and wanted to return to Avignon under a French pope, but the Roman mob had other ideas. Under obvious threat to their lives, the cardinals chose the Archbishop of Bari as Urban VI. Urban's personality was a drawback, and indeed he was scarcely known to the cardinals; he was the last pope chosen from outside the sacred college. He seemed a throwback to the days of Benedict XII in demanding that the cardinals act as spiritual leaders and not as great princes, but he was also erratic and irascible, in striking contrast to Benedict. Under open urging of King Charles V of France, the cardinals left Rome and elected as Pope Clement VII Robert of Geneva, cousin of Charles V, a man whose major accomplishments had been as a papal general in Italy.

The "great schism" of the papacy was to last until 1417. Europe divided strictly along political lines in choosing popes. England, Italy, and Germany supported Urban, along with most of the Low Countries, while France, Scotland, and the Spanish kingdoms supported Clement. Two separate systems of administration and tax collection replaced the one which was already oppressive. The spectacle of two great church princes hurling celestial thunderbolts at each other was not edifying. For over a century some leading thinkers had espoused the idea that a general council was above the pope, in that it represented the unerring entire body of the faithful, whereas the pope as a man might make mistakes. Even some of the decretalists, commentators on papal legislative letters, admitted that a pope might be a heretic and be deposed by a church council. Henry of Langenstein and Conrad of Gelnhausen, German scholars at the university of Paris in the 1280s, also supported this idea, although more from a national sentiment that the popes had been fleecing the German church than from a general concern over church government. The far-reaching theories of Marsiglio of Padua and William of Ockham also had favored the church council above the pope as the proper form of church government.

But the Great Schism of 1378–1417 was the real impetus behind the tremendous spread of the "conciliar movement." Especially after both Urban and Clement died and were replaced by other men, it became obvious that the schism would be permanent if mediation were not employed. The theological faculty of the University of Paris became a sort of moral arbiter of western Christendom in taking the position that the schism should be ended by a voluntary withdrawal of both popes and the choice of a new one by a council. The English and various fluctuating French court factions supported this position. France withdrew obedience from Avignon, then reinstated it, but under obvious threats the Roman pope finally agreed to a council. Benedict XIII, a Spaniard who was now pope of the Avignon line, refused, but a council was held without him in 1409 at Pisa. It chose a new pope, Baldassare Cossa, who took the name John XXIII. John was known chiefly as a *condottiere*, a hired paramilitary thug who was used by various groups in Italy in lieu of forming a civic militia, rather than a spiritual leader, and both other popes refused to withdraw in his favor. Finally a new council met in 1414 at Constance. Its accomplishments included burning John Hus, a Bohemian who had come under the influence of Wycliffe's teaching during a period of cultural exchange with England when Richard II was married to a Bohemian princess. The council finally chose a Colonna as Pope Martin V in 1417, but disbanded without taking adequate measures to insure church reform. The council did make provision for periodic meetings, but Martin V was able to use his new position to undermine the conciliar movement. After a meeting in the 1430s at Florence, later adjourned to Basel, and the election of a prince of Savoy as antipope, the council was discredited, and at its decease there emerged victorious the so-called "Renaissance papacy" of poisoners and patrons of the arts.

Literature and Art

The fourteenth century in Italy is often termed the "birthplace of the modern world," but this viewpoint seems poorly founded. The last great voice of the Italian Middle Ages is usually considered to be Dante Alighieri (1265–1321), a Florentine who was exiled after a political quarrel in his native city in 1302. Dante was noted for his political works as well as some literary effort of mixed quality before his incomparable *Divine Comedy*. In *On Monarchy* Dante, a firm opponent of papal political pretensions, urged the emperor to return to Italy and claim his political inheritance. His arguments were rather thin, for he tried to justify the world domination of the emperor on the basis that the emperor was Christ's vicar on earth, precisely the argument used by the popes to justify their own temporal supremacy.

Dante's *Divine Comedy* was written in the vernacular of Tuscany, and it helped to make Tuscan the literary language of Italy. Characteristically, Dante wrote a Latin treatise *On the Eloquence of the Vernacular Language* to justify to the educated men of the day his failure to use Latin. The *Divine Comedy* is the story of Dante's journey through Hell, Purgatory, and to the edge of Paradise in the company of Vergil, an allegorical figure representing the wisdom and knowledge of the world. Vergil left Dante in limbo, on the edge of Purgatory, for he could not enter Paradise since he had not known Christ. Dante's guide through Paradise was Beatrice, an Italian housewife who became his "lady" in the courtly love tradition and symbolized beatitude or contemplation. Throughout the journey, which shows much of medieval conceptions of the nature of the heavens, the celestial spheres, geography, and the like, Dante finds his various political opponents.

Frozen in solid ice in the innermost circle of Hell are Judas, who betrayed Christ, and Brutus, who betrayed Caesar, representing the empire.

But after Dante there was a waning of the Italian literary spirit. We are in the heyday of the inaptly named "humanist" movement, a manuscript-hunting craze. The humanists were concerned almost exclusively with classical literature. One of the earliest and perhaps most characteristic of the Italian humanists was Petrarch (1304–74). The humanists honored and revered anything that was ancient Roman, particularly Roman from the Republican period, and despised everything else. The important thing to them was the imitation of Roman literary and political forms, and they hence had a passion for Cicero. This actually took some coherent form in the late fourteenth and early fifteenth centuries as the patriotism of the Italian city became the vogue in literature as well as in politics. But the humanists were sterile, as are most imitators. Petrarch's best works are his sonnets to Laura, his equivalent of Dante's Beatrice. They are in the Italian vernacular and show considerable depth of feeling. Petrarch, however, thought them insignificant and preferred instead his Latin work, particularly an absolutely grotesque epic poem in the style of Vergil. The Italian Renaissance killed Latin as an international literary language. The men of the Middle Ages had adapted classical Latin to suit their own needs and modes of expression. The men of the Renaissance, whose educational standards held sway in the western world until well into the twentieth century, thought that no Latin was worthy of the name unless it was in the form spoken by Cicero. Every work for which the Italian Renaissance is still noted is in the vernacular, particularly the works of Dante and the *Decameron* of Giovanni Boccaccio (1313–75), a man important in the proliferation of Greek studies in Renaissance Italy and a more original and hence less appreciated mind than Petrarch. The *Decameron* is a collection of tales supposedly recounted by ten young men and women who had left Florence to escape the Black Death and spent ten days and nights telling stories at their retreat in the Tuscan hills. These stories are a part of the folk epic tradition of the Middle Ages. Chaucer used many of the same motifs.

Although the Italian Renaissance did not produce much original literature, there were some noteworthy accomplishments in painting and sculpture. Giotto, in the late thirteenth and early fourteenth centuries, painted frescoes which show a new life, away from the somewhat stylized stereotypes of much medieval painting. But the great age of Italian art was only to come in the fifteenth century, with the breathtaking realism and emotion of the works of such giants as Fra Filippo Lippi, Brunelleschi, and particularly Donatello. The courts of the Renaissance city despots were centers of patronage for the fine arts.

If the Italian Renaissance was a stillborn creation in most respects, however, we must not imply that the late Middle Ages were a period of striking originality in the intellectual life of northern Europe. There are numerous general manifestations. We have noted the fate of the Gothic cathedrals, declining into an extremely mannered form, and indeed exaggeration in general seems to characterize the intellectual life of this period. We find peculiar motifs in art, particularly the dance of death, for this age was preoccupied with the mortality of human creatures, and drawings portrayed men in various stages of decomposition with gruesome realism.

The fourteenth century is a period of increased individuality, although not better quality, in the art and literature of the north. Chaucer's portrayal of the pilgrims on the road to Canterbury shows each person supposedly representing the class from which he came, but nonetheless behaving in a way peculiar to himself. Peasant and bourgeois literature continued to grow and to exemplify, if not to glorify, the attitudes and mores of the lower and middle classes. Some of the grossest stories of western literature before the twentieth century were related by the proletarian pilgrims immortalized by Chaucer. The farmer comes through as a human being in literature almost but not quite for the first time in *Piers Plowman,* a peasant epic of late fourteenth century England. The author, William Langland, is an almost anonymous figure, but he was a literate peasant, an almost unheard of phenomenon in the twelfth century. The plastic and decorative arts were now becoming professions, and were represented by persons, not anonymous figures who left their monuments but not their names. The van Eycks of Ghent and a generation later Rogier van der Weyden established a school of Flemish painting noted for its portrayals of weeping madonnas and devotional scenes, but also for a stark realism. The Flemings made the most important late medieval innovation in painting technique by using oils. Numerous painters and writers, many of them quite mediocre, flourished around the court of the dukes of Burgundy in the fifteenth century, for the late Middle Ages saw a decline in quality of literature and art along with an increase in quantity.

The decline is nowhere more apparent than in historical writing. The best historian of the fourteenth century was Sir John Froissart, who also wrote reams of bad poetry. Born in 1337 in Valenciennes, he was a bourgeois who desired above all else to imitate the nobility and become noble himself. He described colorful battles and often exaggerated the size of armies and the glories of particular persons. He had only distaste for town and peasant rebels. He is very shallow in portraying motive. Admittedly, one can say that Froissart is unreliable because many more nonnarrative sources have survived from this time than from the early Middle Ages. Tax records, hearth duties, transactions of local magistrates, accounts, ledgers, statutes, and the like were a commonplace by the fourteenth century, while they are very unusual in the north before 1300 and in Italy before 1200. Were we able to subject earlier historians to the scrutiny possible with Froissart, the late medieval parvenu might indeed seem a model of accuracy. In this, as in so many other aspects, the fourteenth century sees the change to more "modern" forms.

Medieval Music

Forms of musical expression also changed toward more modern types in the late Middle Ages. Medieval music had begun with the so-called plain chant or Gregorian chant, once thought to have been the invention of Gregory the Great. This was simply the chanting of the words of the liturgy along a single note, with only occasional rises or falls in pitch. The music had value only as an accompaniment to the mass. But the custom soon developed of prolonging the final "a" of the alleluia of the mass with a more complicated melody, which as the "sequence" began to take on independent musical value. Separate words were eventually added, and musical notation had developed by the ninth century.

Perhaps the most important source of our knowledge of early music is the musical drama. Old tunes, love lyrics, dances, plain chant, and the like were included with dialogue as the stories of the Bible were set to music and performed by the local populations in the great churches. The earliest surviving of these plays in the *Play of Herod,*

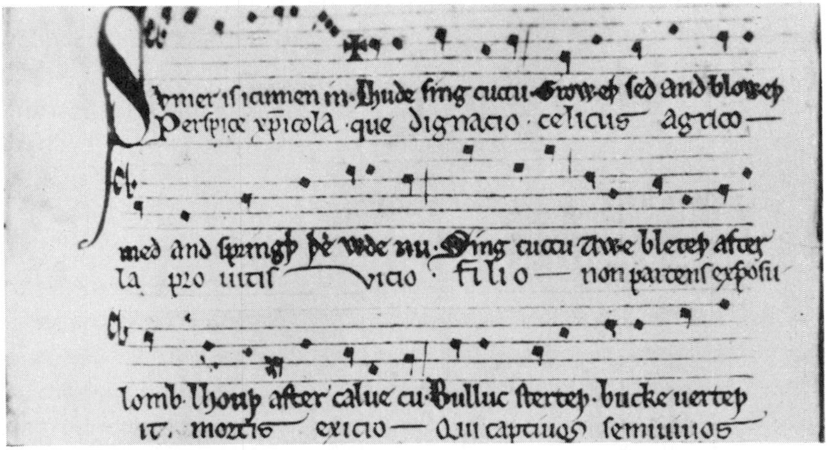

Illustration 28. Medieval music: the English round "Sumer is icumen in"

from the late eleventh century, but the most famous and best is the *Play of Daniel,* composed in 1112 by the students of the cathedral school of Beauvais in northern France. The instrumentation of these plays, as with medieval music generally, was highly percussive, with tambourines and drums playing a not secondary role to the viols. Such music is extremely rhythmical, and was intended to be danced, for the church festivals at which these pieces were performed were occasions of great joy and exhilaration.

Some early musical motifs are also shown in troubadour love poetry, of which some musical manuscripts have survived. Church music in the twelfth and thirteenth centuries also became more sophisticated and increasingly assumed secular melodies, with clear organization of time patterns into definitely established rhythms.

From the central Middle Ages in addition we have manuscripts of some dances which were obviously common in an early period. They were dances of love and fertility, intended to be performed almost orgiastically. At the same time, some of the older love motifs continued and were being refined in the late Middle Ages. By the fourteenth century some composers are important as individuals, particularly Guillaume de Machaut (c. 1300–1377), who composed both masses and love lyrics for court use. The fifteenth century saw the emergence of the Flemish school, which later influenced Italian musical development as the Flemings sought fame and fortune in the

Italian courts. This music is intended for a court audience and is usually extremely melodic and not overly complex, while preserving much of the percussive aspect. As the melody began to supplant rhythm as the essential moving force behind the score in the late Middle Ages, the recorder and stringed instruments, always used in medieval music, became even more prominent.

Religion and Philosophy

The individualism of this age had another side. Sensitive spirits were finding that the only way to lead the Christian life was by withdrawing from worldly concerns and leading lives of quiet piety, with little formal connection with the church. Some manifestations of this were quite primitive, such as the flagellant processions, reflecting the always superstitious mentality of the age, but other forms of expression were quite fruitful. The German Rhineland was noted for heresy in the late Middle Ages, but there was also a totally orthodox strain of mystical preaching, particularly by "Meister" Eckhart, John Tauler, and Heinrich Suso in the early and mid-fourteenth century. Perhaps the most characteristic expression of this form of thought for our purposes is the Brethren of the Common Life, founded by Geraard Groote (d. 1384) of Deventer, in the Netherlands. Groote was a lay preacher, a disciple of a man strongly influenced by Eckhart, who was unhappy with the organized and formalized religion of his day. He founded his organization to gain greater freedom from outside interference and provide a framework for more sincere devotion and charitable work. In contrast to the Béguines, much of the work of the Brethren of the Common Life was in education, for they operated numerous schools in the towns of the Netherlands and northern. Germany, emphasizing the rudiments of learning and the scriptures. The Brethren were a powerful force in the pietistic religious climate of northern Europe in the late Middle Ages, a climate which eventually produced Erasmus and Martin Luther.

At the other extreme, we find the world being justified for its own sake by leading thinkers of the late Middle Ages, although this justification often came from a theological orientation. Even Aquinas felt that man and the world had been created by God for a purpose. He considered the secular state to be natural, and subordinate to the papacy only in matters affecting the soul. But the defense of the state against the papacy was only part of a growing secularization of thought. Aquinas' synthesis of the divine and the human was attacked on philosophical grounds, a fact which seems in a sense to symbolize the growing lack of spiritual unity or security characterizing the fourteenth century, when the entire world seemed to be coming apart. Duns Scotus (1270–1307), a generation after Aquinas, put forth a far-reaching critique which even today is not fully understood, for Duns died young and did not formulate his ideas completely. In one sense Duns Scotus emphasized the individual entity to an even greater extent than Aquinas had done. He argued that the individual was made up of a plurality of forms, but he carried even further Aquinas' emphasis on the unicity of the human form as the soul, seeing the essence of an object as basically its very singular character, its "this-ness." Each of the forms making up the individual was real, and Duns Scotus thus has been considered an extreme "realist."

But Thomas had implied a division of the material and divine worlds in saying that man can know the one through reason and sense experience, but not the other. Duns Scotus denied this division and propounded instead a total, single reality, embracing what Aquinas would call both the material and nonmaterial worlds, and questioned the efficacy of both faith and reason in understanding the cosmos. The world was dominated by God, and particularly by God's will. While Duns did not consider the will prior to or above God, this is a contradiction, for everything which exists was created by God's will, and prior knowledge of the will by God is necessary for creation. Whatever God willed was by definition just, even if it contradicted his previously expressed word. Scotus comes close to making will into a God-force of its own, but he did manage to make a telling critique of Aquinas. God's rule of the world was inscrutable, and in a sense God himself might not know his will prior to the act caused by the will. The entire basis of the moral order might change in an instant.

The most radical attack on Aquinas' position was made in the early fourteenth century by William of Ockham (c. 1300–1349), a Franciscan anathematized by Pope John XXII and given refuge by Louis of Bavaria. Ockham developed far-reaching theories of the supremacy of council over pope in the governance of the church, and argued that the pope should confine himself to his spiritual function and stay out of politics. Ockham taught that unaided reason can never attain eternal truths, or even know general truths apart from matter. The starting point of knowledge is sensory experience, but we have no certain knowledge that even the process of cognition is real. Anything proven by reason must be taken on faith, for only reason can tell us that reason is real, and nothing can be defined in terms of itself. Furthermore, only an act of faith can tell us that the material world, the subject of the reasoning process, is real and not an illusion. Hence we can have no direct or indirect knowledge of God or even of the world through reason, in striking contrast to the view of Aquinas. Ockham differed from Scotus mainly in emphasis and starting point. He began with the world of matter, as did Aquinas, while Scotus began with the nature of God in constructing his system. Yet Ockham was not a skeptic. The individual can attain knowledge of God only through a gigantic act of faith, and Ockham made that act. Two strains of late medieval thought lead directly from Ockham: natural science, with its skepticism of all which cannot be proven empirically, and the all-embracing emphasis on faith, since reason can avail nothing, of the devout Ockhamist Martin Luther.

Most followers of Scotus and Ockham did not measure up to their masters' achievements. There was some speculation of note, such as the works of Nicholas of Cues, Gabriel Biel, Nicholas of Autrecourt, and Pierre d'Ailly, but most late medieval philosophy, apart from that connected with the conciliar movement, is characterized by logic chopping and debates over the meanings of words.

By Way of Conclusion and Transition

Marsiglio of Padua was a thinker of fundamental importance in the late Middle Ages, a man who in a sense represents the transition to the modern world far more than do the Renaissance humanists. Marsiglio was an Italian trained in the Aristotelian tradition at Paris in the early fourteenth century. He fell afoul of Pope John XXII and soon thereafter, around 1316, wrote his *Defender of the Peace*. His fundamental purpose, as he stated it, was to isolate causes of order and discord within the body politic, and his general conclusion was that any interference with the power of the state was dangerous. The temporal power of the church was thus illegitimate. Religion and the church should be matters of private concern to the individual and his conscience, not public policy, although Marsiglio's ideas would allow the state to use the church for civic or political purposes.

Marsiglio evidently had in mind a sort of idealized version of the Italian city-state when he constructed his polity. He spoke at length of the "human legislator," by which he evidently meant the citizenry, a somewhat exclusive term since not all persons living in the towns were citizens by any means, and many towns had a residence requirement of thirty years. The human legislator gave power to the prince, or "principal part" of the state, but the human legislator was the ultimate source of political power. While this obviously shows that Marsiglio thought that some measure of consent was best, he was not a democrat, for laws were to be made not by the entire body of the citizenry but by the "weightier part." He nontheless leaves considerably wider room for participation than most previous thinkers, for the Italian city-state was rather democratic for its day. Marsiglio defines law in terms of a monopoly of coercive power by the prince, for the church cannot coerce submission to its decrees. Marsiglio was a noted conciliarist, denying papal infallibility and even arguing that the enforcement of church decrees is up to the secular power.

Marsiglio's political ideas found no immediate response save from Ockham, and indeed participatory forms of government seemed perhaps more chimerical to many in the fourteenth century than would have been the case in the thirteenth. But nationalism, self-consciousness, decline in power of the church in favor of a more internalized piety, and in a sense a growing secularization of all aspects of society, were preparing the way for the modern age. When printing with movable type finally made obsolete the presuppositions of princes and prelates alike concerning their subjects and their receptivity to ideas, the modern age had surely begun.

SUGGESTIONS FOR FURTHER READING

This bibliography makes no pretense to completeness. It is intended as a guide to the beginning student who wishes to pursue special topics more thoroughly. The list is confined to works in English and emphasizes paperbacks, which are marked with an asterisk. Dates indicate most recent or paperback printing.

I. Political and Institutional Developments

*BARRACLOUGH, GEOFFREY. *The Origins of Modern Germany*. New York, 1963.

——— (ed.). *Medieval Germany*, 2 vols. Oxford, 1938.

*BRØNDSTED, JOHANNES. *The Vikings*. London, 1960.

*BROOKE, CHRISTOPHER. *Europe in the Central Middle Ages, 962–1154*. New York, 1964.

*CHAMBERS, MORTIMER. *The Fall of Rome*. New York, 1963.

*DIEHL, CHARLES. *Byzantium: Greatness and Decline*. New Brunswick, N.J., 1957.

*FAWTIER, ROBERT. *The Capetian Kings of France*. New York, 1962.

*FICHTENAU, HEINRICH. *The Carolingian Empire*. New York, 1964.

*GANSHOF, F. L. *Feudalism*. New York, 1961.

*HASKINS, CHARLES H. *The Normans in European History*. New York, 1966.

*HAY, DENYS. *Europe in the Fourteenth and Fifteenth Centuries*. New York, 1966.

*HERLIHY, DAVID (ed.). *The History of Feudalism*. New York, 1970.

HOLLISTER, C. WARREN. *The Military Organization of Norman England.* Oxford, 1965.

*HUSSEY, JOAN M. *The Byzantine World.* New York, 1961.

*JACKSON, GABRIEL. *The Making of Medieval Spain.* New York, 1972.

JONES, A. H. M. *The Decline of the Ancient World.* New York, 1966.

*LEWIS, BERNARD. *The Arabs in History.* New York, 1960.

*LEWIS, P. S. (ed.). *The Recovery of France in the Fifteenth Century.* New York, 1972.

*LOT, FERDINAND. *The End of the Ancient World and the Beginnings of the Middle Ages.* New York, 1961.

LOYN, HENRY R. *Anglo-Saxon England and the Norman Conquest.* New York, 1962.

LYON, BRYCE. *Constitutional and Legal History of Medieval England.* New York, 1960.

———. *From Fief to Indenture.* Cambridge, Mass., 1957.

*MOSS, HENRY St. L. B. *The Birth of the Middle Ages, 395–814.* New York, 1964.

*MYERS, A. R. *England in the Late Middle Ages (1307–1536).* Harmondsworth, 1952.

*PAINTER, SIDNEY. *French Chivalry.* Ithaca, N.Y., 1957.

*PERROY, EDOUARD. *The Hundred Years War.* New York, 1965.

*PETIT-DUTAILLIS, CHARLES. *The Feudal Monarchy in France and England from the Tenth to the Thirteenth Century.* New York, 1964.

POOLE, A. L. *From Domesday Book to Magna Carta.* Oxford, 1955.

*RUNCIMAN, STEVEN. *Byzantine Civilization.* New York, 1956.

*———. *History of the Crusades.* 3 vols. New York, 1965–1967.

*———. *The Sicilian Vespers.* Harmondsworth, 1960.

*SAYLES, GEORGE O. *The Medieval Foundations of England.* New York, 1961.

*STENTON, DORIS M. *English Society in the Early Middle Ages (1066–1307).* Harmondsworth, 1951.

STENTON, F. M. *Anglo-Saxon England.* Oxford, 1947.

*STRAYER, JOSEPH R. *Feudalism.* Princeton, N.J., 1965.

STRAYER, JOSEPH R. and TAYLOR, C. H. *Studies in Early French Taxation.* Cambridge, Mass., 1939.

*TREVELYAN, G. M. *England in the Age of Wycliffe, 1368–1520.* New York, 1963.

*VASILIEV, A. A. *History of the Byzantine Empire, 324–1453.* 2d ed. Madison, Wis., 1952.

*WALLACE-HADRILL, J. M. *The Barbarian West, A. D. 400–1000.* New York, 1962.

*WHITELOCK, DOROTHY. *The Beginnings of English Society.* Harmondsworth, 1952.

II.   Intellectual and Religious Life

*ANDRAE, TOR. *Mohammed: the Man and His Faith.* New York, 1960.
*BALDWIN, JOHN W. *The Scholastic Culture of the Middle Ages,
1000–1300.* Lexington, Mass., 1971.
*BALDWIN, MARSHALL (ed.). *Christianity through the Thirteenth Cen-
tury.* New York, 1970.
*BARRACLOUGH, GEOFFREY. *The Medieval Papacy.* New York, 1968.
*COHN, NORMAN. *The Pursuit of the Millennium.* London, 1961.
*COPLESTON, F. C. *Aquinas.* Harmondsworth, 1955.
*————. *Medieval Philosophy.* 2 vols. New York, 1962.
GILSON, ETIENNE. *History of Christian Philosophy in the Middle Ages.*
London, 1955.
*————. *Reason and Revelation in the Middle Ages.* New York, 1938.
————. *The Spirit of Medieval Philosophy.* New York, 1936.
*GIMPEL, JEAN. *The Cathedral Builders.* New York, 1961.
*GRUNEBAUM, GUSTAVE VON. *Medieval Islam: a Study in Cultural
Orientation.* 2d ed. Chicago, 1966.
*HALE, JOHN, HIGHFIELD, ROGER, and SMALLEY, BERYL (eds.). *Europe
in the Late Middle Ages.* London, 1965.
*HASKINS, C. H. *The Renaissance of the Twelfth Century,* New York,
1957.
*HEER, FRIEDRICH. *The Medieval World.* New York, 1963.
*HUIZINGA, JOHAN. *The Waning of the Middle Ages.* New York, 1954.
KAMINSKY, HOWARD. *A History of the Hussite Revolution.* Berkeley,
Calif., 1967.
*KNOWLES, DAVID. *Christian Monasticism.* London, 1969.
*————. *The Evolution of Medieval Thought.* New York, 1962.
*LEA, HENRY CHARLES. *History of the Inquisition of the Middle Ages.*
3 vols. New York, 1888. Several paperback abridgements and issues
of selections are available.
LEFF, GORDON. *Heresy in the Later Middle Ages.* 2 vols. Manchester,
1967.
*————. *Medieval Thought from Augustine to Ockham.* Harmonds-
worth, 1958.
*————. *Paris and Oxford Universities in the Middle Ages.* New York,
1967.
MCILWAIN, C. H. *The Growth of Political Thought in the West.* New
York, 1932.

*MOLLAT, G. *The Popes at Avignon, 1305–1378.* New York, 1963.

*MORRALL, JOHN B. *Political Thought in Medieval Times.* New York, 1962.

MORRISON, KARL F. *Tradition and Authority in the Western Church, 300–1100.* Princeton, 1969.

*PANOFSKY, ERWIN. *Gothic Architecture and Scholasticism.* New York, 1957.

*PEVSNER, NIKOLAUS. *An Outline of European Architecture,* 4th ed. Harmondsworth, 1953.

POST, GAINES. *Studies in Medieval Legal Thought. Public Law and the State, 1100–1322.* Princeton, N.J., 1964.

RASHDALL, H. *The Universities of Europe in the Middle Ages,* 3 vols., revised by F. M. Powicke and A. B. Emden. Oxford, 1936.

*RUSSELL JEFFREY B. (ed.). *Religious Dissent in the Middle Ages.* New York, 1971.

SABATIER, PAUL. *The Life of St. Francis of Assisi.* London, 1894.

*SIMSON, OTTO VON. *The Gothic Cathedral.* New York, 1964.

*SOUTHERN, R. W. *The Making of the Middle Ages.* New Haven, Conn., 1964.

*———. *Western Society and the Church in the Middle Ages.* Harmondsworth, 1970.

SUMMERS, MONTAGUE. *The History of Witchcraft and Demonology.* 2d ed. New York, 1956.

*TELLENBACH, GERD. *Church, State and Christian Society at the Time of the Investiture Contest.* New York, 1970.

*TIERNEY, BRIAN. *The Crisis of Church and State.* Englewood Cliffs, N.J., 1964.

———. *Foundations of the Conciliar Theory.* Cambridge, 1955.

ULLMANN, WALTER. *The Growth of Papal Government in the Middle Ages.* London, 1962.

*———. *A History of Political Thought: the Middle Ages.* Harmondsworth, 1965.

*WADDELL, HELEN. *The Wandering Scholars.* New York, 1961.

*WATT, W. MONTGOMERY. *Muhammed: Prophet and Statesman.* Oxford, 1964.

*WIERUSZOWSKI, HELENE. *The Medieval University.* Princeton, N.J., 1966.

III. Economy and Society

*ADELSON, HOWARD L. *Medieval Commerce.* Princeton, N.J., 1962.

*BAUTIER, R. H. *The Economic Development of Medieval Europe.* London and New York, 1971.

*BLOCH, MARC. *Feudal Society,* 2 vols. Chicago, 1961.

———. *French Rural History. An Essay on its Basic Characteristics.* Berkeley, Calif., 1966.

*BOISSONNADE, PROSPER. *Life and Work in Medieval Europe.* New York, 1964.

BRUCKER, GENE A. *Florentine Politics and Society, 1343–1378.* Princeton, N.J., 1962.

*———. *Renaissance Florence.* New York, 1969.

The Cambridge Economic History of Europe, vols. I–III. Cambridge, 1941–1965.

*CARUS-WILSON, ELEANORA. *Medieval Merchant Venturers.* London, 1967.

*COULTON, G. G. *Medieval Village, Manor, and Monastery.* New York, 1960.

DOLLINGER, PHILIPPE. *The German Hansa.* Stanford, Calif., 1970.

DUBY, GEORGES. *Rural Economy and Country Life in the Medieval West.* Columbia, S.C., 1968.

*HASTINGS, MARGARET. *Medieval European Society, 1000–1400.* New York, 1971.

HERLIHY, DAVID. *Medieval and Early Renaissance Pistoia.* New Haven, Conn., 1967.

——— (ed.). *Medieval Culture and Society.* New York, 1968.

*HOLMES, URBAN T. *Daily Living in the Twelfth Century.* Madison, Wis., 1952.

*HOMANS, G. C. *English Villagers of the Thirteenth Century.* New York, 1970.

HOYT, ROBERT S. (ed.). *Life and Thought in the Early Middle Ages.* Minneapolis, 1967.

*LANDER, J. R. *Conflict and Stability in Fifteenth Century England.* London, 1967.

*LATOUCHE, ROBERT. *The Birth of Western Economy.* New York, 1966.

*LOPEZ, ROBERT S. *The Commercial Revolution of the Central Middle Ages, 950–1300.* Englewood Cliffs, N.J., 1971.

*LOPEZ, ROBERT S. and RAYMOND, IRVING W. (eds.). *Medieval Trade in the Mediterranean World.* New York, 1955.

*LUCHAIRE, ACHILLE. *Social France at the Time of Philip Augustus.* New York, 1967.

LUZZATTO, GINO. *An Economic History of Italy from the Fall of the Roman Empire to the Beginning of the Sixteenth Century.* London, 1961.

*MISKIMIN, HARRY A. *The Economy of Early Renaissance Europe, 1300–1460.* Englewood Cliffs, N.J., 1969.

*Molho, Anthony (ed.). *Social and Economic Foundations of the Italian Renaissance.* New York, 1969.

*Mundy, John H. and Riesenberg, Peter. *The Medieval Town.* Princeton, N.J., 1958.

Neilson, Nellie. *Medieval Agrarian Economy.* New York, 1936.

Nicholas, David. *Town and Countryside: Social, Economic, and Political Tensions in Fourteenth-Century Flanders.* Bruges, 1971.

*Pirenne, Henri. *Early Democracies in the Low Countries.* New York, 1963.

*———. *Economic and Social History of Medieval Europe.* New York, 1937.

*———. *Medieval Cities. Their Origins and the Revival of Trade.* Princeton, 1969.

*———. *Mohammed and Charlemagne.* New York, 1957.

Roover, Raymond de. *Money, Banking and Credit in Mediaeval Bruges.* Cambridge, Mass., 1948.

*———. *The Rise and Decline of the Medici Bank.* New York, 1967.

*Rörig, Fritz. *The Medieval Town.* Berkeley, Calif., 1967.

Rostovtzeff, M. *Social and Economic History of the Roman Empire.* Oxford, 1926.

*Thrupp, Sylvia L. *The Merchant Class of Medieval London, 1300–1500.* Ann Arbor, Mich., 1948.

*——— (ed.). *Change in Medieval Society. Europe North of the Alps, 1050–1500.* New York, 1964.

*——— (ed.), *Early Medieval Society.* New York, 1967.

*Trevelyan, George M. *Illustrated English Social History.* Harmondsworth, 1964.

* Waley, Daniel. *The Italian City-Republics.* London, 1969.

*White, Lynn, Jr. *Medieval Technology and Social Change.* Oxford 1962.

*Williams, Gwyn. *Medieval London: From the Commune to Capital.* London, 1963.

*Ziegler, Philip. *The Black Death.* Harmondsworth, 1970.

ILLUSTRATION CREDITS

1. Universitetets Oldsaksamling, Oslo.
2. Royal Commission on Historical Monuments. National Monuments Record.
3. J. K. St. Joseph, Cambridge University Collection, copyright reserved.
4. Drawing by the Dorsey Press after model in F. L. Ganshof, *Over Stadsontwikkeling tusschen Loire en Rijn gedurende de Middeleeuwen* (Antwerp, 1941), by permission of Standaard Boekhandel, Antwerp.
5 and 6. From *The Bayeux Tapestry*, edited by Frank Stenton, published by Phaidon Press, London.
7. Cliché des Musées Nationaux, from manuscript of Gregory the Great, *Moralia in Job,* in Musée des Arts et Traditions Populaires, Paris.
8 and 12. Bodleian Library, Oxford. Ms. Bodley 264, fo. 81, 171 v, the *Romance of Alexander,* illuminated by Jan de Griese, 1339–1344.
9. Cliché C. G. T. Photograph Dedé. From Official Belgian Tourist Bureau.
11 and 15. Official Belgian Tourist Bureau.
13. Bibliothèque Nationale, ms. français 22297, fo. 449.
14. Bibliothèque Nationale, ms. Arsenal 5062, fo. 149 v.
16. Dr. Harald Busch, courtesy German Tourist Information Service.
18. Burkhard-Verlag, Ernst Heyer, Essen.
20. Frau Helga Schmidt-Glassner.
22. French Government tourist office.
26 and 27. Copyright Bibliothèque royale Albert Ier, Brussels, ms. 13076/77, fo. 16 v, 24 v.
28. British Museum, London, Harley ms. 978, fo. 11b.
10, 17, 19, 21, 23, 24, 25. D. Nicholas.

INDEX